A
MEMOIR

Russell E. Train
1801 Kalorama Square, NW
Washington, D.C. 20008

Russell Errol Train (1920-   ) and Aileen
Bowdoin Train (1925-   ), c. 1980

A
MEMOIR

by

Russell E. Train

PRIVATELY PUBLISHED : 2000

To
Aileen,
without whom my life
would not have been
worth writing about

Table of Contents

Preface

This book of memoirs has been written as a companion to *The Bow-doin Family* and *The Train Family,* all three books written and published by me concurrently.

What started about six years ago as an effort to update and, in some respects, to enlarge upon *John Trayne and Some of His Descendants,* written and privately published by my aunt Susan Train Hand in 1933, soon expanded to include an account of the Bowdoin family of my wife, Aileen. As I worked on those subjects, I found that, when writing about persons and events with which I was personally familiar, a good deal of my own life tended to creep into the product. Accepting the reality of that fact, I decided to bite the bullet and write an autobiography as well.

Originally, I assumed that all three efforts would end up as parts of one volume, but that expectation quickly evaporated as the true scope of the enterprise became apparent. I then decided to write three volumes of one book which I tentatively called *Family Portraits.* However, aside from the marriage of Aileen and myself, there is little connection between the Bowdoin and Train histories other than early New England roots, and I reluctantly concluded that in most cases the audience for the three volumes would be quite different. Indeed, few outside my own immediate family will have an interest in all three books. As a result, each of the three volumes is published as an independent unit.

So much for the evolution of the enterprise of which these memoirs are an integral part.

Each of the Bowdoin and Train family books contains extensive credits to various sources upon which I relied in their writing. In this *Memoir,* the principal source is my own recollection, increasingly unreliable. My wife, Aileen, has been a constant help and, indeed, much of my life is also the story of her life.

As to acknowledgments, I have a major debt to Catherine Williams, who has typed and retyped my drafts and redrafts. For her diligence and patience I am enormously grateful. I am likewise grateful to Aileen for many of the photographs in the book.

It is customary, I know, to extend thanks to one's editor. In this case, as will become readily apparent, I have been my own editor.

Russell E. Train
Washington, D.C.
March 1999

Introduction

I have endeavored to set out in this memoir as full an account of my own life as I think my readers can reasonably be expected to endure. However, it is not just a record of my own life, since I use the opportunity to write about my grandmother Train, my aunt Susan Train Hand and uncle Augustus Noble Hand, my aunt Grace (Dargee) Train Whitney and my uncle Myron Whitney, my Savage cousins, and my Payson/Parker cousins, among others. Of course, many of these individuals also appear in this book's companion volume, *The Train Family*. In that connection, it is important that these reminiscences be read together with the chapters devoted to the lives of my grandparents, parents, and the Hands as well as those chapters in *The Bowdoin Family* devoted to my wife Aileen's parents and her own early life.

Since both *The Bowdoin Family* and *The Train Family* set out in detail the lives of forebears in North America, this memoir largely ignores family history. Aileen and I both descend from early colonial stock, John Trayne having emigrated from Scotland in 1634 and Pierre Baudouin, a French Huguenot, in 1685, both settling in the Massachusetts Bay Colony.

From then on, the two family histories diverge radically. Based in Boston, Pierre Baudouin's son James Bowdoin built one of the largest mercantile fortunes in the colonies. The latter's son James II became a major political leader in the Revolutionary and post-Revolutionary War period, serving as the second governor of Massachusetts. He was also a "man of the enlightenment" and a founder and first president of the American Society of Arts and Sciences. When his son, James III, Jefferson's minister to Spain, died without issue, the Bowdoin line passed through James II's daughter, Elizabeth, Lady Temple, and thence through her daughter Elizabeth, wife of Thomas Lindall Winthrop, to their daughter Sarah, who married George Sullivan, son of early Massachusetts governor James Sullivan. Their son, George Richard James Sullivan, great-great-grandson of James II, graduated from West Point, changed his name to Bowdoin, settled in New York City, married Frances (Fanny) Hamilton, granddaughter of Alexander Hamilton, and conducted a successful law practice.

George Richard James' son, George Sullivan Bowdoin, became a partner in J. P. Morgan and Co. and an intimate of Morgan. George Sullivan's son, Temple Bowdoin, Aileen's grandfather, was also a partner in J. P. Morgan. Both men and their families were prominent New Yorkers who played significant roles in the business, social, and philanthropic lives of the city. Aileen's father, George Temple Bowdoin, an only surviving child, made his home in New York City and at Oyster Bay, Long Island. Unsuccessful in his one business venture, he focused his energies on sailing, shooting, enjoying the company of his friends, and, particularly during his marriage to Emily Ligon, a very active social life. With their three daughters, Aileen (Train), Helen (Spaulding), and Judy (Key), the Bowdoin family once again ran out of male heirs.

The history of the Train family is very different in many respects from that of the Bowdoins, not the least being that they had no lack of male heirs. Thus, while nowhere a common name, Train descendants are scattered throughout the country. The first five generations of Trains in America—John I (the settler), John II, John III, Samuel I, and Samuel II—were farmers who settled initially in Watertown, now part of Boston, and then moved west to Weston. The home of Samuel II still stands in Weston and is a substantial white, frame colonial structure.

These were people of modest means and modest educations. They were devout and the Bible was probably the principal and perhaps the only book in their homes. Life on the edge of the wilderness was doubtless hard, and for these early Trains it would have been a constant struggle to provide for their numerous progeny. Their world and their horizons were largely confined to the community around them, and military service may often have provided their only glimpse of a wider world. Trains fought in King Philip's War, the French and Indian War, and the Revolution. Trains were at Lexington, Saratoga, and Valley Forge.

With American independence and the end of the eighteenth century, the pattern of life for the Trains began to change and horizons broadened. Charles Train, the son of Samuel II, graduated from Harvard in 1805, and, caught up in the religious revival that swept New England at the time, became a Baptist minister and the pastor of the First Baptist Church of Framingham. He also served several terms as a member of the state legislature. His son Charles Russell Train graduated from Brown University and Harvard Law School, served as a member of Congress during the Civil War, left his seat to volunteer as an officer with a Massachusetts regiment, and fought at Antietam. He later served seven terms as attorney general of Massachusetts and established a successful law practice in Boston.

Charles Russell's son Charles Jackson Train, my grandfather, graduated from Exeter and then the Naval Academy in 1865. He built his home in Washington. He died suddenly in China in 1906 while commander in chief of the U.S. Asiatic Fleet. His son Rear Admiral Charles Russell Train graduated from the Naval Academy in 1900. He married Errol Cuthbert Brown of an old Washington family and there they made their home and brought up my two brothers, Cuthbert and Middleton, and myself.

So much for family background. I have generally adhered to a chronological order in describing events but have not hesitated to depart from that pattern where convenient. I have probably accorded as much space to trivia as to important milestones in my life. However, since this account is being privately published for primarily a family audience, I have not felt it necessary to produce a more commercially acceptable product. Thus, I have tried to make a record that is as complete as I can make it rather than emphasizing readability.

A major participant in this memoir is, of course, my wife, Aileen Bowdoin. Our marriage not only is the central fact of my own life but also provides the connecting link between the Bowdoins and the Trains that gives these companion volumes their rationale. I do not attempt to cover Aileen's early life here because the essential facts have been set out in *The Bowdoin Family*, in the chapters on her father and mother, George Temple Bowdoin and Emily Ligon (Bowdoin) Foley, and in the chapter devoted to Aileen and her two sisters.

One area in which I go into considerably less detail than I might involves my experience with environmental matters both in government and in the private sector. Since that experience has been integral to my career and is in some ways unique, it deserves fuller treatment than is appropriate here. As a result, I have provided what I hope is an adequate summary of that aspect of my life but leave to another day a more extensive account.

When writing a memoir, I am sure that one's memory can be highly selective. Thus, I have doubtless overlooked no event that makes me look like a hero or even merely casts me in a favorable light while conveniently forgetting anything negative. So be it. Overall, however, I think I have given a reasonably honest account.

One of the unusual aspects of my civilian public service, which spanned the years 1948-1977, is the fact that, coming from the voteless District of Columbia, I had absolutely no political base in any normal sense whatsoever. Despite that handicap, I was the beneficiary of political appointments at a fairly high level throughout most of that period.

As I have set down the events of my life, I have been constantly struck by the role that mere chance and happenstance seem to have played, and I remain amazed at the unexpected turns my life has taken. Nevertheless, one does make choices as opportunities arise, and I firmly believe that, to a large degree, we chart our own course in life. We are not helpless pawns with a predestined fate.

No matter how you look at it, life is a fascinating, unpredictable game. That's the fun of it! And, let's face it, I have been a very, very fortunate guy.

Biographical Summary

Born Jamestown, Rhode Island.	June 4, 1920
Graduated St. Albans School, Washington, D.C.	1937
Graduated Princeton University.	1941
Military service, World War II	July 1, 1941-January 1946
Graduated Columbia University Law School.	1948
Admitted District of Columbia Bar.	1948
Attorney, Joint Committee on Internal Revenue Taxation, U.S. Congress.	1949-1953
Clerk (Chief of Staff), Committee on Ways and Means, U.S. House of Representatives.	1953-1954
Married Aileen Ligon Bowdoin.	1954
Minority Advisor, Committee on Ways and Means.	1955-1956
Head, Legal Advisory Staff, Treasury Department.	1956-1957
Judge, U.S. Tax Court.	1957-1965
Founded African Wildlife Leadership Foundation.	1961
Founding director, World Wildlife Fund.	1961
President, The Conservation Foundation.	1965-1969
Member, National Water Commission.	1966-1968
Chairman, Task Force on Environment for President-elect Nixon.	1968
Under Secretary, Department of the Interior.	1969
Chairman, Council on Environmental Quality, Executive Office of the President.	1970-1973
Administrator, Environmental Protection Agency.	1973-1977
President, World Wildlife Fund-U.S.	1978-1984
Chairman, World Wildlife Fund-U.S.	1985-1994
Chairman Emeritus, World Wildlife Fund-U.S.	1994-present

A
MEMOIR

My father, Charles Russell Train,
Captain, U.S.N., Rome, 1918

My mother, Errol Cuthbert Train,
and my brothers, Middy and
Cuth, c. 1916

CHAPTER 1

Childhood

MY BROTHERS and I grew up in Washington, D.C., in the aftermath of World War I in an era marked by Prohibition, the Depression, and World War II. My parents, Charles Russell Train and Errol Cuthbert Train, and my two older brothers, Cuthbert (Cuth) Russell Train and Middleton (Mid or Middy) George Charles Train, had spent the World War I years in Rome where my father was the naval attaché at our embassy. I have always understood that he had the longest continuous tour of service in the war zone of any U.S. naval officer. My parents loved Italy and made friends there among the American community with whom they remained close for the rest of their lives, not to mention numerous Italian friends.

While the war and Italy seemed as far away as the moon to me as a child, there were constant reminders of Italy in our family life. Much of the furniture in our Georgetown house had come from Italy. Except for family portraits, the paintings on the walls were Italian. Alabaster lamps from Italy hung from the ceiling of the drawing room. Much of our table china had come from Italy. We were apt to have spaghetti for lunch on Saturdays—still my favorite food—and the occasional gnocchi or risotto. Finally, my parents would break into Italian at the table from time to time—both for the fun of it and, I suspect, to cut me out of the conversation.

For most of my growing up, I was the lone child at home. Both my brothers were considerably older—Cuth by 11 years and Mid by 7. They were away at college and at boarding school by the time I was 6 or 7. As a result, I never really experienced the sibling rivalries and interactions common to a more closely-aged family. Indeed, I have been struck by how much time I spent as a child either alone or without contemporary companions. I was in no sense a neglected child, as

At Jamestown, 1923.
From top: Cuth, Mid, and the author

I was always the recipient of loving care and affection, but I was, in effect, an only child for much of the time. Moreover, the children of the friends of my parents were mostly older than I. To this day, I am quite comfortable being by myself and amusing myself by such lone pursuits as reading, writing, walking, and book collecting. As a boy, I was a stamp collector.

Launching in Rhode Island

I WAS BORN at Jamestown, Rhode Island, on Narragansett Bay, on June 4, 1920, a little over a year after my parents' return from five years abroad. They were both 40 at the time, and I like to think that my arrival on the scene was part of their homecoming celebration. Be that as it may, I always understood that I was born in the midst of a violent thunderstorm. I have never liked them since.

My father, a Navy captain, commanded a squadron of destroyers at

At Jamestown, 1923

the time and in those days our Navy was concentrated on the Atlantic Coast. His ships were based at Norfolk, Virginia, and came north with the fleet to summer station in Narragansett Bay. The Navy was a good life in my grandfather's and father's days. My grandfather had graduated from the Naval Academy in 1865 and had died at Chefoo, China, in 1906 while commanding the U.S. Asiatic Fleet. My father had graduated from the Naval Academy in 1900.

Jamestown was mostly a summer community on Acushnet Island off Newport and reached then by ferry. My parents rented two different cottages there during the summers of 1920-1923, and I was born in what was known as the Old Green Farm.

As might be expected, I have essentially no recollection of those summers at Jamestown. Curiously, when Aileen and I got married, I learned that her previous husband, Edward Travers, had also been born at Jamestown, where his father had been the summer rector of the Episcopal church. What must the odds be on such a coincidence!

I have driven through Jamestown numerous times over the years, as it is now connected to the mainland by bridges and provides the most direct highway route between Newport and Providence. In the early 1970s, when I was chairman of the Council on Environmental Quality

Displaying my best golf form, 1924

in the Nixon White House, I represented the federal government in ceremonies turning over an old coast artillery site on the southern tip of Acushnet Island to Rhode Island for dedication as a state park. It was nice to have that further association and reassuring to know that our nation no longer felt threatened by a hostile invasion of Narragansett Bay.

While I have never thought of myself as anything but a Washingtonian, news articles have occasionally referred to me as "a native of Rhode Island." Thus, when I was named to the U.S. Tax Court by President Eisenhower, one or more Rhode Island newspapers reported the appointment as involving a "native son." This led the state's lone congressman and a Democrat, Aimee Forand, to call me and say, tongue-in-cheek, "Russ, I think it's great that you are becoming a judge but I object to you being charged to my patronage!"

Washington Roots

WHEN OUR family left Jamestown at the end of the summer, presumably around Labor Day, it was to return to Washington, where my

With Mid, 1925

parents had rented a detached red brick house at the northwest corner of Connecticut Avenue and R Street. The entrance faced on R and the address would have been 2001 R. It was a fair-sized house, as it would have had to have been to accommodate our family of five plus a children's nurse, a cook, and perhaps other staff. The house has been gone for many years, and the corner site has been occupied successively in recent years by Schwartz' Drug Store and now a Starbuck's coffee shop.

The house was certainly convenient to my grandparents' houses. My Brown grandparents lived three doors north at 1710 Connecticut while my grandmother Train's house at 1642 Connecticut was one door below R Street. Thus, both my parents had grown up in Washington and within a few doors of each other. My grandfather, Rear Admiral Charles Jackson Train, U.S.N., had made Washington his home. His own father, Charles Russell Train I, had been a member of Congress from Massachusetts during the Civil War but had never moved his family to Washington. However, on my mother's side, my great-great-grandfather, Obadiah Bruen Brown, had come to Washington in 1807 when the city was in its infancy, and he had made a considerable name for himself as a clergyman, educator, entrepreneur, and politician.

Our R Street house had been the home of Major Marcellus Bailey, a bon vivant and close friend of my grandfather Train. It was there that one warm afternoon around the turn of the century my grandfather and Bailey sampled an experimental drink concocted by Bailey of gin, lime juice, sugar, and crushed ice in a tall glass. They found it excellent, so much so, in fact, that they immediately repaired by carriage to the Chevy Chase Club—no small journey in those days—where they introduced the drink in the men's bar. It was an immediate success and, to this day, a "Major Bailey" is a staple at the Club.

Naturally, I knew nothing of this particular history until it was related to me by my father many years later. In any event, to correct an incorrect version of the origin of the "Major Bailey" which appeared some years ago in *Gourmet* magazine, I wrote a letter to the editor which was published. In that letter I attributed my own sunny disposition at least in part to the salubrious circumstance of the invention of the "Major Bailey" in the house in which I spent my earliest and most formative years.

Move to Georgetown

IN 1924, my parents bought a new home at 3015 Que St., N.W., in Georgetown, where they lived for the rest of their lives and where my brothers and I grew up. The house was a large Italianate Victorian "villa," as described in architectural histories,[1] and shared a common wall with a twin house at 3013 which belonged to the Nicolson family.[2] In those days, a front porch stretched the width of both houses, separated in the center by a wooden railing. The house was of three stories, with high ceilings on the first two, thick brick walls and a cupola on

1. See, for example, Scott, Pamela, and Lee, Antoinette J. *Buildings of the District of Columbia.* Oxford University Press, New York (1993), p. 410.
2. Grandparents of Aileen's and my friends, Alice (Mrs. Robinson) McIlvaine and Stratton (Mrs. David) McKillop.

3015 Que Street, N.W., Washington

top, full basement below. It was one of eight houses, built in four pairs, each pair being quite different, known as Cooke Row, built in 1868-1869 by Henry David Cooke, a Georgetown banker.

Moving to Georgetown must have been a wrench for my parents. My guess is that real estate was cheaper in Georgetown at the time and that this was a decisive factor in their move. They paid $17,000 for the house, a good portion of the money borrowed. I always understood that among the other houses they had looked at was Dumbarton Oaks, a short distance away on R Street, for which something like $37,500 was being asked. Of course, in those days, Dumbarton Oaks was an old Victorian house in which John Calhoun had once lived. It had not yet achieved the Georgian magnificence it later attained under the ownership of Mr. and Mrs. Robert Woods Bliss with their Carter's Little Liver Pills fortune.

Cuth and Middy were already students at St. Albans School, but I was still a small child when we moved to Georgetown. My nurse was Verena Leonhardt, who was a beloved fixture in all our lives for at least

Verena Leonhardt, beloved nurse for my brothers and me and later housekeeper for our parents, shown many years later with my son at a family celebration, 1965

40 years. Her older sister, Frieda, had taken care of Cuth prior to my family's going to Rome in 1914 but had left to be married and her place had been taken by Verena. They were Germans from the little town of Schopfheim in the Black Forest of Baden. Verena had accompanied the family to Rome but when war broke out she had returned to Germany to avoid internment.[3] After the war, she rejoined the family in Washington, became a U.S citizen, and remained with my parents as housekeeper and general factotum until shortly before they died. She was affectionate, loyal, unfailingly honest, faithful to her Lutheran upbringing, and incredibly hardworking.

Our cook at the time and for a good many years was Sarah Nelson, a large, cheerful black woman who initially lived in the basement in a small cubbyhole of a room off the kitchen where she managed a woodstove. Her daughter, Ruby, came in the afternoons to serve tea and dinner. In 1928, when I suspect my parents were feeling a bit more plush and perhaps had profited a bit from the bull market, they built a kitchen wing on the back of the house, putting the kitchen on the same level as the dining room and adding a sleeping porch—basically,

3. I happened to write this portion of my account on December 7, 1994, the anniversary of Pearl Harbor and the U.S. entry into World War II. Aileen and I were on a Russian icebreaker, heading southeast through the heavy pack ice of the Weddell Sea on our way to visit the emperor penguin rookeries on the coast of Antarctica.

an unheated room with casement windows—over the kitchen. The sleeping porch is where we three boys slept, winter and summer, until Cuth and Mid went away to school or college. I remember to this day how frigid my bed was when I got into it on cold nights. There were, of course, no electric blankets. Verena made blue wool foot bags for all three of us. They were about four feet long, which was ample for me to get entirely into at the time.

Friends and Neighbors

AFTERNOON TEA was a never-failing ritual at our house. My mother would take a nap in her room in the early afternoon, write letters, pay her bills, call friends and then come down for tea in the drawing room at 4:30. She sat on a large red sofa, the tea table before her laden with an elaborate silver tea service, which the maid carried in on a tray and set before her. There would be a three-tiered cake and sandwich stand ("caddy") just to the right of the tea table and my preferred spot was a large armchair within easy reach of the food.

Tea was the time that friends came to call, perhaps close neighbors as well. Lidie Mitchell, Susan Jay, Colonel Louis (Louie) Little, Katherine Dunlap, Connie Jordan, and Cornelia Lane were among the regulars. Years later, after Aileen and I were married, her father, George Bowdoin, would call on my parents at teatime when he was in town. My mother thought very highly of George, in no small part because she considered that he had beautiful manners.

Aunt Lidie Mitchell had been a childhood friend and bridesmaid of my mother's. She was married to Washington's foremost surgeon, Dr. Jim Mitchell, and was a frequent caller with a snuffling pug dog. It was only years later that my mother learned that Aunt Lidie's home life was desperately unhappy and that this fact helped explain the frequency of her visits.

Louie Little was a retired colonel in the Marines and married to Elsie Cobb, a well-known New York decorator. They had lived all over the world from Paris to Peking. His visits for tea by himself that I recall must have been years later after she died. In any event, he was always accompanied by a white Sealyham dog who matched his master's courtly manners by ceremoniously and vigorously wiping his feet on the doormat before entering the house. The Littles lived in a handsome, white frame house at 3010 O Street, N.W., where Paul and Phyllis Nitze later lived for many years.[4]

Katherine Dunlap was the widow of my godfather, Marine General Hal Dunlap. He had been killed while they were visiting France around 1930 when a cave with prehistoric wall paintings collapsed. He and Aunt Katherine had left the cave but their guide, a local farmer's wife, was still inside. Uncle Hal went back in the cave to rescue her and the roof collapsed on him. He was said to have been slated to be the next commandant of the Marine Corps and there is a statue of him at Quantico.

My mother was always partial to Marine officers. In those days, graduates of the Naval Academy could elect to transfer to the Marine Corps and those near the bottom of the class often did, suspecting that their career in the Navy would be handicapped by their class standing. My father, in fact, stood quite low in his class, as did his closest friends, such as Frank Berrien and Hugo Osterhaus. (Standing was entirely determined by academic grades.)

Connie (Mrs. Eldridge) Jordan was a lively widow who lived three doors above us in Cooke's Row. Her house was distinguished by having a square tower that rose from the front door and was said to be the inspiration for the murder mystery novel *The Thirty-Nine Steps* by Mary Roberts Rinehart, who lived at 2419 Massachusetts Avenue in a house now occupied by the Embassy of Zambia. Connie always wore black and white and usually a broad black straw hat. Likewise, she always wore a single white carnation, the daily gift of a former Spanish ambassador who had been her devoted admirer. Connie entertained at lunch every Sunday.

---

4. There is a photo of Louis Little as a young man (although already a colonel) sitting on steps in Peking with Wallis Simpson, later the Duchess of Windsor, in about 1925. Vickers, Hugo. *The Private World of the Duke and Duchess of Windsor.* Abbeville Press, New York (1996), p. 126.

One house nearer than Connie Jordan's was that of Colonel and Mrs. Henry Latrobe Roosevelt (Harry and Eleanor). He was a Philadelphia cousin of the president and was an Assistant Secretary of the Navy. (This, of course, was before the consolidation of the services into the Department of Defense.) The Roosevelts became good friends of my parents, and their children, particularly their daughter Eleanor, of my older brothers. Eleanor later married Reverdy Wadsworth, a close friend of Mid's, who was the son of Jim Wadsworth, a member of Congress and former senator, from Geneseo, New York. The latter's father had also been senator from New York and had appointed my father to the Naval Academy in 1896. (Jim Wadsworth was married to the daughter of John Hay, Lincoln's private secretary and later Secretary of State in the McKinley administration. Hay was a friend of my Brown grandparents and provided my mother with a card of introduction when she visited Europe. The Wadsworth daughter, Eve, became a noted nightclub singer in New York and married Stuart Symington, later Secretary of the Air Force and senator from Missouri. Their son, Jim Symington, a former member of Congress from St. Louis and chief of protocol, inherits his mother's musical talent. A practicing attorney, he is also "Proctor" of the Alibi Club.)

Across Que Street and slightly further west was a large red brick house, the home of Marine General and Mrs. William Wright, the parents of Admiral Gerauld (Jerry) Wright and Marge Key, mother of my late brother-in-law, Al Key (married to Aileen's sister, Judy). Mrs. Wright, known as Ma, was a strong-willed, frequently profane lady.

Later on, Donald and Catherine Hiss (he a brother of Alger), good friends of the family, lived close to the Wrights. Also, across the street at about 3010 was Charlie Baer's cleaning establishment that we patronized for years and, next to it, Jenkins' Market which we did *not* patronize. Never to my knowledge did anyone from our household purchase anything from Mr. Jenkins, who lived in a row house next to his shop. I can only imagine that there had been some disagreement or affront that occurred when we first moved in. In any event, our marketing was done, mostly by Verena in those days, at the Piggly Wiggly next to Morgan's Drug Store at 30th and P. The Piggly Wiggly is now an antique shop. When the Piggly Wiggly disappeared, my mother transferred her marketing to the Safeway north of R on Wisconsin, known widely as the "Social Safeway."

When my mother did the marketing, she generally drove to the store except when gasoline was rationed during World War II. However, we were seldom a two-car family. There was a succession of cars but the only one I recall from my early days was a large green Studebaker with red-spoked wheels. Years later when Mid was living at home after college and before the war, he kept a car in the drive referred to as the "Brown Bomber," a somewhat disreputable-appearing vehicle whose front passenger seat was propped up on a pair of bricks.

Naval Duty

OF COURSE, my father was on sea duty a fair amount of the time, and, once Cuth and Mid were both away at college or boarding school (Princeton and Choate, respectively), my mother and I constituted the family at home. When we moved to the Que Street house, my father was stationed at the Navy Department in Washington, then located in World War I-era, so-called "temporary" buildings or "temps," stretching along the south side of Constitution Avenue from 17th Street west. (It was not until the Nixon administration that they were finally torn down. Nixon reportedly said he didn't want them replaced by simply more vacant parkland but by something with more public utility such as the Tivoli Gardens amusement park outside Copenhagen. He got more parkland.)

Sea duty in the 1920s meant the Atlantic Fleet and my father's ships normally were based at Norfolk or Hampton Roads, Virginia, with a summer station in the north such as Narragansett Bay. He commanded a transport ship, the U.S.S. *Henderson*, from October 1924 to June 1926, and took Cuth and Mid on a winter cruise to the Caribbean on her. Then he received command of the *Utah*, our oldest battleship at the time. I recall the *Utah* being off Annapolis on a Fourth of July in either 1927 or 1928, and my mother and I visiting the ship. I remember hating the banging of the salute gun. I was always "gun-shy" of loud bangs, whether from thunder, firecrackers, or large guns. Doubtless that is why I ended up in the field artillery in World War II.

Even when on sea duty at Norfolk, my father usually managed to get home on weekends. He would take the Norfolk boat Friday night to Washington, arriving home on Saturday morning in time for break-fast. On Sunday evening, Mother and I would drive him back down to the dock on Maine Avenue—now all seafood restaurants—for a 7:00 p.m. departure. The attendant at the gangway would greet him as a regular passenger. Years later, in 1955, shortly after Bowdy had been born, Aileen and I took the same overnight boat down the Bay to Nor-folk with our car on board, fully loaded for Hobe Sound, Florida. It was a delightful way to travel—small, snug, white-painted cabins, and a good dinner served by white-jacketed stewards. It was on that par-ticular trip that we first visited Beaufort, South Carolina, to see the homes and graves of my Cuthbert forebears and also Charleston and Middleton Place.

Early French Instruction

MY FIRST experience with any form of group instruction was at the age of five when I attended Madame Bouchard's French class at her house on New Hampshire Avenue, a half-block north of Dupont Cir-cle. My fellow sufferers in this ordeal were Orme Wilson, John Da-vidge, and Henry Ellis—all of whom were close friends of my youth and, except for Henry Ellis, of my later life. John died unexpectedly in 1980 and Orme in 1990. Henry I have not seen for many years, although we talked by phone not long ago, and he lives in Massachu-setts. Why our parents thought it made sense for us to receive instruc-tion in French when we had not yet learned to read or write English is a puzzler.

Anyway, we suffered through that episode and survived. I learned precious little French and never did develop any facility with foreign languages. I studied French all through school up to and including my

With Orme Wilson, c. 1925

sophomore year at Princeton and never learned to speak or write it at more than a very rudimentary level. That had something to do with the way languages were taught in those days and a lot to do with just plain intellectual laziness on my part, I am afraid.

We children gathered with our nurses in the afternoons, often at Sheridan Circle, and then later almost always in Montrose Park about three blocks away from my house. I have always guessed that my friendship with Orme was founded on the friendship between Verena and his nurse, Helen Taylor. We probably started playing together at Sheridan Circle while my family still lived at Connecticut and R because Orme's family lived at that time on R just west of Florida Avenue.

Potomac School

AT THE AGE of six, I entered Potomac School, located on the south side of California Street midway between Connecticut and Phelps Place. I had not gone to kindergarten, which I imagine my parents considered a waste of time and money. Our grandchildren today start in nursery or pre-school when they are about two! I do think that they tend to be far better informed about a wide range of subjects than I was at a comparable grade level although they cannot seem to spell and do not seem to learn much about geography. Perhaps if you master computers, these deficiencies make no difference.

With Orme, Sheridan Circle,
Washington, 1926

When I attended Potomac, it was coeducational through the fourth
grade, following which the boys went off to other schools. Girls could
continue through the eighth grade. I went through the first and second grades with reasonable ease and a decision was made to have me
skip the third. This was a somewhat fateful decision because it meant
that on the average I was at least a year younger than my classmates
from then through college. Given the fact that I was probably fairly
slow to mature, both physically and socially—a "late bloomer" is the
way I would prefer to think of it—the age differential gave me something of a handicap all through school. I don't think parents thought
too much in those days about the social consequences of such decisions, but I know that, as a result of my own experience, I was always
sensitive to the matter when it came to my own children's education.

Verena walked me to Potomac, and I presume back, rain, snow, or
shine. Down Que Street and across the "Buffalo" Bridge (now officially Dumbarton Bridge), around Sheridan Circle, over R to 22nd
and then up the 22nd Street steps to S, up Phelps Place and right on
California to the school. Crossing the Que Street bridge, I could look
over the south side and see just below me on the west side of Rock
Creek car barns and a round house for streetcars. The space is now
occupied by a large apartment house. A little further south at P and
22nd Street, where a filling station has now stood for many years, was
a large public riding stable. From there, horses could be ridden down

to the bridle path along Rock Creek. On the whole, however, there has been remarkably little change in the visual appearance of that route over the years.

While I do not remember much about those daily walks, I do remember one morning at 22nd and R when the large Slocum house on the northwest corner (now the Pakistan Chancery) was on fire and there were a number of fire engines at the corner. Among these was one of the old pump vehicles carrying a red, tower-like boiler to generate pressure although, of course, the water itself came from the hydrants along the street. There was an alarm box on that corner and it is still there, although I imagine it has been inoperable for many years. It certainly is unpainted and rusty. In the case of fire, one opened the box and pulled the lever and then waited for the fire engines in order to direct them to the fire. That system was, of course, a great temptation for false alarm addicts, but it was on the whole respected and not abused by the public.

My route to and from school passed right along the boundary of what is now Kalorama Square at S and Phelps Place where Aileen and I have lived since 1978. When I walk our Labrador retriever in the late afternoon and before going to bed at night, I am retracing steps I was first making over 70 years ago. Most of the buildings along the way have remained unchanged over the years, but I feel no jog of memory as I walk along. The Kalorama Square condominium town houses occupy the site where the Holton Arms School gymnasium stood for many years. The school proper was located in the large red brick building in the 2100 block of S Street—until recently the national headquarters of the Scientology "church." The brick house with white columns located on the Phelps Place side of the Scientology building, now an English language institute, was in my youth the home of Mr. and Mrs. Jack Biddle. He was a banker and a great friend of my father's. The two of them used to go duck hunting together. Their son, Sam, was one of Middy's closest friends. In later years, after World War II and before he married, Sam would walk to and from work past my Brown grandparents' house on Connecticut. If he saw Grandmama in her accustomed position in the bay window, he would bow and smile. As a result, she invariably referred to him as "sweet, smiling Sam."

Prior to being the site of the Holton Arms gymnasium, the Kalorama Square property had held a frame octagonal house, built by Leroy Tuttle in the 1880s. It was quite a landmark when I walked that way as a boy and I remember it well. Leroy Tuttle was the father of Adelaide Morgan who, with her husband Carroll Morgan, were great friends of my parents and lived opposite the Chevy Chase Club at 1 Quincy Street, now owned by our friends Frank and Patricia Saul. Leroy Place that intersects with Phelps Place was named for Tuttle's family.

I don't recall whether we stayed at Potomac for lunch or not. I do know that on Fridays my mother picked me up in the car before lunch. She would already have picked up my grandfather Brown at his office, and I climbed into the back seat. We drove back to Que Street for lunch, which invariably featured fish, which Grandpapa loved—halibut, flounder, or shad in season. I don't think "boned" shad existed in those days, and I recall a steady procession of small fish bones appearing from Grandpapa's mouth as he chewed, to be plucked away and deposited on his plate. His Friday luncheon with us was a fixture, and it gave my mother a regular opportunity to visit with him. Moreover, hardly a day passed that my mother did not stop at 1710 to see her own mother, usually in the late morning.

I remember very little about my time at Potomac. I remember some of my classmates. John Davidge was in the fourth grade when I entered it. Orme was away in Argentina where his father was in our embassy (when Peter Jay was U.S. ambassador). I remember all my teachers: Miss Rice, the head of the school, in the first grade; Miss Hoover (whose father was "Ike" Hoover, the chief usher of the White House) in the second; and Miss Ruprecht in the fourth. The latter also taught our daughter Nancy in the fourth grade at Potomac some 28 years later. I remember standing at the blackboard in the fourth grade, struggling unsuccessfully with an arithmetic problem. I remember several school plays and having to dress up variously as a Pilgrim, a Dutch boy, and a Revolutionary War soldier. In the latter role, I had my longest and only lines: "To arms! To arms! The British are coming!" I remember "shop," in which I turned out various ramshackle constructions such as a footstool, which I gave my parents for Christmas. It was also in "shop" that I almost cut off a finger with a hand jigsaw, thus giving early warning of a technological ineptitude that has dogged me all my life.

One reason that Verena walked me to school was that my mother was not an early starter in the mornings. She invariably had breakfast in bed at 7:30—a poached egg on toast, of which she cut off and discarded the white. My father would have breakfast in the dining room in his wrapper—orange juice, oatmeal, two fried eggs, bacon, toast, and coffee, plus the *Washington Post*. Other than at breakfast, I do not remember him being a big eater, but he did love his breakfast. He also exercised fairly regularly—squash and tennis in season, a practice he did not pass on to me. I believe that I ate breakfast either in the dining room or in the pantry, probably at 7:00. I remember hot cereal—oatmeal, cream of wheat, and wheatena, upon which I put large amounts of sugar. Always lots of milk, "to build my bones." When I was ready for school, I would go in to say good morning to my mother and to be inspected. That makes her sound rather distant, which she wasn't. She was warm and affectionate and always took a meticulous interest in my welfare—my health, appearance, performance at school, etc. I always felt that I had a close and easy relationship with her.

By the time I was 7 or 8, and my father was away at sea, I ate dinner regularly with my mother in the dining room. Before dinner, we listened to the radio, an arch-shaped Philco. "Amos and Andy" was a favorite program. When my father was there, we invariably listened to Lowell Thomas and the news. Gabriel Heater was another newscaster that I remember.

CHAPTER 2

Adirondack Summers

MY FAMILY had no regular summer home and my summers, starting in 1923 or 1924, were spent at Elizabethtown, New York, in the Adirondacks, with my father's sister Susan Hand, and her husband, Augustus Noble Hand, at that time federal judge for the Southern District of New York and later of the Second Circuit Court of Appeals.

For one or two summers, my family rented a frame house at Elizabethtown that belonged to the Hands. There I made an unforgettable contribution to the family's general well-being and happiness. I had apparently been in the car when it stopped for gas at a filling station. Somewhat later, moved as always by a spirit of helpfulness, I took the garden hose, turned on the water, removed the car's gas tank cap, and proceeded to fill the tank with high-test water. I was doubtless extremely proud of my effort and very disappointed with the lack of enthusiasm with which it was greeted, particularly by my father.

After my father went to sea again in the fall of 1924, the family gave up having its own house in Elizabethtown, and the Hands took me under their wing for the summers. For the next five years, I spent about three months a year with Aunt Sue and Uncle Gus in the old red brick Hand mansion. I would take the train north from Washington with Grandma T, my Train grandmother. She was partial to the old B&O (Baltimore & Ohio Railroad) which had no access to New York City proper and only went as far as Jersey City. From there we transferred to a ferry to New York and thence by taxi to Grand Central Station where we boarded the "Montrealer" for the overnight trip north, getting off at Westport on Lake Champlain in the early morning.

I remember little of those trips except, once, losing my shoes when they fell out of the open window after I had gone to bed in a lower berth. I was pretty small when that happened, and I cried bitterly over

With my mother, Elizabethtown, 1926

the loss. When I was probably a bit older, I would enjoy lying in a lower berth, shut in by the heavy green curtain, watching the darkened countryside rush past. If it was a moonlit night, it would look as if the fields were snow-covered. Then waking a bit to mysterious stoppings and startings in the dark. All in all, it was a romantic way to travel. We would be met by Mr. Egglesfield, who owned the garage/filling station in Elizabethtown where I had doubtless learned how to fill a gasoline tank, and who drove us the ten miles to Elizabethtown in a Dodge touring car.

The Hand house, certainly the grandest in Elizabethtown, had been built in 1840 by Uncle Gus' grandfather, Augustus C. Hand, who had moved to Elizabethtown with his law practice from Shoreham, Vermont, across Lake Champlain—a town that also had associations with my Grandma T's Tomlinson family. The house was surrounded by quite a large property with a barn and icehouse. A horse and a cow tenanted the barn, the cow being led up the hill behind the house to a pasture on the upper part of the property and led back down again in the evening for milking. The white horse was principally useful in pull-

The author, c. 1926

ing the large rotary lawn mower driven by the farmer, Ernest Smith, who lived with his family in a house at the further end of the lawn, near the cutting and vegetable garden. I recall barrels of apples stored in his cellar. One of my favorite pastimes was riding on Mr. Smith's knee on the mower and helping hold the reins of the horse. The ice-house was a new experience with its blocks of ice cut from a pond and buried in insulating sawdust. It was always deliciously cool on hot summer days. As needed, Mr. Smith unearthed a block of ice from the sawdust, hung it with ice tongs so it could be wiped clean of the sawdust and then took it to the house in a wheelbarrow to replenish the icebox.

There were thick woods running down to the Bouquet (Bo-ket) River, reached by a path that led over a stile, all of this a wonderful playground for a small boy. There was croquet with my grandmother and Aunt Sue and, later, mountain climbs and picnics in the marvelous Adirondacks. There were Sunday morning walks to the small Episcopal church on the hill to hear Dr. Pittman preach. My parents would spend my father's vacation with us, driving from Washington in two long days. I can remember now the excitement of seeing them drive up to the front door. Then there would be tennis at Keene Valley, golf at the nine-hole Cobble Hill course where I learned to caddy, excursions with my father while he painted an oil landscape, and other welcome variations in my activities.

My father loved to paint but had had little formal instruction. However, he had an artist's eye for landscape and color and gave me a heightened appreciation of color at an early age. He would ask me what color I saw in a stretch of water and I would say, "Gray." Then he would proceed to point out the blues and greens, the yellows and purples in that same bit of water. Unfortunately, aside from a few experiments, I have never taken up painting (although I have equipped myself for a start on watercolors), but I know those brief and infrequent times when I was with my father when he painted made a great difference throughout my life in my awareness of color in the world around me.

Aunt Sue and Uncle Gus Hand

AUNT SUE was probably about 50 as I first remember her. She was an intelligent, affectionate, cheerful person and had a wonderful sense of humor, doubtless inherited from her father. (Neither she nor her brother or sister inherited his musical talent.) She was a devout Christian and conservative in terms of proper behavior. She was well read in classical literature and was probably already embarked on her researches into the Train family history. She had no athletic skills insofar as I can recall; I never saw her ride, swim, play tennis or golf, or do any extensive walking. She did join me at croquet on occasion. She read, chatted, sewed, or knitted, wrote letters, picked flowers in the cutting garden—I particularly remember masses of sweet peas in a riot of color—and did all the other chores incident to running a fair-sized household.

Uncle Gus was one of the most distinguished jurists in the country. He was a tall, heavy man whom I recall as slightly leaning forward as he walked. (My grandfather Brown gave the same impression of tilting forward and then having to move his feet to keep from falling down. It must have been somewhat risky to come to a sudden halt.) I have a photo of an oil portrait of Uncle Gus in his judicial robes, heavy browed, very serious, and somewhat daunting. Fortunately, he smiled frequently, loved a joke, and laughed easily. I can see and hear him laughing now, his whole body heaving with his chuckles. He brought his workload from the court with him to Elizabethtown and was usually busy for much of the day in the "Office"—a one-story, brick edifice, with at least three large rooms, built by his grandfather, Augustus, as his law office and used by his father, Richard, as well. There were complete sets of the federal and New York state law reports along the walls and woodstoves in each office. His law clerk frequently came to stay to work with him. (See *The Train Family* for a fuller discussion of the Hands.)

As imposing as Uncle Gus was, he was affectionate and welcoming to me as a child. I slept in the little bedroom directly over the front door and next to Aunt Sue and Uncle Gus' bedroom. In the early morning, I would sometimes go in their room—I assume by invitation—and climb into the big four-poster bed between them. Uncle Gus' mustache was an impressive and bristly adornment and being in bed with him was a bit like being in bed with a bear. Aunt Sue would usually get up and leave us, and Uncle Gus would tell me stories of camping in the Adirondack wilderness as a boy with his cousin Learned Hand, of huddling around the campfire while panthers screamed in the darkness about them—heady stuff for a six-year-old!

Serena and Bill Savage

THE HANDS had one child, a daughter, Serena, my only first cousin. She was much older, graduating from Bryn Mawr in 1927. She was full of fun and a great favorite in the family. I recall her having a houseguest on one occasion, a classmate from Bryn Mawr—Cornelia Otis Skinner, the famous writer and stage actress. Serena married William Lyttleton Savage in the summer of 1925. Cuth was an usher, and I remember the reception in the garden of the Elizabethtown house, the men in the wedding party all in dark coats and white pants.

Bill and Serena had three children: Arthur, Sue, and Serena. (See *The Train Family* for a fuller description of the Savage family.) With the sudden and totally unexpected death of their mother, from a brain aneurysm, at the early age of 49, these three became my closest cousins. Art, a lawyer in New York, became a leader in the conservationist battle to protect the Adirondacks. Sue, like her mother a Bryn Mawr graduate, was one of the first two women trustees of Princeton and she and I served on the board together. Her husband, T. Guthrie Speers, is a Presbyterian minister and was pastor of the church in New Canaan, Connecticut, for many years. He has recently retired and they now live in Center Sandwich, New Hampshire. Serena lives in Baltimore and is married to Jerry Baum, who, after a career in business, now directs a foundation whose principal focus is the education of inner-city youths. Serena is in business.

Aunt Eleanor and Uncle Phil Parker

THERE WERE houseguests, usually family, who came for one to two weeks. Aunt Eleanor and Uncle Phil Parker were regulars. She was the daughter of Althea (Aunt Attie) and Gilbert Payson. Aunt Attie (whom I never met) was a sister of my grandfather Train. Therefore, Aunt Eleanor Parker was a first cousin of my father and Aunt Sue. Her husband, Uncle Phil, was a Massachusetts state judge, and he was a tall, silver-haired, rather austere-looking man who wore pince-nez on a long black ribbon. He and Uncle Gus enjoyed a lot of legal talk. Their visits were my first introduction to the Payson/Parker family connection. They lived in Brookline, a suburb of Boston, and summered with their clan at Pochet Island on Cape Cod, which I later visited.

Learned Hand

ANOTHER VISITOR was Uncle Gus' first cousin Judge Learned Hand, one of the best-known jurists in the country.[1] He and Uncle Gus had been brought up practically as brothers and sat together on the Second Circuit Court of Appeals for many years. Learned was a charismatic presence under any circumstance, and he was never too grand to talk to a small boy of perhaps 5 or 6. I remember one occasion when he and I took a walk together down the sidewalk that ran in front of the Hand property in Elizabethtown and was separated from it by a low, dry, stone wall. Old sugar maples grew along the wall and spread their contorted roots toward the sidewalk. Cousin Learned held my hand and, pointing to the roots, proceeded to describe to me how the fairies came out to play among those roots in the moonlight. The image has never left me.

Many years later, when I was a judge of the United States Tax Court, I saw Learned Hand at a banquet of the American Law Institute at the Mayflower Hotel in Washington. He was old and beginning to fail at the time, although not enough to keep him from singing several lines from Gilbert and Sullivan's "Trial by Jury" from the dais during dinner. In any event, before dinner, I went up and introduced myself and he promptly confused me with my father. "Judge Hand," I said, "I am Russell Train and I am a judge of the United States Tax Court." "That's odd," he said, "I always thought you were an admiral in the Navy!"

Cuth and Mid were also with us off and on during those summers in the Adirondacks. Mid went off to camp a couple of years at Camp Wachusett on Lake Winnipesaukee in New Hampshire (run by the Reverend "Pop" Henderson, chaplain and athletic coach of St. Albans School), where Mid won the Camp Spirit Award for which he was teased for years after. They had friends of their age in the Elizabeth-

---

1. For a recent and definitive biography with many references to A. N. Hand, see Gunther, Gerald. *Learned Hand—The Man and the Judge.* Alfred A. Knopf, New York (1994). The book has a foreword by my friend the late Justice Lewis F. Powell, Jr.

Adirondacks, 1929.
(The foot is impressive.)

town neighborhood, particularly within the Wadhams family. Mrs. Wadhams was Uncle Gus' sister and her children, Dick, Marcia, Liz, and Jimmy, were all friends. Jimmy was the nearest to me in age but was still several years older. Actually, as I am sure has already become apparent, I had few regular playmates of my own age during these summer vacations. I became accustomed to occupying myself.

Cuth did a lot of mountain climbing and became enamored of the Adirondacks, eventually buying a house at Keene Valley in the high peak region. Always gregarious, he had a host of friends in the area.

Elizabethtown was a busy place at the time. The county seat of Essex County, it was also a summer resort with several rambling, white two- or three-story frame hotels. At one—the Deer's Head Inn—I got an early haircut. On the street where the Hand house stood was a drugstore with a "fountain" and little round tables where you could enjoy a chocolate ice cream soda. A banana split was more daring, and I wasn't old enough for that. There was a hardware store and, up a long, narrow flight of wooden stairs, a photographer's studio. I think

Mr. Underwood was his name, and I can still remember the smell of the chemical developers he used. Further along was the post office and Grandma T and I would walk there to get the mail every weekday. When Uncle Phil Parker was staying, there was always a pink-wrapped *Boston Transcript* in the mail. The pace of life would doubtless seem pretty torpid today!

CHAPTER 3

Early Youth

IN THE FALL of 1928, Herbert Hoover was elected president and the time was arriving for great changes in the United States and the world, not least in the Train family. Hoover did a post-election trip to South America and the battleship *Utah,* my father commanding, was ordered south to pick up the president-elect and his party, including Mrs. Hoover, at Montevideo, Uruguay. The assignment was a fateful one for my father. He liked the Hoovers and they liked him, and they spent about two weeks together on the homeward voyage. There was a small press party on board as well, including the dean of Washington political columnists, Mark Sullivan, with whom my father developed a warm friendship. (Sullivan's son, Mark, Jr., married my friend John Davidge's older sister Martha.)

St. Albans School

IN THE FALL of 1929, I entered St. Albans, an Episcopal school on the Washington Cathedral close. With the exception of Form II (eighth grade) when I was at St. George's in Newport, I spent the next eight years at St. Albans, graduating and going to Princeton in 1937. Cuth had graduated in 1927 and was already in his third year at Princeton. Mid had gone to Choate and would have been then in the Fourth Form, the only one of us to go away to boarding school (although I boarded from time to time at both St. George's and St. Albans). Mid was small for his age, and for some reason my parents decided he would add height if he went away to school. I never understood the logic of that but, in fact, he did add a few inches quite quickly while at Choate.

The Reverend Albert Hawley Lucas, an Episcopal clergyman from

Philadelphia, was headmaster of St. Albans the entire time I was there. He came the same year I did, but to those of us in the Lower School he remained a pretty remote, austere figure. I did not really get to know him until I was in the Upper School. He was big, red-haired, quick-tempered, and demanding of the students whether on the athletic field or in the classroom. (By the way, it occurs to me that, given my current gray or even white hair, my family may not realize that I, too, was once red-headed. My father occasionally called me "Red-top" or, less often, "Carrot-top.")

Many of my male classmates from Potomac were in my St. Albans class. Orme and his family were back from Argentina, and he was in the class, as well as John Davidge, Henry Ellis, Cary Grayson, Tom Wright, and others. Alfred True was our form master, well liked by boys and parents alike. He soon became headmaster of the Lower School.

Father's White House Duty

ON THE COMPLETION of his tour of duty with the *Utah*, in 1929, my father was ordered back to Washington as President Hoover's naval aide. This position had a heavy ceremonial aspect but in those days it also provided an important link between the president and the Navy. (There was a parallel military aide, Colonel Hodges.) There was no National Security Council. Indeed, Hoover was the first president to have a telephone on his desk. My father's office was in the connecting link between the White House proper and the West Wing and occupied space now filled by the press room. His staff included several young naval officers whose duties largely revolved around the various social events at the White House. My parents frequently attended state dinners and became friends with a number of senior officials, such as Charles Francis Adams, Secretary of the Navy. On occasion, they accompanied the Hoovers to Rapidan Camp (now Camp David) in the Blue Ridge Mountains where Hoover enjoyed trout fishing.

Since I was at school during the days, I was mostly aware of the fact that my parents had to go to a lot of official parties. My father was a stickler for being on time for dinners and became extremely impatient with my mother over the matter. I recall one such episode when they were going to the Italian Embassy for dinner. My father had had to get himself into full dress uniform (comparable to white tie and tails) with medals, etc. He paced the downstairs hall while my mother completed her preparations before her dressing table. As time passed, my father became more and more irate, his shouted exhortations for greater speed more and more profane. When they finally arrived at the Italian Embassy and approached the receiving line, my father in all his full-dress, bemedaled glory, my mother looked down and said to him quietly, "You are wearing your bedroom slippers!" And so he was. I guess that evened the score a bit—but only for a time. Patience was not my father's long suit.

Buses and Streetcars

ONE OF THE perks of my father's job as naval aide was that he was entitled to a Navy steward who was, in effect, our driver, and he drove me to school in the mornings. I think he also helped serve the table. I also went to school by bus and streetcar although that would have been when I was a bit older. There was a bus stop close to our front door, and I would take a bus to Wisconsin Avenue where I changed to a streetcar which dropped me at the corner of Massachusetts, right by the school. Streetcars, later augmented by buses, were a principal means of transportation around Washington when I was growing up. There are not many reminders of the streetcars now but O Street west of Wisconsin Avenue in Georgetown is still cobbled and the old tracks are still evident in the middle of the street.

I recall my grandmother Train describing the service when she first lived on Connecticut Avenue and there were horse-drawn trolleys. When she wanted a ride downtown, she would hang a signal of some sort by her front door which the trolley conductor would see on his way up the avenue. When he got to Florida Avenue, which was the end of the line in those days and only one long block further north, he

Old horse-drawn trolley similar to the one that went up Connecticut Avenue to Florida Avenue (Boundary Road) in about 1885, passing both my grandparents' houses

unhitched the horses from the front end of the trolley and hitched them onto the other end and started back down Connecticut. When he came abreast of 1642, he would stop and wait while my grandmother left her house and climbed aboard. Or he would take a package downtown for her. Then and in my youth, the streetcars went around Dupont Circle on the west side. Much later, they were put into a tunnel under the circle. The tunnel is still there but used by auto traffic.

Sports, Particularly Baseball

I WAS GENERALLY a mediocre student and a terrible athlete. Football was compulsory in the Lower School and I hated it. Ditto basketball in the winter term. I was skinny and underweight and most contact sports left me decidedly the worse for wear. Perhaps for that reason I rather enjoyed baseball although I was never much of a star. Soccer was usually fun, probably because I was reasonably fast on my feet. Finally, in the Upper School, I peaked my athletic career by making the tennis team, continuing a long family tradition of devotion to that game.

Baseball was more familiar territory to me than most of the other sports because my father used to take me to games at Griffith Stadium, then the home field for the old Washington Senators, just off 9th and U Streets, a site now part of Howard University. In his own youth, my father had gone with his father to watch the Washington team play when its home field was on Capitol Hill, close to where the Supreme Court is now located. That must have been in the late 1880s and early 1890s. I remember many of the Senators whom I saw play—Joe Cronin, Joe Judge, Buddy Myers at short, Cecil Travis, "Goose" Goslin, and, of course, the great pitcher Walter Johnson (the "Big Train"). Obviously, not all of these played at the same time, as my memory of Senator ball games extends over a number of years. Of course, all this was before the introduction of night baseball.

When my father took me to the ball game, often accompanied by my mother, it was probably on a weekend. We usually sat in the second tier on the first base side. These were always wonderful occasions—the chatter of the players, the roar of the crowd, peanuts (in their shells), popcorn, hot dogs, and soft drinks hawked by vendors in the aisles and then passed or sometimes thrown to the customers. We each kept a meticulous record of the progress of the game on our scorecards. I enjoyed every moment at the ball game. When, under the influence of television, most games came to be played at night, it became difficult to take kids because of the late hours involved. Then, of course, the Washington franchise moved to Minneapolis-St. Paul and the Senators became the Twins. The magic was gone and my interest in baseball faded. Many years later—probably in 1985 or thereabouts—when I happened to be in San Francisco, my friend Walter Haas, who had bought the Oakland A's, asked me to the season's opening game with him and his wife, Evelyn. I sat next to Joe DiMaggio, who autographed my scorecard, and the whole occasion was full of pleasurable nostalgia.

Lindbergh and Other Heroes

SPEAKING OF DiMaggio reminds me that there seem to have been a lot of heroes when I was growing up—Gertrude Ederle, who swam the English Channel, Babe Ruth, Charles Lindbergh, Amelia Earhart, and Admiral Robert Byrd, among others. As Hoover's naval aide, Father got to meet and know a number of such celebrities when they were greeted ceremoniously by the President and Mrs. Hoover. In 1927, when Lindbergh returned in triumph from France on a U.S. cruiser, I stood on the bank of the Potomac at Bolling Air Force Base and cheered as Lindbergh's ship headed for a berth at the Navy Yard. (Today, the Bolling base has been largely converted to non-commissioned officer housing. It is located directly across the Potomac from National Airport.) A day or two later, I stood at the corner of 30th and Que Streets in Georgetown, a few yards from our house, and again cheered Lindbergh as his motorcade came over Que and turned down 30th on its way across the river to Arlington to lay a wreath on the Tomb of the Unknown Soldier—a standard observance for such celebrities.

Today, our heroes—and they are usually more celebrities than true heroes—are largely drawn from the world of entertainment and professional sports, and the latter is probably part of the entertainment world as well. It is primarily in such a field that an individual can keep his or her image before the public sufficiently long to achieve what passes for celebrity status. Obviously, when I was growing up we also had larger-than-life celebrities in the sports and entertainment worlds. But we also had some true heroes—men and women who pursued goals above and beyond our common human experience. Charles Lindbergh was one of these—despite his isolationist views at the outset of World War II. Forty years later I was to get to know Lindbergh quite well when we served together on the board of directors of the World Wildlife Fund.[1]

1. Lindbergh served on the WWF board from 1964 to 1973. He had become deeply concerned over environmental issues, which he tended to see in planetary terms. At the time I knew him, he was a vice president of Pan Am and did a lot of global flying in the exploration of new air routes. He used to say that, over the years, he had observed the slowly shrinking green areas of the Earth during these flights. He became involved in specific wildlife issues such as whaling off the coast of Peru and the conservation of the rare monkey-eating eagle of the Philippines. He and his wife, Anne Morrow Lindbergh, went on safari to Tanzania with our friends Amyas and Evelyn Ames.

Lindbergh was not happy with the executive management of WWF and seemed to feel that I was a kindred soul in that regard. He spent a night with us on one occasion in about 1967 at our house on Woodland Drive. He was tall, balding, and remarkably youthful looking. I always found him very friendly and agreeable but serious and certainly lacking much sense of humor. Bowdy, then aged 12, met him and Lindbergh autographed a model plane construction kit of the *Spirit of St. Louis* for him. His pas-

Life at School

I MOVED STEADILY through the Lower School at St. Albans although seldom without some difficulty, particularly in algebra, and I was blessed with good and, usually, patient teachers—Mr. True in Form B, "Pop" Jarman in Form A, and Mr. Smith in Form I. After school—and that meant after athletics—it was my regular custom to go with Orme Wilson to his home, first at 2415 California Street and then at 2374 Massachusetts Avenue, to play. The Wilson chauffeur, Davis, picked us up at school in a rather grand Pierce Arrow limousine, and my parents would pick me up at the end of the afternoon at the Wilson house in whatever car we owned at the time. Other boys would join us: John Davidge from his home on Rock Creek Drive (now the Canadian Embassy residence) although he was studious and usually was doing homework, which the rest of us put off until evening; Philip Fell, the stepson of Ogden Mills, who was Under Secretary and then Secretary of the Treasury in the Hoover administration, succeeding Andrew Mellon as Secretary; and John Mitchell, son of the Army Air Force hero Billy Mitchell, who lived on Massachusetts Avenue just above Dupont Circle, where the Embassy Row Hotel now stands.

---

sion for privacy was proverbial. On a somewhat later occasion when he wanted a discussion with me, I ended up going to his home in Darien, Connecticut, for the night with him and Anne, an interesting visit. He had met me at the old Eastern Airlines shuttle at LaGuardia, a tall, unmistakable figure, and driven me to Darien in his Volkswagen Beetle. In 1978, several years after his death, Aileen and I visited his grave in a little churchyard on the cliffs of the remote Hana Coast of Maui in the Hawaiian Islands, a beautiful, peaceful spot. He had had a small house there—actually an A-frame—next door to the property of his old boss, Pan Am Vice President Sam Pryor. Aileen and I had dinner there with his widow, Anne, and his daughter, Reeve. (We had also visited Pryor at his home on Maui where he lived with a group of pet gibbons. Several of these were buried—with appropriate monuments—in the same cemetery as Lindbergh and also Mary Tay, Pryor's late wife. Her mother from Pittsburgh was the sister of the Travers grandmother of Nancy and Emily Train, so we had a family connection. Sam's sister was the redoubtable Permelia Reed of Hobe Sound, Florida.)

In 1986, at a ceremony in Minneapolis, I was the recipient of the Lindbergh Award given annually by the Lindbergh Foundation. The award is given "to an individual who has made an outstanding contribution to the achievement of a balance between technological progress and the preservation of our natural environment."

John Mitchell was a boon companion and an incorrigible rule-
breaker. He was always awarded the largest number of demerits in our
class and regularly spent his entire Saturday mornings in study hall at
school. I recall at about age 11 constructing a crude still on the top floor
of his house. We fermented grape juice and yeast and then boiled the
concoction, drawing off and condensing what we were convinced was
alcohol. We each carried a small bottle of the stuff to school and
dumped it into our iced tea at lunch and succeeded in acting reasonably foolishly afterwards. We did not get caught on this occasion and,
while I suspect we failed in actually producing much, if any, alcohol, it
strikes me that the whole endeavor reflected a laudable spirit of enterprise. John died when a very young man, and the world lost an original
spirit.

CHAPTER 4

Cape Cod and the Whitneys

THE SUMMER of 1930, when I would have been 10, I spent with my aunt Grace (Dargee) T. Whitney (1874-1950) and her husband, Myron W. Whitney, Jr. (1874-1958), at their farm on Cape Cod. It was an important summer for me. I learned to swim, ride a horse, fish, crab, sail a boat, and I smoked my first cigarette. I also spent about two weeks with my Parker and Payson relatives at Pochet Island on the east, Atlantic Ocean, side of the Cape.

Dargee and Uncle Myron Whitney

DARGEE, CHRISTENED Grace after her mother, was an older sister of my father, situated in age between him and Aunt Sue. I believe the name "Dargee" had been bestowed by her niece, Serena Hand, and none of my generation ever knew her as anything else. Uncle Myron Whitney came from the Cape and graduated from Harvard in the Class of 1898. He was a singer and, after a successful career on the concert circuits, taught singing in Washington from a studio at the corner of 17th and H Streets where the New Executive Office Building is located today, across 17th Street from the Metropolitan Club. He was a tall, strikingly handsome man, gentle in manner, even self-effacing, very reserved but with a fine sense of humor. He and Dargee had no children and lived with my grandmother Train at 1642 Connecticut Avenue until the latter's death in 1938 when they bought their own house on O Street in Georgetown.

Having no children herself, Dargee was always very warm and affectionate with my brothers and me, and she was a great favorite of ours.

She had a rather bubbly sense of fun—much like her sister, Aunt Sue. She also possessed the strongly aquiline nose of her brother and sister (and nephews). (In this connection, I must report that my father's Naval Academy class book, called the "Ditty Bag," published in an era that gave little or no thought to "political correctness," declares his nickname at the Academy to have been "Ike.") A portrait of Dargee as a young woman by her Washington artist-friend, Alice Barney, shows her in an exotic, romantic mood, but that may have been more a reflection of the artist than of Dargee. (Alice Barney's house on Sheridan Circle now belongs to the Smithsonian. She was engaged to be married at one time to Henry M. Stanley, the famed African explorer.)

Dargee was an enterprising person. She had her own car and always did the driving for herself and Uncle Myron. I do not recall ever seeing him drive except on Cape Cod where traffic was minimal. She also had owned one of the early electric cars, one of those contraptions where you sat up front as if in a buggy and steered with a tiller. On one occasion when she was driving the electric down the long Massachusetts Avenue hill about where the British Embassy is today, she suddenly saw one of her front wheels running down the hill ahead of her. I do not recall what happened next. At a much later date, when in her fifties, she learned to read Sanskrit and Arabic and translated Persian manuscripts in the collection of the Freer Gallery, whose director, John Lodge, a younger brother of Henry Cabot Lodge, the powerful senator from Massachusetts, was a great friend of the Whitneys. Her translations were done with "such poetic skill" that she was employed by the Freer for that purpose and became a member of its Near East Department.

There is a remarkable account of Myron Whitney singing in 1899 at the reception for Julia Ward Howe, the author of "The Battle Hymn of the Republic," in Boston at the Boston Theater. She had written the hymn during the Civil War and was now in her eighties. A reporter wrote: "You could see the splendid white head trembling; then her voice joined in as Whitney sang: 'In the beauty of the lilies, Christ was born across the sea,' and by the time he reached the words, 'As He died to make men holy, let us die to make men free,' the whole vast audience was on its feet sobbing and singing at the top of its thousands of lungs."[1]

Since Uncle Myron had only graduated from Harvard one year earlier in 1898, I am uncertain whether he is the Myron Whitney referred to in the above account or whether it was his father, also a noted singer. In any event, there is no question but that five years later, on January 15, 1904, Uncle Myron sang at a White House musical, together with Pablo Casals, cellist, and Ward Stephens, pianist. The program, which was published in the *New York Times* magazine section, February 18, 1971, in an article on President Nixon and the arts, clearly lists "Myron W. Whitney, Jr., basso." Of course, Casals became a world-famous cellist and many years later, in a much-publicized event, played at the Kennedy White House and was introduced on that occasion by the First Lady, Jacqueline Kennedy.

In the secret life of his imagination, I think that Uncle Myron rode the open range of the early West, tall in the saddle, and a fast draw with his six-guns. Beside his chair in the library on Connecticut Avenue, there was always a pile of Western pulp magazines, and he never seemed to tire of them. He rolled his own cigarettes, and I can see him now carefully tapping tobacco out of a Sir Walter Raleigh tin into the folded paper held in his left hand, then moistening one edge of the paper with the tip of his tongue and rolling it all neatly into a cigarette cylinder, which he then inserted into a holder. He smoked with the holder firmly clenched in his teeth.

Once Uncle Myron and Dargee had gone to the Cape for the summer, he moved into his own world where he was in charge. Their house was an eighteenth-century "Cape Codder," built by a Whitney, with low ceilings, a sloping roof, and dormer windows on the second floor. The exterior of the house was gray-weathered shingle with white trim. Red roses climbed up against the gray walls. An old barn stood close by, tenanted by a Jersey cow and a horse, both of which had been

1. Tharp, Louise Hall. *Three Saints and a Sinner. Julia Ward Howe, Louisa, Annie and Sam Ward.* Little, Brown and Company, Boston (1956), pp. 359, 360. I am indebted to Robert (Pete) L. Walsh, Jr., for providing me this material.

The old
Whitney house,
Sandwich, Cape cod

rented for the summer. A buggy was housed in a shed at the end of the barn. There was even a dog, courtesy of a Wianno friend who bred championship Welsh terriers. Unlike in Washington, where they lived essentially as guests of my grandmother's, here Dargee and Uncle Myron enjoyed their own home and independence.

Edward, Man of All Work

AN INTEGRAL part of their household was Edward, a middle-aged black man from Middleburg, Virginia, where he had lived all of his life and worked on a horse farm. He was bowlegged and walked with a sort of rolling gait which I took to be the result of spending a lot of time on horseback. Edward milked the cow, took care of the horse, tended the vegetable garden, did the cooking, waited on the table, cut wood, and did about anything else that needed doing. I spent quite a bit of time with him as he did his chores, including trying my hand at milking the cow—never very successfully.

With Edward's help, I saddled the horse and he saw to it that the girth was tight enough. I would go for rides by myself, lasting an hour or so, down the country roads and along the "wood roads" that ran into the surrounding pine forests. There almost never was any traffic to worry about. I assume that all of this had been preceded by a reason-able amount of riding instruction in the pasture. In any event, those rides by myself were a welcome bit of independence for a ten-year-old, and I thoroughly enjoyed them. The Whitney house stood on a knoll and the last hundred yards or so of the lane were uphill and I liked to do this at a canter. The only time I remember Uncle Myron ever speak-ing crossly to me was when he met me coming up the lane with the horse all lathered with sweat. He said that the horse was out of condi-tion and should not be worked so hard. He doubtless was right. Edward and I rubbed the horse down and cooled him off before putting him in his stall. (Curiously, while I have been allergic to horses for many years, I do not recall any such reaction when I was a boy.)

On Sundays, Edward would get drunk. The farm was in the middle of the Cape, south of Sandwich (which was the post office), just east of Wakeby Pond, and several miles north of Mashpee, the little village which was the center of the Mashpee Indian tribe. On Sunday morn-ings, after he had done his morning chores, which I am sure included cooking and serving breakfast, Edward would change into his Sunday clothes, hitch the horse up to the buggy and head for Mashpee with me sitting beside him. We would creak down the lane at a walk and then, once on the tarred county road, break into a trot for the trip to Mashpee. The latter comprised a small general store and little else that I recall. Edward would hitch the horse near the store under a tree and then go inside, to reappear briefly with the Sunday papers which he gave me. He would then disappear into the store for an hour or so while I read the comics. I never went inside myself but remained dis-creetly on the buggy, aware of various rather dark-skinned individuals of what I imagine were African-American and Native American ancestry—labels that would have been meaningless to me then—entering and leaving the store.

When Edward finally came out, his habitual rolling walk had an added distinct weave and he tacked his way over to the horse, which he unhitched. He climbed aboard the buggy, took the reins, clucked to the horse, and we were homeward bound. It would not be long before Edward would nod off and teeter alarmingly from side to side to the motion of the buggy. He slept most of the way. Fortunately, we seldom met other vehicles and, in any event, the horse knew the way home as well as Edward did. Once we were back at the barn, Edward would unhitch the horse, water him, put him into his stall, feed him, put the buggy away and disappear into his own room to sleep. Perhaps it was after one of these Sunday excursions and after he had recovered enough to read his paper that I joined Edward and had my first cigarette. I don't think I enjoyed it very much, and I did not really start to smoke until my freshman year at college.

Prohibition

THIS ACCOUNT of Edward's day off is as good a point as any to bring up Prohibition. Obviously, the liquor that Edward consumed at the Mashpee store had to be illegal, as the country was still in the throes of Prohibition in 1930, and it was probably locally produced "moonshine." Edward never mentioned liquor or the fact of his drinking and never offered any explanation of how he spent his time in the store, but I certainly knew what was up. Of course, I was too young to be affected by Prohibition but was aware of its existence. (Cuth and Middy, on the other hand, were both experienced with bootleg liquor and speakeasies.) My parents had returned from Rome in 1919 to find that the Eighteenth Amendment had been adopted "while the boys were away." When they were leaving for Europe, my father had stored a couple of cases of liquor at Uncle Gus and Aunt Sue's apartment on West 9th Street in New York City. I don't think he cleared this with Uncle Gus who discovered to his horror when the Eighteenth Amendment passed that he, a federal judge, was harboring contraband in his home. Neither Uncle Gus nor Aunt Sue drank and both were pillars of rectitude. How the parties resolved this knotty problem, I don't know.

My parents were moderate drinkers and basically enjoyed a drink before dinner throughout their adult lives. My father would usually have what he called a "toddy" which was made in an "old-fashioned" glass with a lump of sugar, Angostura bitters, bourbon with water and ice to taste, and a slice of lemon peel. My mother liked a gin martini "straight up" with a bit of lemon peel and she called her evening cocktail her "little fellow." My father would make it in a small shaker, pour the martini, and then, when that was finished, my mother would have the "heel tap," which was the remains in the shaker. After I was grown, my idea of a before-dinner cocktail was the same "toddy" which my father drank and which, in my case, later evolved into the simpler bourbon "on the rocks." Later yet, I made a bold move into vodka martinis, likewise "on the rocks," which remains my cocktail of choice.

During the Prohibition years, my father had a bootlegger named George who would arrive at our front door in Georgetown in the evening with a golf bag. On George's admission to the house, the golf bag would miraculously disgorge its cache of liquor, mostly bourbon, scotch, and gin.

While in Rome, my parents had developed a taste for wine at dinner. Refusing to be frustrated by Prohibition, my mother set up a winery in what we called "the packing room" on the third floor of our Georgetown house. The room was primarily used for storing trunks and suitcases but my mother installed some large pottery crocks and she and Verena filled them with a mysterious concoction of grapes, orange juice, orange rinds, lemons, raisins, yeast, and other ingredients which I do not recall. Cheesecloth was secured over the top of the crocks to protect their contents from insects. After fermentation, the contents were strained through cloth, tasted, and bottled. The "wine," which was clear and golden in color to my eyes, was served at the table—usually only for festive occasions—from two-foot-tall, long-necked, glass decanters from Italy which had silver handles and bases. The wine always seemed to be appreciated but, of course, there wasn't much choice at the time. One lasting memory of my mother's winery is that the fermenting mash would produce gases as it "worked." Large bubbles would suddenly rise to the surface with a very audible "harumpf" sound which could be clearly heard on the floors below. This vinous flatulence from upstairs was often startling to visitors.

In 1930, the year of which I am writing, Prohibition had almost run its course. With the election of FDR, the Eighteenth Amendment was repealed in 1933. The country was subjected to 3.2 beer for a couple of years and then in 1936 federal law permitted any form of alcoholic beverage. Of course, individual states could, and some did, impose various restrictions.

Life at the Farm

DARGEE AND Uncle Myron introduced me to many new activities. I have already mentioned riding. Another was fishing, which they loved. Somehow they seemed to have access to rowboats on most of the good fishing lakes and ponds on the Cape. These were largely uninhabited in those days. Dargee and Uncle Myron would drag a minnow net along the shallows to procure our bait and then we would fish for smallmouth bass and yellow perch. I had a rod and reel, and it was great fun. On at least one occasion, we trolled for snappers, which were young bluefish, from a catboat, sailing back and forth in Buzzards Bay near the southern entrance to the Cape Cod Canal. We used hand lines and Uncle Myron handled the boat. There was no motor. It was exciting and hot work when we hit a school of feeding snappers. We caught a large mess of them.

A related activity was crabbing in the saltwater inlet at Marston's Mill. Here again there seemed to be a rowboat ready for us and we used a crab net from the stern of the boat. Uncle Myron would take the oars and back the boat toward a likely spot while I stood on the stern seat with my net poised. When I saw a crab, we would sneak up on it and I would scoop it out of the water (hopefully) and drop it into a bushel basket behind me. Cleaning the cooked crabs on the dining-room table back at the farm was the least fun part of the enterprise—a lot of work and a lot of mess.

Swimming was another first for me. We would drive to Peter's Pond and change into bathing suits behind the car. And I mean suits. Both Uncle Myron and I wore wool outfits with straps over our shoulders and a sort of skirt around the bottom. I remember that mine scratched like hell. Peter's Pond had a clean, sandy bottom, and I was shown how to swim in water only waist deep. I learned to do a very staid breast-stroke and sidestroke and to this day that is my repertory in the water. Neither of my instructors knew anything about the crawl. I also swam at nearby Wakeby Pond where cousins of Uncle Myron had a camp with a dock. My second cousin Grace Parker Luquer and her husband, Lea, had a summer house on the shore at Cotuit and we occasionally went there to swim and picnic.[2]

The Sandwich farm was a remote place—but I suspect that most places in the country were fairly remote then. The old house stood on a knoll with fields and orchards nearby and pine woods enclosing the whole. There was no traffic, audible or otherwise, nearby. In the eve-nings, in particular, it was very quiet. After supper we sat in the "par-lor" to the right of the front door as you entered. There was no elec-tricity and we relied on kerosene lamps and candles. The center of the room was occupied by a square table with a large oil lamp. Uncle Myron sat in a rocking chair on one side—reading his Westerns—and Dargee and I sat on other sides, all depending on the one lamp for illumina-tion. Dargee introduced me to the card game Russian Bank and she and I had many a spirited game around that old lamp.

I had begun to read a good deal. Of course, there was no television and I do not recall a radio at the farm. I read quite a few of Uncle Myron's Westerns, and I am sure there was a summer reading list from school that I had to work through. None of those books stick in my

2. Lea was a teacher and at the time I believe he was headmaster of the Asheville Country Day School at Asheville, North Carolina. They had three children, Grace, Shippen, and Peter, all younger than I. Gracie was an extremely pretty young girl with high coloring that I can remember today. The next time I saw her was 60 years later at Bill Savage's funeral service at the Princeton University Chapel. Her hair was gray but she had the dramatic good looks promised by the young girl I remembered. She is married to Edward W. Madeira, Jr., and they live in Wayne, Pennsylvania. They have three daughters, Martha, Melissa, and Amanda. Shippen (who is Lea Shippen, Jr.) is married to Giovenella Chierebetta and they have four children. Peter is married to Deborah B. Morgan and they live in Devon, Pennsylvania. I have met them at con-servation meetings in Philadelphia. They have a daughter, Heidi, whom I met in about 1993 in Hobe Sound and who is working for a conservation organization, and also a son, Peter, who lives in Massachusetts.

mind, but I do remember lying in a hammock near the well in front of the house reading John Galsworthy's *Forsythe Saga*—or at least a portion of it. I am sure it was way over my head.

The Whitneys' Deaths

SHORTLY AFTER World War II, the old Whitney house on the Cape was burned to the ground, presumably as the result of blueberry pickers setting fire to the woods to promote a good crop the following spring. Fortunately, the Whitneys had returned to Washington at the time and no one was hurt. The loss seems particularly hard because Dargee and Uncle Myron asked so little from life and the old farm meant so much to them. In any event, they bought a house at Castine, Maine, at the suggestion of their old friend Mary Winslow, and there they spent their remaining summers. Dargee died there in 1950 and Uncle Myron in Washington in 1958, both after very short illnesses. They are both buried in Castine. On her death, her brother-in-law, Augustus N. Hand, wrote these words in the Elizabethtown, New York, newspaper: "I have never known a happier marriage than that of Mr. and Mrs. Whitney, nor a life more full of useful work, stable friendships, and enduring goodness than hers." They were both wonderful people who added much to my life.

Pochet Island

IN MID-AUGUST, I went to Pochet (pronounced "Po-chee" with the accent on the first syllable) Island to spend two-plus weeks. Located on the Outer Cape at the head of Pleasant Bay above Chatham and near East Orleans, its post office, Pochet lay just inside the great Atlantic beach from which it was separated by a narrow marsh. It was the summer stronghold of the Payson/Parker clan to whom I was closely related. It could be reached with some difficulty by a track through the marsh and that is how major transportation problems were solved. However, the usual mode of arrival was via rowboat from Barley Neck where Uncle Russell Payson lived. (His grandfather, Samuel Gilbert Payson, had been president of Manchester Mills, said to have been the largest textile mill in the world at that time. He had made the first land purchases in the area.) There certainly were no motor vehicles on Pochet.[3]

Pochet was a fairly bleak, treeless island extending a mile or more in length, with steep bluffs dropping into Pleasant Bay on the western side and falling away gradually into marsh on the seaward side with dunes and the Atlantic beach beyond. Bushes reached above my head and there were grassy paths leading through them. Up until about 1915, the island had been burned regularly and kept in grass for sheep and cattle. There were few structures: the Old House, a small eighteenth-century farmhouse that had been moved there many years before and was uninhabited; the New House, a three-storied, shingled house that had been built by Gilbert Payson in 1886; Rough House, a large, one-room structure which had bunks; and the boathouse on the shore. The latter contained a large stock of shorebird decoys which would now be worth a fortune to collectors.

Payson/Parker Relatives

LET ME ESTABLISH the relationships first. My great-grandfather, Charles Russell Train, had, among other children, a daughter named Althea (1847-1926), Aunt Attie, but known to her own children and grandchildren as "Ba." She married a textile manufacturer named Gilbert Russell Payson (1840-1891). They acquired Pochet Island and also proceeded to have a number of children: Gilbert Russell, known as Russell (1868-1939), Eleanor (1873-1956), Samuel Cushing (1875-1950), and Charles Clifford, known as Clifford (1877-1949). These were all

3. The only source of historical information that I have is a mimeographed paper by Charles H. Thomsen, *Pochet*, Barley Neck Point (June 1985). The paper is illustrated by photographs and contains a "Pochet Island Family Tree."

first cousins of my father, so they were close relatives. I knew all of them. Aunt Eleanor was married to Massachusetts lawyer and judge Philip Stanley Parker (1868-1939), as I mentioned earlier, and they had Philip, Grace, Eleanor, and Frances. (For full names and dates, see *The Train Family*, Chart 4, a genealogical table for the Payson/Parker family.)

My second cousin Eleanor (known to the younger generation within her own family as "Aunt Jim") drove me from the Whitney farm down the Cape to East Orleans and thence out onto Barley Neck. There, I am sure, we called briefly on Uncle Russell, Aunt Eleanor's older brother. His wife had died many years before, and he lived the year round by himself there on Barley Neck. Ruddy-faced, white-mustached, he was full of fun and of stories for a ten-year-old. He took me clamming and introduced me to clam chowder, which he made himself. On a later occasion, sitting with Uncle Russell and several other men at his dining table, I reached for a bottle of what looked like water only to discover it to be gin—which was another new experience for me. Uncle Russell was vastly amused and said: "Your father will enjoy hearing about this!" Uncle Russell would have been 62 at the time. He very likely rowed Eleanor and me and our gear over to Pochet on our arrival.

Adventures with Eleanor

ELEANOR WAS 28 that summer and how or why she got tagged to take care of me, I do not know. She took me sailing and rowing and exploring around the island, and she was great fun to be with. To this day, I remember her with tremendous fondness. She is gone now, having died in 1992 at the age of 90, but my memory of her is in shorts and battered sneakers at the tiller of a sailing dinghy, short, dark hair blowing in the breeze.

She and I sailed one day down to Hog Island which also belonged to the family and was situated below Pochet in Pleasant Bay and very much smaller. Legend had it that Captain Kidd, the redoubtable eighteenth-century buccaneer, had sailed his full-rigged ship from Nantucket Sound up Pleasant Bay past Pochet and then back out Nauset Inlet to the sea. One could not do that today (or when I was there in 1930, for that matter) as much of the way has filled in. Family legend had it that he stopped at Hog Island and buried a substantial treasure there. Many of the family—and, I suppose, others—had dug for that treasure.

Uncle Russell told me that he had once gone to Hog Island to dig for the treasure and had done so on a full moon, which is apparently propitious for such matters. He said that he had actually uncovered a chest but that, just as he was about to pull it out of the ground, he had been confronted by a tall man "with a red bandana around his head, a black patch over one eye, a cutlass in his hand and *teeth like barrel-staves!*" This description was rendered in a voice that rose to a crescendo with the last phrase. Uncle Russell said that he had dropped his shovel and run to his boat, pursued by the apparition swinging his cutlass at him. He got away and said he had never been able to find the spot again. Powerful stuff for a ten-year-old! Eleanor and I sailed there, walked the island, dug a bit here and there and found nothing. But then, there was no full moon!

Other Memories of Pochet

IT'S FUNNY the things you remember of a time so many years ago—and it makes me nervous about what my grandchildren will remember of me! I remember the breakfasts in the dining room at the New House at Pochet, particularly the fresh-baked biscuits with butter and marmalade. I think I used to eat these as long as the maid would bring them or until Aunt Eleanor told me that I had had enough. There was also my first experience with blueberry muffins—moist and laden with freshly picked blueberries. I remember reading Baroness Orczy's *Scarlet Pimpernel,* which I loved, and I believe one or two other of her books, not as good.

Most of all, I remember going to the bathroom. There was only one toilet in the New House, located on the main floor in sort of an addition right outside the living room. I think that was the problem. I was not used to going to the bathroom close to other people, even when they were cousins. You have to sort of see the picture. There we all were around the table and the one oil lamp in front of the fireplace. The silence would have been deafening. Aunt Eleanor would probably suggest it was time for me to go to bed. Should I then go straight out to the john—and tinkle audibly to the crowd? Or should I go up to my room and use the chamber pot thoughtfully placed there? The latter was the obvious choice and the one I made until someone—probably Aunt Eleanor—suggested I use the toilet except in real emergencies. To compound the problem, I ate a lot of candy in the evening, which apparently had a sort of diuretic effect.

Labor Day weekend was the highlight of the Pochet summer as members of the Payson/Parker clan gathered from far and wide. Eleanor's sister Frances, called "Frannie,"[4] was there and her brother Philip. There was a game of Murder in the pitch-black interior of the Old House, a traditional New England clambake on the shore, and a tennis tournament on Uncle Russell's court when Aunt Eleanor was my partner.

I have not been back to Pochet since that summer. I do not imagine that it has changed much although I believe a couple of small houses have been added. It was a "Proper Bostonian" kind of a place with everything kept very simple. I have been back in the area several times. In 1969, when I was Under Secretary of the Department of Interior, I spoke at the dedication of the Cape Cod National Seashore Visitor Center at Provincetown—along with Tip O'Neill, later Speaker of the House of Representatives. On that occasion, Aileen and I stayed in a house that was owned by the National Park Service on the beach near Eastham. I recall that we walked down the beach to the Outermost House, made famous by Henry Beston's book of that name. Several

4. Frannie lives in La Jolla, California, and is over 90. I have telephoned her and found her well and cheerful. Eleanor had lived with her in La Jolla until her death in 1992. Frannie had worked as a scientist at the Scripps Oceanographic Laboratory at La Jolla and had taught history for several years at Foxcroft School, Middleburg, Virginia, when Aileen was there as a student about 1940.

years later, Aileen and I spent a summer weekend with Anne and
Elliot Richardson at Eastham. It was Elliot's birthday and there was a
cocktail party and among the guests was a cousin of mine with Pochet
connections. There are today a hundred or more living descendants of
Uncle Gilbert Payson and Aunt Attie Train Payson. The Pochet "clan"
still gathers at the island for Labor Day weekends, and Pochet is still
the "glue" that binds the family together.

CHAPTER 5

Washington and Newport

I DO NOT recall how I returned to Washington after Pochet. Most probably I took the train—the "Federal"—getting on at Providence. On the way north, I had traveled with Uncle Myron, first by day train from Washington to New York and then by boat overnight on one of the vessels of the Fall River Line, getting off at Fall River, Massachusetts, where I imagine Dargee met us by car. Perhaps we did the same thing on the reverse trip. The next time I remember taking the Fall River boat was from Boston to New York with several college classmates after a Harvard-Princeton football game at Cambridge. I think that on that occasion, my roommate and I had hitchhiked to Cambridge from Princeton. Travel was definitely more interesting in those days!

After the Cape Cod summer, I returned to Form A at St. Albans, taught by Mr. ("Pop") Jarman. Life continued on an even keel, and I moved on the following year into Form I. Algebra was introduced, taught by "Pop" Henderson, school chaplain and football coach. He was a wonderful guy and beloved by all the students, but any affection I felt for him did not extend to algebra. Math was not my thing. He also taught Sacred Studies, a far less demanding subject, and certainly requiring little of the analytical and logical capacity that math did, and I usually did well in it. Unfortunately, Sacred Studies was not as important in the curriculum, having little relevance to the ultimate goal of college entrance.

Dancing Class

I MUST HAVE started going to dancing class a year or two earlier. When I first went to dancing class it was at Miss Hawke's at the Play-

The author, 1931

house on N Street, just west of Connecticut Avenue. So far as I know, she ran the only dancing class in Washington at the time—at least the only one of which families such as mine were aware. The facade of the house is still there, but it is a facade only and has been incorporated into the front of an office building. Miss Hawke was a redoubtable, bosomy figure, corseted into a tight black evening dress, pearl choker around her neck, white hair piled on top of her head, and with long white gloves up to her elbows. She greeted each of us formally as we arrived. We learned to fox-trot and to waltz as well as the niceties of dance floor behavior—how to ask a girl to dance, how to hold her, how to lead, etc. I can remember the sweaty palms, the damp backs, to this day.

After a couple of years at Miss Hawke's, a rival dancing class was opened by Mrs. Shippen at her house two doors down from ours on Que Street. This was too convenient to pass up, and I transferred to the Shippen class, as did most of my friends. There was less formal instruction and more actual dancing practice. Also, critically relevant to the whole operation, puberty had begun to arrive, with some of us more precocious than others in this regard. Being generally a year younger than my peers, I was on the less precocious side. Nevertheless, it was a common observation that the girls were on average much more enthusiastic about dancing class than the boys, most of whom looked upon it as a damn bore.

This attitude led to a regrettable but memorable incident on one occasion. On that particular dancing-class evening, I said good-bye to my parents, went down the street and into Mrs. Shippen's house, met three or four like-minded social dropouts—all male—and led them out the back door, through the garden, and into the alley and thence to freedom. Living in the close neighborhood, I was on *terra cognita*. Where we went then, I have no idea—perhaps to a movie at the old Dumbarton Theater on Wisconsin Avenue. It makes no difference. The important thing was that we had beaten the system—or thought we had. Of course, all I had to do was to be back home at the appropriate hour. The others, who presumably had to be picked up by parents, had a somewhat trickier time, but I believe all made it. When I walked into my house, I was asked the usual question: "How was Mrs. Shippen's?" I gave the usual answer, "Fine," and did not elaborate further, but doubt that I ever did. All was well and good until the Fates decreed that my mother was to encounter Mrs. Shippen on the sidewalk the next morning. "How is Russell?" said Mrs. Shippen. "Is he sick?" "Not at all," said my mother. "Why do you ask?" "Because," said Mrs. Shippen, "he wasn't at dancing class last night."

When I was confronted by the damning evidence on my return from school that day, I confessed all. I had always been taught that to tell the truth was one of the cardinal virtues—as it is. I think I tried not to implicate my co-conspirators and, to their credit, I doubt that my parents urged me to. That I was appropriately punished is certain, and I never pulled that stunt again.

However, a close replica occurred several years later. The Argentine ambassador and his American wife, Madame Espil, gave a "sub-debutante" dinner and dance for her daughter at the Argentine Embassy at the northwest corner of New Hampshire Avenue and Que

Street.[1] Following the seated dinner and during the interval while males were separated from females before repairing to the ballroom—a custom no longer politically correct but one that is not without its convenience—several of us young men simply retrieved our overcoats and left by the front door. We walked a few blocks east to the Lucky Strike Bowling Alleys on 14th Street where we bowled until it was time to go home. Once again, I was caught and I had to sit down and write a letter of apology to Madame Espil. (I dated her daughter, Louise Stillwell, a couple of times and she later married Randall Hagner.)

This was all pretty mild stuff and probably showed no serious criminal bent. However, both stories do reveal a certain deviousness on my part which has not been widely recognized by others but which has served me well from time to time.

Let me return briefly to dancing class for a serious comment. However much we may have griped at the institution, most of us did learn to dance, which is more than I can say about most of my children's generation, at least in terms of ballroom dancing. To try to lead the average young woman in a simple two-step or a waltz is often like trying to lead an obstinate wrestler. To be fair, I am hopeless at rock 'n' roll! A related complaint is that many young people do not really seem to know how to behave at a dance. Many of the men fail to dance with their dinner partners and many of the women seem to want to dance only with their husbands—if at all. All of this is too bad and a great loss. A dance with good music and attractive people has to be one of the most enjoyable of social occasions. Of course, I am spoiled by having a wife who is a marvelous dancer.

---

1. The same intersection where in about 1952 while driving her mother, Emily Foley, Aileen had had to put on the brakes very suddenly to avoid an accident. Emily was thrown forward and knocked unconscious by the windshield. Police and ambulance arrived and Emily, still unconscious, was laid out on a stretcher. Aileen was asked to provide certain vital statistics about her mother. When Aileen was asked about her mother's age, Emily sat bolt upright and said, "It's none of their goddamn business," and then sank back into unconsciousness.

Overnight at the White House

IN MID-1932, just as my school year at St. Albans ended, my father left his job as naval aide to the president and was transferred to the Naval War College at Newport, Rhode Island, basically a one-year course in naval tactics and strategy. He was in the junior class, made up mostly of captains. There were several contemporaries of my father at the War College who went on to become household names in World War II—Ernest King, "Bull" Halsey, and William Spruance, among others.

The plan was for my mother to drive to Newport accompanied by Mid and myself, while my father took the train. (Cuth was leaving for a sailing cruise with friends.) There was big excitement when President and Mrs. Hoover invited us three boys to spend the night before our departure at the White House. The invitation was extremely thoughtful, as Mrs. Hoover was aware that trying to close our house with three sons in it would be hard for my mother. I do not recall the logistics of the occasion, except that we all had dinner at the Littles'. We three boys then went to the White House and were escorted to the Andrew Jackson bedroom where Cuth and Mid were to share the great Victorian double bed, and I was to sleep in a small bedroom that opened off the room. I think I got to sleep reasonably promptly but Cuth, showing a fine sense of historical opportunity, stayed up for hours writing letters to his friends on White House toilet paper.

The next morning we breakfasted with President and Mrs. Hoover on the portico on the back of the White House looking out across the Ellipse toward the Washington Monument. (The portico did not then have the upstairs level added in President Truman's time.) There were just the five of us, and I sat on the president's right. He was extremely friendly and chatty, and Mrs. Hoover was always a very warm, outgoing person. However, I think that what made the greatest impression on me were the tall glasses of fresh California orange juice. I had never seen anything quite like those large glassfuls before. Many years later, Barbara Bush gave Aileen and me a tour through the White House

With my father on the steps of
4 Redwood Street, Newport,
Rhode Island, 1932

bedrooms, including the Andrew Jackson bedroom. In early 1997, I
had an occasion to tell Hillary Clinton about my night at the White
House and barely resisted the temptation to say that it had not cost me
anything.

At Newport, my parents had rented a green, frame house on Redwood Street, separated from Bellevue Avenue by a vacant lot and situated directly opposite the Redwood Library. The house, which is no
longer there, had a large garden stretching along Redwood Street
behind a privet hedge. (I was responsible for mowing the lawn, raking
the leaves in the fall, and trimming the hedge.) The house was not
large but had at least five bedrooms—one occupied by Sarah Nelson,
our cook, who had accompanied us from Washington—and was on a
par with most of the homes in the neighborhood occupied by naval
friends. In fact, I recall it being more attractive than most. In any event,
in that summer of 1932 when I was just 12, my friend Philip Fell, Secretary of the Treasury Ogden Mills' stepson, had arrived in Newport
harbor on Mills' grand steam yacht, *Avalon*. Philip invited me on

board, and I invited him to our house for lunch. Afterwards, I walked with him back to the landing to take a launch to the yacht. Walking down the hill toward the harbor, Philip suddenly turned to me and said, "Gee, Russ, I never knew your family was so poor!"

Family Finances

I HAVE NO idea what I said. I certainly realized that there was an enormous gap between Ogden Mills' circumstances and those of the Train family but the fact is I had never given the matter any particular thought. I suppose to somewhat lesser degrees much the same could be said about the family circumstances of most of my friends. Yet I never thought of us as being poor. Cuth and Middy were both at Princeton; I was about to enter St. George's from St. Albans, both top-flight preparatory schools. We had servants in the house and my parents belonged to the proper clubs, etc., in Washington and had hosts of friends. And, of course, there was never any discussion of money in the family that I can recall. (I exclude from that statement occasional discussions of my 25-cent-a-week allowance.)

Looking back on it all, I realize that my parents had a very tough time making ends meet. Aside from my mother's allowance from her father and the dividends from a small stock portfolio, there was very little income beyond my father's naval pay. Moreover, while he was a very senior captain, having been in that grade since at least 1914, he was being paid a commander's pay under the severe economy measures which our government had instituted to combat the budget deficit caused by the onset of the Great Depression. In fact, when my father was promoted to rear admiral later that year, his pay remained that of a commander. I do not ever remember hearing a complaint on that score from either of my parents. It makes one think a bit about attitudes today when the economy is strong, unemployment is at a historically low level, the budget is in surplus and yet no one would dream of asking the American people, let alone government employees, to make any sort of sacrifice.

I think that the education of their sons was probably my parents'
only extravagance. They never traveled—aside from a summer visit to
the Hands in Elizabethtown or later to Atlantic City. I never knew my
mother to take a taxi; she always took a bus. I recall once—it could
have been just before we went to Newport or perhaps later when the
Depression was really biting deep into the country—when I heard my
parents talking together in the drawing room. The large double door-
way into the room from the hall had heavy curtains, called portieres,
and these were drawn together. This was unusual and I was curious. I
pulled the curtain open a crack—just enough so I could see in. My
mother and father were sitting close together on the bench in front of
the fireplace. All I heard was a fragment of conversation and it was my
mother saying, "I could sell my ring." She must have been referring
to her engagement ring, an emerald surrounded by small diamonds,
which she loved and was never without. I let the curtains close and
stole away, but I never forgot the scene or the words. I don't believe I
ever told my parents what I had overheard.

Without being maudlin about it, the memory is one that always fills
me with tenderness, gratitude, and love toward my parents. They
would have been in their early to mid-fifties at the time. Later when
their own parents had gone, their circumstances eased considerably
although their lifestyle remained pretty much the same.

The Subject of Sex

ALONG WITH no mention of money, there was certainly never any
discussion of sex. Unlike today, when no subject is off limits at the
family dinner table, sex just did not ever rear its head in any family discussion. And in private? My father never once raised the subject with
me, ever. Moreover, since my brothers were so much older than I, I
never learned a thing from them either. It's a wonder that I have had
children and grandchildren. Perhaps this insulation from the facts of
life explains why I did not marry until I was 34. It took that long to
learn the essentials.

All of this reminds me of the time I imparted the facts of life—at least so far as I knew them at age 47—to my son Bowdy, then aged 12. In the summer of 1967, Aileen and I had rented Paul Moore's camp in the Adirondacks, a 5,000-or-so-acre wilderness with lovely lakes, forests, brooks, and mountains.[2] We had all four children with us. I decided that the time had come for a man-to-man talk with my son. I broached the idea of an overnight camping trip for the two of us— being careful not to reveal my secret agenda. We hiked to a distant lake, transferred to a canoe cached there for just such occasions, and paddled across the lake to a rocky promontory where we set up camp. We cooked supper over the fire, told stories and talked generally, and then rolled up in our sleeping bags under the stars. I slept fitfully, rehearsing the discussion I planned for the next day.

We were up at dawn, skinny-dipped in the lake, had breakfast and broke camp. We boarded our canoe and this time I was careful to take the bow paddle so Bowdy would not see me turn brick red as I raised the subject of sex. I told him everything I knew, absolutely everything. I cannot now recall just what I said but I remember clearly his inter- jecting from time to time: "Gee, Dad, I *know* all that!" Anyway, it was a great occasion for male bonding and we both survived the ordeal.

Preparation for St. George's

I WAS TO enter St. George's as a day student in the fall of 1932. While most of the boys at the school were boarders, the school had a helpful policy toward the sons of naval officers on duty in Newport and accepted a few of us as day scholars. One of the entrance requirements that I had to meet was one year of Latin or its equivalent. Since I had had no Latin as yet at St. Albans, I had to pursue "the equivalent" which, in my case, involved Mid spending about an hour a day trying to drum some elementary Latin into me—"amo, amas, amat, amamus, amatis, amant," "hic, haec, hoc," etc. Poor guy. This would have been

2. Paul Moore was Episcopal bishop coadjutor of Washington at the time and later bishop of New York.

the summer of Mid's sophomore year at Princeton, and I am sure he had a lot better things to do, although the family must have paid him fairly generously to ease the pain. I did scrape into St. George's thanks to him although Latin never did become one of my best subjects.

The summer was pretty uneventful. I joined something called the "Sea Scouts" at the U.S. Naval Training Station next to the War College. We wore white, pseudo-sailor uniforms, did close-order drill on the parade ground, carrying wooden rifles, and what else we did I do not recall. Tied up alongside the parade ground was the U.S.S. *Constellation*, sister ship of the *Constitution*. I learned that my grandfather, Charles Jackson Train, had commanded the *Constellation* as a training ship and had taken her on at least one cruise in the 1880s. He had also gone to the Naval Academy during the Civil War when it was located at Newport to avoid the risk of Confederate attack in Chesapeake Bay. So there were a number of family associations with Newport—not to mention the fact that I had been born only a short ferry ride away at Jamestown.

The Newport Scene

MY PARENTS were definitely not part of the grand summer society of Newport, although they did have friends in that world. The only Washingtonian that I remember was Countess Laszlo Szychenyi (Gladys) who lived at the Breakers, the grandest of all the summer "cottages," which she had inherited from her father, William K. Vanderbilt, who had built the house. Countess Szychenyi was a friend of my parents and I remember visiting the Breakers but that's about all I do remember. Szychenyi himself was the Hungarian ambassador and was a tall man with a black patch over one eye.

In those days, one left calling cards, and I recall driving around with my mother on this mission. She would drive the car, doubtless a somewhat elderly, economy model, pull up to the front door of the targeted mansion, and I would get out with the cards and ring the doorbell. There was a fixed code involving whether the card of both husband

and wife was used plus the card of the actual caller, and a corner turned down conveyed a special meaning. None of this means anything to me now nor did it then. It is part of a world long gone. Of course, my mother was not calling upon people at random but only those with whom there was some association. Thus, we "dropped" cards on Mrs. Cornelius Vanderbilt because she was my friend Orme Wilson's great-aunt, the sister of Mr. Wilson's father. The Wilsons would have written that we would be in Newport. (Mr. Wilson's father, Richard Thornton Wilson, had married Caroline Astor, the daughter of William Waldorf Astor, and another sister married Robert Goelet.)

I still remember Mrs. Vanderbilt's butler. His look at our car indicated clearly that it was not up to his standard. I am not sure that he looked at me at all but simply extended a small silver card tray a few inches in my direction. I deposited the cards and fled into the car. In due course, my mother was invited to tea with Mrs. Vanderbilt and enjoyed meeting her. She was the grande dame whose picture was invariably on the front page of the papers showing her arriving for the season's opening of the Metropolitan Opera in New York. We also dropped cards on Mrs. Alexander, the aunt of my mother's good friend Susan Jay. Mrs. Alexander was also a grande dame but much easier and Mother always enjoyed being with her. (Mrs. Alexander was the grandmother of our friends Liberty Aldrich Redmond, Sylvia Whitehouse Blake, and Charlie Whitehouse, and the great-aunt of Susan Mary Jay Alsop.)

We were not members of Bailey's Beach, which in any event would have been too pricey for my family. We went to Third Beach on the Seconnet River, along with the other Navy families. We walked to beautiful old Trinity Church on Sundays, and I was fascinated by the box pews. (In 1945, Aileen married Edward Travers at Trinity Church.) Many years later, when Aileen's mother and stepfather had a summer house at 4 Red Cross Avenue in Newport, we would visit them for a weekend every summer. On those occasions, we generally swam and lunched at Bailey's Beach. We had a number of friends whom we enjoyed seeing but we usually found that a short dose of Newport was all we needed.

At St. George's

IN THE AUTUMN, my father took me hunting for pheasant. I don't believe I bagged one but I shot the tail off one that flushed right in front of me. I was so excited that I never got the gun to my shoulder but shot from the hip.

My parents introduced me to bowling and took me to the movies with them. With my mother, I went for walks on the Cliff Walk after the big houses were closed for the season. We also walked along Second Beach, just beyond St. George's. Father gave his talk "Random Recollections" at the Redwood Library, the only autobiographical effort I ever remember him making.[3]

My year at the school was not a great success. Being a day student at a boarding school just about guarantees that you remain an outsider. There were only about three of us and our parents took turns carpooling us back and forth to school. I did make a few friends who later were in my class at Princeton. There were the usual mandatory athletics and, once again, football showed me to least advantage. On my particular team I played center, which was odd because I was probably the lightest and skinniest boy on the team. Probably no one else wanted the job. Predictably, every time I passed the ball back, I was overrun and mashed into the ground. In any event, that was my last year of football.

My father made rear admiral sometime during that school year, to great family delight, and was ordered to the West Coast to take command of a division of light cruisers. My mother planned to follow him in due course and live on the West Coast for the duration of his tour of duty. As a result, I became a boarder at St. George's for the spring term, and I enjoyed those two or three months. St. George's is a beautiful school located on a hill at Middletown just east of Newport and overlooking the curving sweep of Second Beach and its dunes. The chapel is lovely and its fine Gothic tower dominates the school and its

3. Published in its entirety in Susan Train Hand's *John Trayne and Some of His Descendants* (privately published, 1933), pp. 174-192.

hilltop. Altogether, the spring and the greater sense of belonging which came with boarding gave me a much more positive attitude toward school.

Almost forty years later, our daughter Errol entered St. George's in the fall of 1974, three years after it had become coeducational. When she graduated in 1977, I gave the commencement address in the chapel, a moving experience for me and probably ghastly for her. One other time while she was there, I gave an illustrated lecture on African wildlife to the school in the study hall.

CHAPTER 6

Crossing the Continent

AT THE CLOSE of my own school year in the spring of 1933, I returned to Washington where my mother was closing our house and packing for the West Coast. The plan was for her and us three boys to drive across the continent and to join my father in Seattle, a great adventure in those days.

The car was loaded with all of our gear for the summer. There probably was not much of a trunk in the back, and luggage was tied down to a rack on top. There were running boards, and at least one of these held more luggage along the side. Various nooks and crannies inside the car were stuffed with gear as well. We must have looked like a family of Okies fleeing the Dust Bowl.

Our route: the first night with friends in Williamsport, Pennsylvania; then Cleveland, Ohio, where I watched enviously from my hotel window as my older brothers entered a burlesque show across the street; a lake steamer from Cleveland to Duluth, with stops at Detroit and Mackinac Island and passage through the Sault Ste. Marie Canal; Devil's Lake, North Dakota; Culbertson, Montana; Kalispell, Montana, from where we toured Glacier National Park; Spokane, Washington, where a gas station attendant, bemused by my mother's Eastern accent, said, "Are you from the old country, lady?"; Seattle.

The trip took about twelve days. From Duluth west, most of the route was a gravel road. Three hundred miles was a good day's run. There were no fast-food outlets, and we would usually eat at a soda fountain in a drugstore where we could get a sandwich and a milk shake. Likewise, there were no motels, and we stayed in small hotels in the towns through which we passed. In some cases, the latter comprised little more than a rail stop, a grain elevator, and a main street. It was a memorable trip for all of us. My own travels had never gotten beyond Washington to New England, and that was pretty much true for Cuth and Mid as well. Now we had traveled from coast to coast and seen much of the Great Lakes, the Great Plains, the Rockies, and finally the Pacific Coast. And we had seen all of this vast expanse of the country from relatively "close-up." Crossing the Plains was monotonous at times but that too was part of the experience. And on those northern plains we saw a sight then common but now virtually vanished from the landscape—large communities of prairie dogs with many of them standing upright on their mounds to watch us go by.

Possibly the biggest dividend for me was the rare opportunity to spend some protracted time together with my two brothers. Cuth had left Princeton the year before with the Class of 1932, having slipped from his original Class of 1931. I do not recall how he had been occupying himself since leaving college. He had spent the summer of 1932 with several college friends, sailing a boat up Lake Champlain and into the St. Lawrence, down the latter and around the Gaspé Peninsula and Cape Breton and down the Atlantic Coast to Mount Desert Island and Northeast Harbor, Maine. Middy had completed his junior year, and I suspect that he and Cuth must have found the continuous exposure to their 13-year-old kid brother pretty wearing.

My father gave us an enthusiastic welcome. No longer a deskbound sailor but a seagoing admiral with a flagship and a division of four light cruisers under his command, he was a different man. We went (without him) to Mount Rainier, where Cuth actually stayed and climbed the mountain with a guide while the rest of us indulged in more mundane excitements such as sliding down the icy mountainside wearing britches with paraffin-coated seats.

Later, from Tacoma, my mother and we three sons went to Victoria, British Columbia, for a couple of nights, taking the ferry from Port Angeles on the Olympic Peninsula across the Strait of Juan de Fuca to Vancouver Island. We stayed at the mammoth Empress Hotel and visited the world-famous Bouchart Gardens. In the summer of 1994, after fishing for a week with Bill and Jill Ruckelshaus and Jerry and Lynne Grinstein for rainbow trout on the wild Blackwater River of British Columbia, Aileen and I went to Vancouver and then to Victoria—my first visit since 1933. While the Empress had been a citadel of British gentility when our family had stayed there, it was now overrun with package tour groups. We stayed elsewhere but visited the Bouchart Gardens, which we found crowded but colorful. We enjoyed Victoria immensely and thought the Royal British Columbia Museum of Natural History one of the best museums we had seen anywhere.

Large numbers of our Pacific Fleet—battleships, cruisers, destroyers, and I believe either the *Lexington* or *Saratoga,* our principal aircraft carriers—were in Puget Sound. They were to move as a body down the coast to San Francisco and then on down to San Pedro and Long Beach near Los Angeles. My father had wangled permission to carry Mid and me on board the *Concord,* his flagship. Cuth drove to San Francisco with Mother.

We sailed from Port Angeles in the Strait of Juan de Fuca and I can still feel the excitement of that foggy day. My father's division of light cruisers—the *Concord, Trenton, Omaha,* and *Minneapolis*—led the entire fleet down the coast. He had given me his cabin and probably had bumped the ship's captain out of his. Mid shared a cabin with one of the officers. While the cabin in which I bunked was not large, it opened into a much larger cabin that was my father's office and mess room. It was all dark paneling and gleaming brass with comfortable chairs and sofa and polished mess table—all presided over by a Filipino steward's mate. Thinking back on it, I have to wonder whether my father was trying to seduce me into a naval career!

It must have been about a three-day cruise. I got all over the ship, including the bridge, and, as the admiral's brat, I can only imagine that I was well taken care of. We did not simply steam dead ahead for three days, but the ships undertook various maneuvers, and the signal lights were constantly blinking from ship to ship.

It was a great experience which was capped by our entrance into San Francisco Bay. It was a beautiful, clear day with a strong breeze blowing directly into our faces. This would have been of little note except that we were accompanied by our earliest aircraft carrier, the *Langley.* She was a converted collier with a small flight deck supported by upright girders. Somehow, she was ahead of us as we entered the bay. The wind caught her, and she was unable to hold her course but fell off and slowly drifted under the Golden Gate Bridge—then newly completed—and down upon the entire Pacific Fleet advancing into the bay. The magnificent order and discipline that had been maintained since Puget Sound evaporated as ships scrambled out of the way. The big concern was that she might drift into one of the bridge supports but she did not. Eight or more years later, she was destroyed by the Japanese as she tried to ferry a load of P-40 fighter planes to the beleaguered Dutch at Batavia (Djakarta) in the East Indies in the stark, early days of World War II not long after Pearl Harbor.

In San Francisco, we stayed at the Canterbury Hotel, a small hostelry that is still there. Cuth and I made a one-day round trip to Yosemite National Park which is the only time I have been there. It was a grueling trip without much time in the park proper, and I remember that the temperature reached 120° F in the narrow, dry valleys through which we drove to the park. It was like driving through a furnace. Of course, there was no air conditioning. Once we got there, El Capitan was hard to forget.

From San Francisco, we drove south to Long Beach—apparently our tickets on my father's ship had expired. At Long Beach, my parents had rented a large apartment at the Riviera Hotel, and I slept in a Murphy bed that pulled down from the wall. There was a fine beach but the currents were tricky, and on one occasion it took my mother, eventually aided by Cuth, to pull me in from a riptide carrying me down the shore. Visits to ships of the fleet in my father's resplendent admiral's barge, lunch aboard the carrier *Saratoga*, and drives to Pasadena to see our Brown relatives—these were some of the activities that kept us busy. Finally, it was back across the continent by train for my brothers and me, a trip I do not remember, my mother remaining on the West Coast for the next two years.

CHAPTER 7

Last Years at St. Albans and European Trips

I RETURNED TO St. Albans for the Third Form, and I boarded for two years. It was the reverse of the St. George's experience in that St. Albans was principally a day school and boarders were very much in the minority. There were two long dormitories, each with a row of cubicles along both sides. Classes, athletics, dinner, and study hall did not leave much time for idleness. In my Third Form year, I had a crystal set radio with earphones to which I could listen in bed. Arthur Godfrey was a favorite performer, and he had been a radio operator on the *Utah* when my father commanded her. Later on, he always was a friend when my father needed help for some cause he undertook, such as Children's Hospital.

Perhaps in my Fourth Form year I started my principal extracurricular involvement, the *St. Albans News,* the school newspaper. Ferdinand Ruge—Mr. Ruge to several generations of students—was the faculty advisor for the *News* and I did a lot of work with him. My classmate Bill Jackson (son of Deputy Attorney General, Nuremberg prosecutor, and Supreme Court Justice Robert Jackson) eventually became editor-in-chief and I was managing editor. It was a demanding activity and often required late hours when a deadline was imminent. I enjoyed the writing and became a passable editor. I learned to proofread galleys, write heads, lay out the paper, and eventually do the "cut and paste" job before going to press. The *St. Albans News* won most of the national prizes for a scholastic newspaper, such as that given annually by the Columbia University School of Journalism. Looking back on it, I credit Mr. Ruge and his insistence on quality for the success of the paper. He was also an exacting teacher of English, and I think whatever facility I have for writing clear, grammatical English is largely due to him. A good many years later he also taught Bowdy at St. Albans.

(A quarter of a century after I left St. Albans and had founded the African Wildlife Leadership Foundation, I decided that we needed a news bulletin to send our members. My model for the *African Wildlife News* was the *St. Albans News* which I had helped produce so many years before. I even employed the same commercial press. A federal Tax Court judge by that time, I used the same skills except in this case I had to do it all myself, as I had no helpers—and, especially, no Mr. Ruge.)

Weekends were the tough time for boarders. Fortunately, I had grandparents in Washington and frequently had Sunday lunch at my grandmother Train's. Among the latter's letters to her daughter Susan Hand which I have read was one that expressed worry about me because I was so quiet when I came to lunch. However, in a later letter to Susan, she said that I reminded her of my grandfather because I was a good conversationalist and was interested in many things! Orme Wilson had left St. Albans for St. Mark's, and I had fewer friends my age in town. In any event, the time passed and eventually my father was transferred back to Washington. Thus, I was able to return home for my last two years at St. Albans, graduating in 1937. Old friendships, such as with Cary Grayson and Richard (Ritchie) Henry Lee, remain from those days.

Having been at best an indifferent student over the years, I had a brief scholastic flowering as I left the school. St. Albans had an excellent record of college acceptances for its students. The headmaster, Canon Lucas, was very protective of that record and did not like to provide a recommendation to a college if he did not think the student could make it. Likewise, he did not recommend a student to take particular college board exams if he thought he would make a poor grade. I was trying for Princeton, which he had clearly decided was over my head, and I took all the college boards I would need despite his negative recommendation. To make a long story a bit shorter, I crammed like hell for those exams and, to use an expression of my father's, "I knocked the eye out of them."

That summer at Bar Harbor with Orme, I went to see Lucas at his summer home at Southwest Harbor, also on Mount Desert Island, and he ate "humble pie." I had plainly surprised him, and he graciously admitted it and warmly congratulated me. It was one of those small triumphs that one savors.

European Trips

STARTING IN 1934 and ending with the start of World War II in September 1939, I spent four summers with the Wilsons in Europe—first in Berlin, then two summers in Prague, and finally, following a summer spent mostly in Bar Harbor, a summer in Brussels. Those summers—like the one spent driving across the continent and seeing the West Coast—provided an eye-opening breadth of experience at an impressionable stage of my life.

We were in Berlin in the summer of 1934 as the phenomenon of Hitler and Nazism unfolded. We were in Czechoslovakia during the summers of 1935 and 1936 as fear of German expansionism gripped that country. And we were in vulnerable Belgium in the summer of 1939 as the war clouds were about to burst. We visited the great museums of London, Paris, Berlin, Munich, Dresden, and Prague. We saw the changing of the guard at Buckingham Palace and toured the Tower of London. We visited Versailles and Potsdam. We went to bullfights in Spain. We visited St. Paul's and Westminster as well as the cathedrals of Notre-Dame, Rheims, Rouen, Amiens, Chartres, and Compiègne.

We toured landscapes from the Bay of Biscay to the Adriatic to the North Sea. We went to the opera in Prague and the music festival in Salzburg. We stayed at some of the great watering places of Europe, such as Carlsbad and Baden-Baden. We had guest memberships at the best country clubs, such as the Blau-Weiss at Berlin and the Royal Leopold at Brussels, where we played tennis and swam. We went to

In Berlin with Orme, 1934

the 1936 Berlin Olympic Games where we saw and heard Adolf Hitler receive the Nazi salute of 100,000 raised arms and the Sieg Heils from 100,000 throats. I had seen him once before in 1934 right after the burning of the Reichstag—one of the events used to whip up anti-Jewish feeling in Germany.

On at least two and perhaps three occasions, Cuth escorted Orme and myself across the Atlantic to Europe, where he then disengaged from us and pursued his own interests, which included climbing the Matterhorn one summer. Learning experiences came in different forms. Once, crossing on the brand-new French liner *Normandie*, the three of us were traveling second class. Cuth left Orme and me unchaperoned one evening, while he was the guest for dinner of a Washington girl in first class (a daughter of Dwight Davis, donor of the Davis Cup). I got thoroughly intoxicated on red wine at dinner and had to retire below to our cabin, where I proceeded to be violently sick. I ended up on the floor of the cabin, quite unable to rise. Suddenly, while I was in this dignified posture, the door opened and there was Cuth with his dinner date. I was introduced, smiled wanly from my prone position, and they left rather hurriedly. It was not one of my greatest moments. I must have been just 15 at the time.

It seems too bad to leave those summer experiences on such a sorry note. They were, in fact, quite extraordinary times that left a deep imprint. The Wilsons were wonderfully kind and generous in making such opportunities available to me, and I owe them a very large debt of gratitude. Mrs. Wilson became almost a second mother to me, and I held her in great affection.

One recurring question—at least to me—is why I never looked for a summer job and, indeed, why my parents never suggested that I find one. I am not talking about when I was a schoolboy but rather later when I was an undergraduate at Princeton. It never seemed to occur to anyone, which is probably as much a commentary on the times as anything else. Moreover, I don't recall Cuth or Middy ever taking a summer job either—other than the time that Mid spent an hour or so a day in Newport trying to teach me a bit of Latin. Actually, there was only one summer that I was largely unoccupied and that was the summer of my freshman year in 1938. The summer of my sophomore year in 1939 was spent in Europe, and during the summer of my junior year in 1940 I spent six weeks at R.O.T.C. summer camp at Madison Barracks, near Watertown, New York, on Lake Ontario. I really did spend a pretty feckless summer at the end of my freshman year, spending much of it at my grandparent Browns' house on Connecticut Avenue. My parents were again on the West Coast, where my father commanded a division of three battleships, with his flag on the *Tennessee*. (This was to be his last sea command.) In their absence, there was really no one to stir me up.

Chapter 8

College and World War II

I know that my father had always hoped that I would go to the Naval Academy. Certainly, he and my grandfather Train had established a fine naval tradition. Neither Cuth nor Middy had been likely candidates—Cuth because of bad eyesight and Mid because of his short stature. I knew I was the last hope, and I postponed a decision until my senior year at St. Albans, in large part, I suspect, because I hated to disappoint my old man. It was a tough decision, and I was only 16 at the time. To his credit, my father never tried to pressure me in any way to go to the Academy. He knew I knew that he hoped that would be my decision, but both he and my mother made it quite clear that the decision was mine. I was influenced by several things.

First of all, of course, both my older brothers had gone to Princeton and had had a marvelous time. Second, it seemed to me that the Navy had changed enormously—certainly since my grandfather's day but also during my father's career. It had grown very much bigger and, while they had both enjoyed a close association with most of their fellow officers, that sense of a close-knit society had changed tremendously. Also, while I had been brought up very much aware of the Navy tradition in the family, my life and my friends were not those of a typical Navy "brat." My life had been almost entirely in Washington and much of it devoid of Navy associations. I still remember the moment when I told my father that I did not want to go to the Academy. I could see that it hit him hard but he made no effort to argue the matter.

I have never regretted the decision. The Navy would have provided a more ordered, disciplined life from which I might have benefited up to a point, but I doubt that it would have been a good fit. At the same time, my career at Princeton was hardly exemplary.

Princeton freshman, 1937

A Freshman at Princeton

NO CLASSMATES from St. Albans accompanied me to Princeton. In
fact, there was only one other freshman from Washington and I did
not know him. Basically, I had no friends to start off with, a situation
very different from that of most of my classmates from the big prep
schools who came with a core group of friends. To compound the
problem, I was a year younger than most of my classmates. I brought
no athletic skills with me although I played a bit of tennis my first
year. I was a pretty miserable physical specimen in any event and was
required to take "Doc" Swinnerton's "body-building" course my first
term. On the other hand, I took to cigarettes and beer (and, not infre-
quently, hard liquor) with enthusiasm. Looking back on it all, it is easy
to see that this sort of behavior was a natural reaction to what was
doubtless a pretty strong sense of social insecurity.

My big achievement that first fall was to participate with another
classmate—John L. Lewis, Jr., the son of the renowned labor leader—
in "stealing" the clapper of the bell in the tower of Nassau Hall, a peren-

nial freshman escapade. We were not caught and later returned the clapper anonymously to the authorities.

As might be imagined from all this, my achievements on the academic side left a good deal to be desired. In fact, midway through my first year, I was summoned to Dean Radcliffe Heermance's office in Nassau Hall. He was dean of freshmen and director of admissions and had had somewhat similar dealings with both Cuth and Middy. He came straight to the point and opened the meeting by stating "Russell, under present circumstances, there is absolutely no way you can ever become a sophomore." I do not recall the rest of the conversation, but the dean's statement had what I suppose was the desired effect. I galvanized myself, pulled up my grades in the spring term, and did, in fact, become a sophomore.

R.O.T.C.

ONE OF THE best early decisions I made was to sign up for R.O.T.C. (the Reserve Officers Training Corps). In part, I think that I saw R.O.T.C. as a bit of a propitiation for not going to the Naval Academy. Since Princeton did not have a Navy R.O.T.C., I necessarily ended up in the Army Field Artillery. And, even in 1937, it seemed increasingly likely that there would be a major war and that the U.S. would eventually be drawn in. What I had already seen of the tensions in Europe and the rapid re-armament of Germany doubtless contributed to this sense.

The equipment with which we trained was strictly World War I vintage: horse-drawn caissons and "French 75s," then still the basic light artillery weapon of the U.S. Army. One advantage that came with our obsolete equipment was riding. We had regular riding instruction, including jumping, on the rather tired old Army remounts. I still had not developed the allergy to horses which afflicted me later.

Several of those who were in the R.O.T.C. program had signed up because it gave them access to horses for polo. A few had even brought their own horses with them. Two of my good friends were enthusiastic polo players—one of them a sophomore-year roommate, Whitney Bowles—and I developed an interest in the sport. I spent time in the practice cage, sitting on a wooden frame and swinging a mallet at a ball. The bottom of the cage was sloped so that a hit ball would roll back into position for another shot. After a while, I tried the real thing in the riding hall where indoor polo games were played. It was quickly apparent that polo was not my thing. I always explained my lack of talent by saying that I could ride a horse and could hit a ball with the mallet but couldn't do both at the same time. In any event, I kept in touch with the game as a sort of non-playing assistant manager. My father came to Princeton and spent several days during which he watched a polo match and met and talked with a number of my friends.

Debutante Parties

DURING CHRISTMAS vacation my freshman year, I began to attend debutante parties—usually a dance but sometimes a tea—at which young ladies were presented to society by their parents. I went to a few such parties in New York, one in Bar Harbor, but mostly in Washington. The girls were usually 18 when they came out and most of the young men who attended their parties were that age or older. Thus, as usual, I was about a year ahead of myself. I think I spent more time around the bar than on the dance floor at most of those parties. During my sophomore year, more girls came out who were my contemporaries and whom I had known as I grew up.

Most of the winter "deb" parties in Washington were given at the Sulgrave Club, and we joked about how many consecutive evenings we had been there. I remember one coming-out party at the White House for Eleanor Roosevelt's niece. There was a receiving line but the president did not join it. I remember him in his wheelchair watching the dancing in the East Room, but I did not meet him.

Hard liquor was not served—I imagine out of sensitivity over serving alcohol to minors in the White House. However, I soon noticed that members of the Roosevelt family seemed well supplied with drinks and I quickly solved the problem. When Father had been Hoover's naval aide, he had a yeoman named Clanch. The latter had risen rapidly since then and had become chief usher of the White House, the general factotum who basically ran the White House social logistics. I went to his office which was in the vestibule of the White House, immediately to the right of the main entrance as you came in, and explained the problem to him. He told me to go and wait just inside the entrance to the Red Room. This I did and soon a waiter arrived with a tray covered with a large napkin. He approached, lifted a corner of the napkin and "Presto!" there was a scotch and soda. I had learned to crack the Washington special-interest system!

Clubs and Roommates

AT COLLEGE, I tried out for the "Daily Princetonian," or "the Prince," as it was generally known. Either I did not make it or my interest flagged and I left the competition. A major event in sophomore year was the selection of students for membership in the various upper class eating clubs. There was the horrendous "bicker week" when you stayed in your rooms in the evenings and were called on (or not) by representatives of the clubs. I made the Terrace Club which, on a social ranking of 1 to 10, would have been about a 3. I had only one good friend who joined with me, Jack Monzani, and at the end of our junior year I resigned my membership. As a result, during senior year, I was either a guest for dinner at someone else's club or, frequently, had dinner on my own in the bar of the Nassau Tavern—the "Nass." I think this story of my club experience pretty well exemplifies my lack of social success at college.

I had two roommates my sophomore year, Whitney Bowles and Ed Holden. We had become friends as freshmen. Whit was a polo player which was probably one reason I became interested in the sport. His home was in northern New Jersey and he was a great-grandson of Samuel Bowles, who had been a famous editor of the Springfield,

Massachusetts, *Republican* and a friend of my great-grandfather, Charles Russell Train. Whit had gone to Lawrenceville before coming to Princeton. Ed came from New York City and his family had a summer house at Quogue, Long Island. He had gone to Kent School in Connecticut where he had been coxswain on the crew. However, his principal outdoor interest lay in sailing.

Whit went back to rooming by himself in our junior year and eventually left Princeton without graduating. His father had been killed at the close of World War I just prior to Whit's birth, and he had been brought up under the strong influence of Roger Baldwin, a prominent liberal and pacifist, who was practically speaking a surrogate father to Whit. When war came, Whit registered as a conscientious objector. He refused to make any easy compromises and his case went all the way to the Supreme Court, which ruled against him. Knowing him as well as I did, I know that no lack of courage was involved but a matter of strong personal principle which he simply would not compromise. I lost touch with him until after Aileen and I were married when he came once to our house in Washington.

Ed Holden and I remained roommates for the rest of our time at Princeton. We were very compatible, as we seemed to share all the same bad habits. We smoked like chimneys, drank whenever we could afford it, took little exercise, and avoided study as much as we could. His father, Arthur C. Holden, was an architect in New York, and he and Ed's mother had a house in the East 70s where we usually stayed after a night on the town. We would take the train into the city and our favorite haunts were jazz hangouts along 52nd Street and in Greenwich Village where we listened to such jazz greats as Duke Ellington, Count Basie, Bix Beiderbecke, and Zutty Singleton. These excursions were mostly on weekends and not all that frequent, as both Ed and I suffered from a chronic shortage of funds. At one stage, he succeeded in selling a sailboat, a Star class boat, and he generously saw to it that I too enjoyed the proceeds as long as they lasted.

Ed subscribed to the *New Yorker* while at college, and I became an inveterate reader although I find few of its cartoons today either funny or comprehensible. He introduced me to the world of James Thurber, whose writings and drawings continue to delight me, although Thurber himself is long gone.[1]

I do not now recall what Ed did during the war and our paths did not cross during those years. After the war, he worked for the New York *Daily News*. I saw him on several visits to New York, and he was very much the same laid-back, entertaining guy. He made a rather ill-assorted marriage which did not last and then suddenly became ill and died.

His father, known as "Ace" Holden, had been a member of the Class of 1912 at Princeton and was his class alumni secretary for many years until he was the only member of his class left. He became the oldest living alumnus and lived to about 102. When I had my fiftieth reunion, he and his nurse led the P-rade in a golf cart and he later came to my own class gathering.

A short while before that, he had telephoned me in Washington out of the blue. I had had essentially no contact with him since my graduation. He told me then that he was over a hundred and then asked, "Do you remember Miriam?" That was Ed's mother and I replied, "Of course." (She had been one to take up "causes" and Ed would laugh and say that when you visited his family's house there might well be an Indian weaving a basket in the corner of the living room. I never saw one.) Ace then said, "Well, she died about 35 years ago and I decided to marry the girl I always had wanted to marry in the first place. I did. [Pause] She died about 20 years ago." Our conversation sort of petered out after that.

1. I have an original Thurber drawing inscribed by him to Charles Laughton, the actor, on his birthday. The cartoon, which depicts a man and a woman wheeling in inimitable Thurber style through space, is entitled "Marriages are Made in Heaven." Thurber usually stayed in London at the Stafford Hotel and stayed there for fairly protracted periods. A number of his letters collected and published after his death are dated at the Stafford. The latter is where I always stay in London but unfortunately the records which would show which room Thurber used have been destroyed.

Outbreak of War

WORLD WAR II began shortly before the beginning of our junior year in the fall of 1939 and radically changed our prospects, although, as I have said, war in Europe had seemed inevitable to many of us for some time. Not only did war seem inevitable, but I also assumed that the U.S. would ultimately enter the war and should. Orme Wilson and I had spent that summer in Brussels with his parents. Joseph Davies was our ambassador but, with his wife, Marjorie Merriweather Post, was absent the entire time we were there—pretty surprising in view of the level of tension in Europe and the vulnerability of Belgium. Orme's father was chargé d'affaires that summer and we heard a lot of political talk.

We played a great deal of tennis and by this time Orme was clearly my superior on the court. We played regularly at the Royal Leopold Club outside Brussels and entered tournaments at Spa in the Ardennes and at Ostend, Zeebruge, and La Zoute on the coast. As August advanced, and the gorgeous dry summer waned, Belgium began to call its military classes[2] to the colors. Orme and I advanced rapidly in our tournaments as our opponents were called up. Finally, in our last tournament of the season at Ostend, Orme and I defaulted rather than win the doubles trophy by the forced departure of our opponents.

Early in September, we returned home. We drove from Brussels to Le Havre where we boarded the U.S. Line's S.S. *Washington* for New York. The ship called at Southampton and by the time we had reached that port the German panzers had crashed into Poland and France and Britain had declared war. We had to enter Southampton through a minefield and one of the mines had apparently broken loose, delaying our entrance until it had been recovered and secured. Barrage balloons hung over the dock area. Once under way, we moved at our best speed and at night were fully floodlighted to display our nationality. About a day out from Southampton, we heard the news of the torpedo-sinking

2. All troops who are conscripted for training in a particular year belong to the "class" of that year.

of the British passenger ship *Athenia* in the North Atlantic—pretty much on our course. We had a number of friends on board the *Washington*. I think we all felt pretty nervous, but we were young and excited and hid any worries we may have had by partying heavily all the way across.

My Father's Retirement

MY PARENTS returned to Washington from the West Coast. My father had a heart condition that had been growing worse. He had had a fairly severe heart attack several years before following a tennis match at Chevy Chase. Now his physical condition was forcing him to retire on disability and to do so just as the nation began to gear itself up for war. He was recalled to active duty later to head the Navy Relief Society which provided assistance to families of Navy personnel suffering the various dislocations that could occur in wartime. It was an important responsibility, and my father threw himself into it with characteristic enthusiasm. Whatever job he ever had, he always put the best he had into it. He was always determined that his ship be the best—whether in gunnery or whatever. It was no different with the Navy Relief Society. But I can imagine how hard it was for him, having trained all of his life for a war, to find himself sidelined—particularly after the war in the Pacific began and his friends and contemporaries, such as Halsey and Spruance, went on to become great battle commanders. I never heard him complain. At least he was in uniform. He would have made a splendid commander in action and would doubtless have followed Nelson's tactical advice when confronted by an enemy battle fleet: "Go right at 'em!"

Princeton Graduation

COLLEGE PROCEEDED about as usual. The news on the radio and in our newspapers reported on the progress of the war. After the fall of

Poland, the war in the west settled down to a sort of waiting game. R.O.T.C. took on a new reality and few of us doubted that the U.S. would be in the war sooner or later. In the summer of 1940, I spent six weeks at the R.O.T.C. camp at Madison Barracks on Lake Ontario. The First Division—known as the "Big Red 1" from its shoulder patch—was based nearby. Our nearest town was Watertown, where the bar in the Woodruff Hotel was our principal watering spot. The nearest village was Sacketts Harbor which played an important role in the War of 1812. We lived in pyramidal tents, did KP, had calisthenics, drilled, and otherwise got some feel for life in the Army. We had classes and field exercises which involved setting up telephone networks, protecting ourselves from poison gas, serving the artillery pieces, doing vehicle maintenance, etc.

On the road to camp from Watertown was a strategically located brothel known as "Dirty Gertie's." Later, when we had entered the war, and the First Division was in action in North Africa, a ballad sprang up entitled "Dirty Gertie from Bizerte." I always wondered whether Gertie had packed up her girls and somehow moved them from Watertown to Bizerte to stay close to the Big Red 1.

My major at Princeton was political science, known there as "politics," and my senior thesis was entitled "U.S. Naval War with Japan," which certainly proved a timely subject. Obviously, I chose it in large part because of exposure to the topic at home over some time. My father's second tour at the Naval War College had focused on a Pacific war, and, in the various war games, they tested out the strategic concepts that later shaped the course of the naval war in the Pacific. I believe that he was the senior officer in his class at that time and, thus, was apt to "command" one of the fleets engaged in the games. He became a strong believer in the use of aircraft carrier task forces to project air power across the Pacific, opening the way for surface forces to follow. That is pretty much what happened, in fact.

When I was considering a Foreign Service career as I was getting ready to leave active service at the end of the war, my family sent a copy of my thesis to Norman Armour, then an Assistant Secretary of State, who read it and wrote a letter describing it as "prescient." Lest it be thought that I was simply parroting ideas presented to me by my father, I put a lot of research into the development of the thesis, particularly in finding Japanese authors on naval strategy whose writings provided insight into Japanese thinking on the subject. I also researched back files of the *South China News* and other similar sources to see what the Japanese military had been up to in the Far East in recent years, and, finally, by way of background, I did an analysis of Japanese natural resource availability (or lack of it).

In any event, the thesis was well received by my advisor and other reviewers and, wonder of wonders, I graduated cum laude and my thesis won honorable mention for the New York Herald Tribune Prize. I had come a long way from that meeting with Dean Heermance in my freshman year. My parents drove up from Washington and stayed with friends in order to attend the commencement ceremonies. Believe it or not, I partied so late and so strenuously the night before that I simply slept through the entire graduation exercise. How it was possible to be so immature and so irresponsible after four years of college—and so lacking in respect and gratitude to my parents—I will never understand. I still squirm with embarrassment as I write this all down! Pretty much the worse for wear, I drove back to Washington that afternoon with my parents.

I received my commission as a second lieutenant in the field artillery reserve at the same time as I was awarded my degree. I would have been only three or four days beyond my 21st birthday at the time. Almost immediately, I received my orders to active duty which directed me to report to Fort Myer, Virginia, directly across the Potomac River from Washington, on July 1. So on that day began my active service in World War II, service which would last about four years.

CHAPTER 9

Military Service

IT IS SOMEWHAT misleading to devote a special section to my war service because it was largely uneventful, and there were certainly no heroic actions on my part to report. At the same time, those four years represented a fair chunk of my life as well as a time when I began (hopefully) to grow into a more responsible individual.

At Fort Myer, I was temporarily assigned to the 16th Field Artillery—the ceremonial, "White Horse" battalion that performed burials of those entitled to full military honors. I performed no duties with them and was simply assigned on paper while awaiting further orders. These came in a few days, and I was ordered to report to the Field Artillery Replacement Training Center (F.A.R.T.C.) at Fort Bragg, near Fayetteville, North Carolina. About half of my Princeton R.O.T.C. group was also ordered to Fort Bragg and the other half to the Basic Officers' Training Course at the Field Artillery School at Fort Sill, Oklahoma. The latter was the preferred assignment because it generally led in a few weeks to being assigned to a "line" field artillery unit.

Prior to my leaving for Fort Bragg, my father and I went to Stohlman's Chevrolet, an auto dealer located on the south side of M Street in Georgetown, close to Key Bridge, and he bought a car for me. I acquired a two-door, 1939 Plymouth for $300, all of which my father paid. I remained totally impecunious. Becoming 21 had not produced any trust funds or other resources. On the other hand, my Brown grandparents had both died the year before and my grandmother Train in 1938, and my parents were now in relatively comfortable circumstances and reasonably free of financial worry. Having their three sons out of college must have helped in that regard.

Second lieutenant,
Field Artillery, 1941

Fort Bragg

A FEW DAYS later I drove south to Fort Bragg, spending the night
before I reported at a hotel in Raleigh where I recall being horrified to
have my first experience (probably on a Sunday night) of the "dry" laws
scattered across the South. At Fort Bragg, I was assigned to the "cooks
and bakers" battalion. While cooks and bakers were clearly essential to
a rapidly growing army, the assignment did not have a very dashing
ring to it. In point of fact, the culinary training was entirely conducted
by Quartermaster Corps officers and non-coms. We "line" officers were
responsible for the men's basic military training—military courtesy,
close-order drill, calisthenics, personal hygiene, field exercises, weapon
(rifle) care and range firing, etc. It was largely a rehash of much of the
training that I had received in R.O.T.C.

As a second lieutenant, I was responsible for a platoon of 25 or so men, perhaps more. It was not arduous work, and we had the assistance of regular Army non-coms. After six weeks, the trainees graduated from basic training and were shipped out to field artillery units being formed around the country. A new group of trainees would then arrive, and we started all over again with them. How inductees got assigned to a "cooks and bakers" unit was always something of a mystery. If a man had actually been a cook in a restaurant, that was plain enough. However, when I asked one of the cooks in the 750th F.A. Battalion with which I ultimately went overseas how he had been selected as a cook, he replied: "Because I had worked in a factory that made machines that made pretzels." There was the logical way of doing things and then there was the Army way. The big thing in the Army was order and discipline, logical or not, and with a burgeoning citizen army, those were probably the right priorities. My father visited Fort Bragg while I was there, gave a talk to my platoon, and generally enjoyed himself. Looking back, I am always impressed by the opportunities he found, both with my mother and alone, to visit me in college and in the Army.

We officers lived on the other side of the large parade ground from the enlisted quarters but in similar structures called BOQs—Bachelor Officers' Quarters. Each of us had our own room, not much bigger than the cubicles I remembered from boarding school. The F.A.R.T.C. was a wartime, temporary construction, but the main post of Fort Bragg was a permanent facility. There was a fine officers' club to which we repaired, mostly on weekends. Southern Pines and Pinehurst were not far away for additional, civilized recreation.

My boon companion during that tour at Fort Bragg was Jack Monzani, a classmate and good friend from Princeton. Later in the war and subsequently, we failed to keep in touch and Jack died unexpectedly around 1970. Aileen and I ran into his widow and two small children during a visit to Harbour Island, Eleuthera, Bahamas, in 1974.

Pearl Harbor

MOST DRAFTEES had been drafted for one year of service, and that time was up for many of them in October 1941. As rumors grew that Congress might extend the service period, there was a good deal of discontent among the draftees and "OHIO" was their slogan—"Over the Hill in October." Well, Congress extended the period of service but very few made good their threat to go AWOL, and the whole issue became moot when the Japanese bombed Pearl Harbor.

I had flown home to Washington for that weekend and was staying at Que Street. About lunchtime on Sunday, December 7, the day "which will live in infamy," in the words of Franklin Roosevelt in his war message to the Congress the next day, someone called up and said we had better listen to the radio. Thus, we heard the news of Pearl Harbor.

Early that afternoon, my parents and I walked to the Japanese Embassy on Massachusetts Avenue at California Street—the old embassy and not their present mammoth structure on Nebraska Avenue—and joined a small group of perhaps twenty who stood quietly across the avenue from the embassy. Japanese men in dark suits scurried in and out of the door of the left wing. A curl of smoke rose from the chimney, and our group opinion was that the Japanese were disposing of classified documents, codes, etc. One or two policemen stood quietly in the vicinity. The atmosphere had an unreal quality about it. A newspaper photographer appeared in front of us, aimed his camera at us, and said, "Now, everyone shake your fist!" A very few did.

After a while of this, the three of us walked back home and my parents gave me a lift to National Airport where I caught my commercial flight back to Raleigh. I was back for duty with my unit Monday morning. The training routine remained the same as before. It was as if nothing had changed, and yet everything had.

The commanding general of the F.A.R.T.C. was Major General Edwin Parker. I never met him at that time, and he was a distant and godlike figure. A great friend of Mid's from Washington, Charlie

McKenny, was his aide, and he and I got together for a drink now and then. Curiously, years later when I was chairman of the Board of Governors of St. Albans School, General Parker, who had had a distinguished career as a combat commander during the war, was the school's administrative officer. (He also managed Oak Hill Cemetery in Washington for several years.)

Fort Sill

AFTER A YEAR at Bragg, I was ordered to Fort Sill, Oklahoma, to take the Basic Officers' Training Course, reporting there in June 1942. I went home briefly first and then drove to Fort Sill via Bristol, Virginia; Nashville and Memphis, Tennessee; and Tulsa, Oklahoma. I don't really recall how long the course was, perhaps six weeks, perhaps three months. The focus was on gunnery, which was welcome after my cooks and bakers stint. There was nothing particularly memorable about the duty. Fort Sill was home base for the field artillery as Fort Benning, Georgia, was for the infantry and Fort Riley, Kansas, was for the cavalry.

Weekends were spent in Oklahoma City. The state was entirely dry, but liquor could always be procured from the bellboy at your hotel. The alternative was to drive to Wichita Falls, Texas, commonly known as "Whiskey Falls," to acquire a supply of liquor. When I inquired about the rationale of the various dry laws that one ran into around the country, I was told cynically that the dry laws were the product of an unholy alliance between the anti-alcohol clergy and the bootleggers.

Tank Destroyers

AT THE conclusion of the Fort Sill course, I was ordered to the Tank Destroyer Replacement Training Center at Camp Hood (now Fort Hood) between Waco and Temple, Texas. I had hoped to be assigned to a new artillery unit but that was not to be. One had no say in such

Fort Sill, Oklahoma, 1943

decisions, and the rationale always remained mysterious. Camp Hood was the headquarters of the tank destroyer command. Tank destroyers were a recent innovation based on the idea that to counter the German panzers we needed a faster, more mobile gun mount. The Army had already developed armored personnel carriers described as "half-tracks"—wheels in front and tracks on the rear. They were reasonably fast but very lightly armored and the weapon mounted on them as tank destroyers was the old "French 75." The first time tank destroyer units saw action was in North Africa at the Battle of Kasserine Pass. They got badly mauled and beat a hasty retreat—some might say ran. They were heavily outgunned by the German tanks with their longer-range, more powerful, flatter-trajectory 88s—converted anti-aircraft weapons. Ultimately, the tank destroyer concept was abandoned.

I spent about a year at Camp Hood, getting to know Dallas, Fort Worth, Waco, and Temple, Texas, during leisure hours. We were giving basic training to new recruits with a lot of emphasis on vehicle operation and maintenance.

A Parental Visit

A SURPRISE was a visit to Camp Hood by my mother and father. Frankly, I think my father was really curious as to what went on in the Army and that now that he had a son in the Army this was his chance to find out. He arranged their visit directly with General Bruce, the T.D.R.T.C. commander. My parents stayed at a hotel in Temple, and General Bruce entertained my father royally. He rode and probably drove an assortment of armored vehicles and fired a 50-caliber machine gun on the firing range. He watched a gunnery demonstration with the French 75s. In other words, he had a ball. He liked General Bruce, whom he saw quite a bit, and liked the way Bruce ran his command— a taut ship, I am sure he said. I think he left with a good deal of respect for the Army. I saw little of my parents except during our evening meals, but I was thrilled that they had come and that my father had seen so much of our activities. The Army's public relations office knew a good thing when they saw it and a local newspaper headlined: "He's An Admiral And The Son Of An Admiral But He's Proud Of His Son Who Went Wrong And Joined Army."

Mid had been commissioned in the Navy before I went on active duty in the Army. He had taken the officers' course on the U.S.S. *Prairie State* at New York City and had been assigned to a Navy command on Trinidad in the West Indies under Rear Admiral Arthur Radford with whom he developed a close association. Mid then served under Halsey in the Pacific and was stationed for a time at Noumea, New Caledonia. When Radford was transferred to the Pacific and given command of a carrier task force, Mid joined him as flag lieutenant aboard his flagship *Independence*. (See *The Train Family*, Appendix E, for Mid's own account of his war record.)

The Navy finally let Cuth and his bad eyes in, and he was commissioned a personnel officer at the Navy Department in Washington.

I received my promotion to captain while at Camp Hood. Our battalion commander, Lieutenant Colonel McIlhenny, was an avid baseball fan. Our battalion had an officers' softball team, and, on the occasion in question, played a game with the team of another battalion. Old McIlhenny—probably at least 20 years younger than I at this writing—exhorted his team from the sidelines. I don't recall what position I played, but late in the game I stood at the plate and hit a home run, doubtless due to ineptitude in our opponents' outfield, that won the game. The papers for my promotion to captain were forwarded by McIlhenny the next morning.

Louisiana Maneuvers

TOWARD THE end of 1943, I was ordered to the 17th Tank Destroyer Group on maneuvers at Camp Polk, Louisiana. I was there only a short while, including Christmas 1943. I remember now how cold it was in that red clay country of northern Louisiana. About Christmastime, I was temporarily assigned to special duty with the Third Army Provisional Headquarters as assistant G-1. This was the headquarters for all troops on maneuvers. A letter written to my parents on January 1, 1944, said: "I have a few more amenities of life in this new job—a steel cot, mattress, tent with wooden floor, stove, hot showers, etc. . . . We celebrated New Year's Eve as well as possible around a fire in the woods." We had coal stoves in our tents and the coal smoke hung low in the pine woods where we were camped. I was involved in field maneuvers but mostly had an administrative job. This was fortunate because one day a "requisition" came in from higher headquarters directing us to provide the names of several officers to help staff new field artillery units. I seized the oppportunity and submitted, along with the requisite others, my own name to be the operations officer (S-3) of a new heavy (8-inch howitzer) field artillery battalion.

The New Field Artillery Unit

THE 750TH F.A. Battalion, my new unit, was being activated at Camp Hood, of all places. So back I went to Camp Hood, except that

Orme Wilson, Jr., 1944

this time I was no longer in a training unit but with a line, combat outfit. Of course, we would receive mostly raw recruits who would have to
be trained from scratch. As S-3, I was the third-ranking officer in the
battalion, responsible for organizing, scheduling, and monitoring all
training. Actually, the day-by-day training schedule was pretty much
laid out for us and all we had to do was follow it. My new associates
were those with whom I would presumably serve out the war.

Our battalion commander was Lieutenant Colonel John Toman
and our executive officer Major Ralph Cox. In addition to the staff
officer positions, there was a Headquarters Battery to which all the
headquarters enlisted personnel belonged and which was responsible
in the field for establishing and maintaining communication networks—both telephone and radio—and for operating the mapping
and survey functions essential to fire control. The Headquarters Battery commander was Captain Edward A. O'Neill. Ed became my
closest friend. He and his wife, Lo, lived in modest married officers'
quarters on the post and their home was a cultivated oasis for me.

There were three firing batteries, A, B, and C. Each of these was under the command of a captain—although they did not all attain that rank immediately. There was also a service battery which handled supplies as well as vehicle and weapon maintenance that was beyond the capability of the batteries.

The officers were a good group, most of whom had been commissioned through R.O.T.C. We got along well together, although the battalion commander was not well liked. He had been a National Guard officer and, as I remember, had managed a car wash business in Milwaukee. I suspect he felt very insecure and dealt with his insecurity by maintaining a considerable distance from the rest of us. I do not recall a personal exchange with him—other than strictly business—in the two years or so we were together. When not required in headquarters, he would shut himself into his room or tent, as the case happened to be. On Okinawa, after hostilities were pretty much over, occasional movies were shown to our and the neighboring battalion (the 749th F.A.). Places were reserved in the front row for the officers. Our battalion commander evidently felt conspicuous in always arriving by himself and solved the problem by detailing Cox and myself to take turns accompanying him.

On another occasion, also on Okinawa, the island was battered by a vicious typhoon and our battalion's camp was hard hit. When it subsided, we received warning of a possible tsunami, an enormous wave that sometimes follows a typhoon and can wreak tremendous destruction. Our camp was on former agricultural land that gently sloped down to the sea. I had no idea whether we were vulnerable or not and there was certainly no expert opinion available. I suggested to Toman that we move the men to higher ground for the night as a precaution. He replied that he did not think there was any danger, that he was not leaving his tent, and that I could do whatever I wished. Left with the decision, I hiked the entire battalion up onto a nearby and very rocky ridge where we spent a miserable night in driving wind and rain. No tsunami developed and the next morning we returned to camp. But what an odd way to run a railroad!

Either during this period or during my previous tour at Camp

Hood, Mid paid me a visit en route to San Francisco and the Pacific, where he was to join Radford's staff. We both stayed in the hotel at Temple, Texas, over a weekend and caught up on our war stories. My naval relatives were really checking up on me! I am sure I showed Mid around the base. Visiting me was a major detour for him, and I appreciated his doing so. Travel was not all that easy. Planes were crowded, and it was hard to get a seat unless traveling under orders. And, of course, there were no jet planes in those days. DC-3s and DC-4s were the commercial workhorses. Actually, Mid was probably traveling across the continent by train.

At some point I attended the Advanced Officers' Course at Fort Sill but am not certain as to the dates. At Camp Hood, our battalion trained with World War I-vintage 155-mm howitzers—basically companion pieces to the old French 75s. Our weapons would eventually be modern 8-inch howitzers—very large and requiring oversized tracked vehicles to move them. However, none of this equipment was yet available.

Overseas—Oahu and Okinawa

IN JANUARY 1944, when our battalion was about a year old, we moved by train to Fort Lewis, Washington, just outside Seattle, and then by Navy transport to Honolulu where we went into camp at Schofield Barracks, the principal army base on Oahu and about a 20 minute drive from Honolulu and Waikiki Beach. There we finally received our 8-inch howitzers and prime movers and started training exercises on the firing range. This was my first visit to Hawaii, and I found it very beautiful. The steep, forest-clad ridges were unlike anything I had ever seen. We swam from white-sand beaches without a sign of other people. I drove up the Pali Pass road behind Honolulu and had Sunday dinner at least twice with Dr. and Mrs. Morgan, the parents-in-law of my cousin Nancy Brown Morgan, at their beautiful home overlooking the city.

My battalion sailed from Oahu—"shipped out" was the common

phrase—about June 1, 1945. We were on a number of different ships, and I was on an LST (Landing Ship Tank), destination: Okinawa. Only one other officer was on board from the battalion. We had a large number of our enlisted personnel and a lot of trucks. The ship's officers were all reservists and a nice crowd. Okinawa had been invaded March 26. We were not intended to be part of the Okinawa operation but to stage there for the final assault on the main islands of Japan.

The Okinawa operation took far longer than anticipated. Hence, our trip across the Pacific was stretched out for about six weeks. We stopped briefly at Eniwetok and Ulithi on the way and then made a protracted stop off Saipan waiting for Okinawa to be secured. My letters home give some of the flavor of the trip.

June 4 [my 25th birthday] . . . The food of course is superlative. Our men simply cannot get over the comparative luxury of life aboard ship. I must say that I look forward to these ocean jaunts and enjoy them more than anything I know . . . Pretty good library on board and I have been doing a lot of reading—John Dos Passos, Sherwood Anderson, Beard's "Republic," a life of Francis Parkman, etc.—all very intellectual and, of course, some murders.

June 10 . . . the sea continues calm. No unpleasant motion as the sea has been squarely astern and this ship doesn't pitch but when the sea comes from abeam she really rolls. Magnificent sunset tonight—as there is almost every evening. It's the pleasantest time of day—cool and no sun burning your face . . . Fortunately, this type of enforced inactivity doesn't bore me in the slightest. Breakfast about 7:15, read on deck or sit in the con until lunch at 11:30, sleep in my cabin in the afternoon, shower and fresh uniform for supper at 5:15, on deck until dark, cards (cribbage, hearts, bridge) in the wardroom (I have just finished trimming the skipper at cribbage) until after nine, then a large bowl of coffee and to bed where I sleep like a log. As far as I am concerned and as long as the weather and books hold out I could continue this routine indefinitely.

June 28 [Off Saipan] ... We had a Protestant service aboard in the
morning. Very nice—on deck and surprisingly well attended.
Whether it's religion or just a little variety I don't know but the
men really enjoy going to church. More than anything else I think
it makes them feel closer to home ... The big event yesterday was
my bidding and making a grand slam in no-trump, not very significant but still an event of some importance in the wardroom.

Saipan was crowded with Navy ships, and kamikaze attacks were a
fairly regular occurrence. Very few of them were successful but there
was a good deal of anti-aircraft fire from time to time. The island of
Tinian lay close by Saipan and just across a narrow strait to the south.
Unlike Saipan, Tinian was flat and had been turned into a large aircraft base. We watched the B-29 bombers take off and land on their
way to and from their bombing runs over Japan. Coming in to land,
they flew low, quite close to our ship. I took liberty parties ashore, went
to the Navy officers' club, which was an enormous Quonset hut with a
bar about 50 yards long, swam off the ship, went fishing in the strait
between Saipan and Tinian, hitchhiked around Saipan, which had
been the scene of heavy fighting, followed the progress of the Senators
baseball team by radio, and generally kept myself reasonably occupied.
Fishing, I was amazed by the variety and color of the reef fish.

Okinawa was declared "under control" on June 22 although the official surrender did not occur until September. We finally sailed from
Saipan on July 15. My first letter from Okinawa (July 17) says: "The
biggest and best news is the new niece [Lucinda]. I can't think of anything nicer. Give my love to Betty and Cuth. I am delighted to have
been put up for the Chevy Chase Club. I feel very much honored to
have been sponsored by Adm. Hart." Obviously, I was not locked in
mortal combat after we got to Okinawa. "Adm. Hart" was Admiral
Thomas (Tommy) Hart, a close friend of my parents, who had commanded our naval forces in the Philippines at the time of the Japanese
invasion. He had finally gotten his ships away and taken them to the
Dutch East Indies where I think they were all lost in combat. I remember him well.

I was on Okinawa until the spring of 1946 when the war was over. We were camped in the south, below Naha and Itoman. Just to the south of us was a steep, limestone escarpment which had been the scene of bitter fighting not long before our arrival. The last remnants of Japanese resistance had dug in here. The ocean cliffs a bit further south had been the scene of a mass suicide by Okinawan civilians—mostly women and children who had leapt off the cliffs to avoid falling into the hands of the American monsters described by the Japanese propagandists.

Our camp was on what had been open farmland stretching south to the escarpment I mentioned above. We performed a number of patrols to close caves in the escarpment where Japanese soldiers continued to hide. A letter dated August 12 says:

> I have done a good deal of work in them [the caves], trying to get the Japs out and trying to close them with TNT. No small task and actually not much danger. They stay underground generally during the day and come out at night. You would see their fresh footprints outside of the cave in the morning (bare feet with the spread big toe) and still warm fires where they had been cooking. Not at all aggressive and if cornered as apt to use a hand grenade on themselves as on us. I have had several patrols out to get them and haven't done badly. Several prisoners and [some] killed although I personally haven't even shot at one. The men's carbines and rifles do a better job than my pistol[1] except within a few feet. We keep a small perimeter defense out at night which runs just behind my tent. One Jap was killed about 75 yards away last night but I never woke up . . .

Later, when the war was either over or almost so, I secured the surrender of the remains of a Japanese infantry regiment that had hidden away to the north in a valley that had somehow been bypassed. How I got involved in that venture, I do not recall. I remember driving into the area in my jeep with a Japanese-American soldier who called out

---

1. The .45-caliber Colt automatic I carried was the same weapon (Serial No. 3600) that my uncle Cuthbert B. Brown had carried in World War I.

The admiral with his three sons in uniform. Left to right: Father, Mid, Mother, Cuth, Betty, and the author

in Japanese until a Japanese officer suddenly appeared. Through the interpreter, I told him of the emperor's order to surrender and explained that they would be treated honorably, the sick given medical attention, etc. He left and we returned the next day to get the answer which was affirmative. We worked out the details of the surrender, and the next day I returned with a convoy of trucks to pick them all up and drive them to a POW enclosure further north. The Japanese colonel made a short speech. I concocted something to the effect that I accepted his surrender in the name of General MacArthur. He gave me his pistol, which I kept until recently, and I drove him off in my jeep.

Somewhat earlier, when we still expected to have to invade Japan proper, I had attended several invasion-planning sessions at Corps headquarters in the center of the island. I was appalled to discover that our entire battalion would be transported to Kyushu, the southernmost main island, by LCTs (Landing Craft Tanks). Given the relatively small size of an LCT, it would have required about a hundred of them to move the battalion, its heavy howitzers, and vehicles. It seemed to me that the likelihood of the outfit ever arriving and reassembling as a fighting unit was pretty remote.

My letters from Okinawa shed a bit of light on the thinking of those of us in the field. On August 9, 1945, I wrote:

You enclosed certain clippings of David Lawrence and Drew Pearson. As for the former, I don't think much of what he says about Okinawa. Anybody who says that we should have made landings in Southern Oki is a damn fool. I know the coast down here pretty well and it would have been militarily impossible. The cliffs are terrific, the water is extremely shallow for a long way out and outside of that there are continuous reefs. As for the employment of the 2nd Marines their part in the campaign has not been disclosed but in my opinion was highly successful. The columnists aren't told everything thank God and in this case they are criticizing without any basis. He also says that Army-Navy disunity caused a failure to neutralize the suicide plane bases. That's rot. As long as the Japs have any planes they'll always be able to get some through. Their bases are certainly getting a pounding now but it doesn't appear to prevent planes coming over almost every night. I wonder if these so-called military experts know that during the campaign and even now the Japs used their columns in propaganda broadcasts to our troops here. I would suggest that Lawrence stick to political reporting. . . .

The big news here, of course, is the President's announcement of the atom bomb. An extraordinary thing but I don't think it will end the war. Japan will still have to be occupied and I believe we shall have to fight to do it. This in spite of this morning's news that Russia has declared war. Personally I wish she had stayed out. I am afraid I don't trust her motives.

I continued on Sunday, August 12.

It looks this morning as if there will be peace before many hours or days have passed. We received word night before last of the Jap acceptance of the Potsdam ultimatum with the reservation about the Emperor. Ralph Cox and I were entertaining Bob Love and another major in our tent when we heard a lot of firing. We went outside and up north there were tracer bullets crisscrossing the sky and search lights moving back and forth. We thought it was simply an air raid but it slowly dawned on us that perhaps the war was over. The wild shouting and cheering convinced us.

With the dropping of the atomic bombs on Hiroshima and Nagasaki, it was obvious the war would soon be over and that, if we did have to go to Japan, it would not be as part of an invasion force. I felt nothing but relief that we would not have to fight in Japan. God knew how many casualties—on both sides—would have been involved. I certainly never felt the slightest sense of guilt over the bombing. It was the way to end the war.

As I write this some 50 years later, there is revisionist debate going on among some historians over the morality of the bombing. There wasn't much soul-searching among those of us who were poised to invade Japan. Pure and simple—we welcomed the bombings. Moreover, none of us felt particularly warmhearted toward the Japanese. They had started the war with what we all saw as the treacherous, sneak attack on Pearl Harbor. They had perpetrated the horrors of the Bataan Death March and other atrocities that we had read or heard about. We called them "little yellow bastards" and we hated them. It was that simple. All of this is by way of saying that we didn't have any complicated feelings about the atom bombings.

In late April 1994, I visited Okinawa again—and also the island of Ishigaki some 450 kilometers further west. I was on World Wildlife Fund business and was given a dinner by the Okinawa governor, Mr. Ohta, who was leading the political movement to close U.S. military bases on the island. One argument was that U.S. military activities were hurting the environment. I visited some of the bases and found that in fact we were protecting a lot of natural areas—including large tracts of original forest—as compared with much of the rest of the island, which was being turned into a concrete wasteland by Japanese construction companies. I said as much in a television interview. During the same visit, I found the area in the south where my battalion had been camped. Cultivated fields had been restored. The escarpment was still there. However, while it loomed large and menacing in my memory, it seemed quite insignificant in reality.

I came home in the spring of 1946 and was more than ready. Curiously, I remember nothing of the voyage back to the U.S. or where I landed. I do recall that I was the senior officer on a troop train which crossed the continent to Fort Meade, Maryland, and there I was discharged from active duty in January 1946. I had been in the service just short of five years, and it was time to get on with my life. It had been a decidedly unheroic war for me, and I had collected no medals for bravery in action but had dealt with a lot of new situations and people and had, hopefully, grown up a bit.

For a short time, I moved back into 3015 Que Street with my parents. Their routine had not changed. Cuth had been out of uniform for some months and was the owner and president of Fitch, Fox, and Brown, my grandfather's real estate business. Mid was back, had married Audry Campbell the year before, and had now joined the Security Storage Company.

CHAPTER 10

Law School, Career Beginnings, and Marriage

AFTER CATCHING up with my family, including new nephews and nieces, learning to wear civilian clothes again, and making a visit to New York to see my old roommate, Ed Holden, I joined Cuth at FF&B to help in the office. During my months on Okinawa, I thought seriously about a career in the Foreign Service. I had seen a fair amount of the Foreign Service during my summers with the Wilsons in Europe, and my parents had a number of friends, such as Uncle Arthur Lane, who were diplomats. It was a life that appealed to me. Assistant Secretary of State Norman Armour's enthusiastic comments on my senior thesis at Princeton encouraged this interest further. Of course, most of the Foreign Service people whom I had known possessed substantial private means which I most definitely did not. In any event, and for whatever reason, I gradually dropped the Foreign Service as a career. Cuth offered me the opportunity of working with him at FF&B while I considered my options. FF&B provided a wonderful way station as I thought about the future. I don't think I thought seriously about a career in real estate and I doubt that Cuth had that in mind. His was a very personal business that depended heavily on the enormous network of friends that he had in and out of Washington. I doubt that it could have supported both of us.

Columbia Law School

I DECIDED fairly soon that I wanted to go to law school. I had no driving impulse toward a legal career but had distinguished family connections in the law, including my great-grandfather Charles Russell Train and my uncle Judge Augustus Noble Hand. I think I saw a law degree as giving me a strong, professional base from which I could move in a number of directions. The truth is I really did not know what I wanted to do, and law school was an opportunity to postpone decision. Thus, going to law school was both an equivocation and a conscious effort to keep my options open. I still think it was the right approach. Looking back on it, I realize that I never once thought of a business alternative. That is one risk of growing up in a family with a long tradition of public service. You tend to forget that somewhere along the line someone has to make the money to support all that altruism.

I applied to both Harvard and Columbia Law School. Uncle Gus wrote a fine letter of recommendation to Harvard and, as he had been a Harvard overseer and also a former president of the Law School Alumni Association, I felt that his recommendation would carry a lot of weight. In due course, I received a letter of rejection from the director of admissions, Professor Warren Seaver, who wrote that my academic record at Princeton, "despite high friends at court," was insufficient to gain me admittance to Harvard Law. I am sure he was right about my academic record of five-plus years before, but I always resented the rather snide reference to Uncle Gus' letter on my behalf.

Columbia Law wrote me that the class was already filled but that there were about 20 vacancies for which tests would be given late in August. Just before the appointed time, I went to New York and stayed at the empty apartment at 11 East 68th Street of Uncle Gus and Aunt Sue who had not yet returned from their summer home in the Adirondacks. As luck would have it, I came down with a flu bug and a high temperature. I spent 24 hours in bed, dosing myself with massive amounts of aspirin and water and succeeded in sweating the fever out of my body. The next morning, weak but ambulatory, I got up to Columbia and joined several hundred applicants in taking the tests. I knocked the hell out of the tests and won one of the few places remaining for admission that September.

Like the majority of my classmates, all my fees and other costs at

the law school were covered by the so-called "G.I. Bill" that paid the
education costs of returning veterans. It was a great program, administered with a minimum of red tape, and it made a great contribution to
our war generation. I roomed in a dormitory that faced onto Broadway. My room was small and shared with a graduate music student
who fortunately did his homework elsewhere because we had only one
desk. There was a double-decker bunk and I occupied the upper level.

I worked reasonably hard in law school but, when the evening's
work was finally done, usually repaired for refreshment to the West
End Bar & Grill on the other side of Broadway. Oddly enough, Aileen
tells me that her first husband, Ed Travers, was at Columbia trying to
get an undergraduate degree in 1947 and 1948 and spent most of his
time at the West End. Poor girl—to have been married to two natives
of Jamestown, Rhode Island, both of whom were also denizens of the
West End Bar & Grill on Upper Broadway, is a fate no one should be
asked to bear!

Most of my contemporaries at law school were veterans and like me
were anxious to make up for lost time insofar as our careers were concerned. Almost all of us completed the normal three-year law school
curriculum in two years by pursuing our courses during the summers.
Several of us rented an apartment on Morningside Drive for the summers—Jack Castles, Arthur Murphy, Mason Salisbury, Harry Feehan,
and myself. I was pretty relaxed about my class schedule and each summer spent a week or more with Middy and Audry at their summer
home on Coolidge Point, Manchester, Massachusetts. Vacations I
spent at home with my parents on Que Street. From time to time on
Sundays, I went to lunch with Aunt Sue and Uncle Gus Hand. He
took a strong interest in my subjects and seemed to know a good deal
more about them than I did. He had taken on an even larger dimension to me now that I had read some of his opinions and learned of the
universal respect in which he was held by the law school faculty. My
friends were awestruck that I should have such a connection.

Twice during law school I was the guest of Jack Castles at his family's 5000-acre camp in the Ontario wilderness. We flew to Ottawa
and then took a train north to the village of Madawaska from which

the camp took its name and from where we drove and finally boated to the campsite on a large lake named Victoria. There were about twenty smaller lakes on the property.

The camp buildings were of log construction with moss-covered shingle roofs. There were bear and deer in the forest and we fished— mostly for lake trout in the stream running into the lake. Jack's parents made me very welcome, and his father presided over the grill at daily luncheon picnics at various scenic points around the lake. These visits were happy times with the Castles family and friends. Jack's sister, Pat, and her husband, David Acheson, a friend of mine since childhood, were there on at least one occasion.

After we had graduated from law school, Jack and I made a trip to Acapulco, Mexico, for deep-sea fishing.

Legislative Drafting Research Fund

MY MAJOR extracurricular involvement at the law school and one that was to influence my later career was with the Legislative Drafting Research Fund, a nonprofit entity within the law school. The Fund had been organized on the premise that writing effective legislation requires professional training and skill. Over the years, the Fund had done a good bit of legislative drafting for the New York legislature and had been the progenitor of the Office of Legislative Counsel of both the Senate and the House of Representatives in the U.S. Congress. My friend and classmate Jack Kernochan, the senior student member of the Fund (and later a member of the faculty and director of the Fund), persuaded me to join the staff. It was a small group working out of one office but membership was considered an honor just below law review status—an honor which I do not believe was fully supported by my grades.

I recall doing a research paper on immigration law, and I also did an analysis of the development of congressional joint committees as a leg- islative device. Such committees had become increasingly common: the Joint Committee on Internal Revenue Taxation, the Joint Committee on Atomic Energy, the Joint Committee on the Economic Report, etc. During our spring break in 1948, while I was in Washington staying with my parents, I took advantage of the opportunity to visit Capitol Hill and meet with the staff directors of several of these committees. I had an introduction from Whistle and Marne Hornblower to Gordon Grand, clerk of the Ways and Means Committee, who in turn introduced me to Colin Stam, the longtime chief of staff of the Joint Committee on Internal Revenue Taxation.

Joint Committee on Internal Revenue Taxation

STAM AND I apparently hit it off reasonably well, as later that spring I received an offer of employment on the staff of the Joint Committee after I graduated from law school that coming fall. I visited at least two law firms to discuss possible employment—I believe Hogan and Hartshorn and Covington and Burling. At the latter, I was interviewed by Dean Acheson, a somewhat daunting affair. Actually, he was friendly and courteous and made it as easy for me as possible. However, I do not believe I had any illusions about receiving an offer from Covington and Burling. I did have an offer from the Legislative Counsel's Office of the Senate, but it was at a salary less than that offered by the Joint Committee, which was $4200 a year. When I accepted the latter offer, I became one of the highest paid graduates of my law school class. Back in Washington, I lived initially with my parents at 3015 Que Street. I took the D.C. bar exams in the fall of 1948 and was admitted to the bar shortly afterwards.

Thus began my career as a tax lawyer—a career for which my rather mediocre performance in the law school taxation course had given little advance indication. The chain of circumstance that led to the congressional staff position—the Legislative Drafting Research Fund job through Jack Kernochan, the research assignment on joint committees, meeting Gordon Grand, etc.—all brought home to me how much sheer luck or plain happenstance seems to affect our destiny.

Eating lobster with my parents at Atlantic City, c. 1953

For the next four-plus years, I was a member of the Joint Committee staff. The Joint Committee, which had been established by the Revenue Act of 1926, was made up of the three senior members of the House Ways and Means Committee and the Senate Finance Committee. It met formally very occasionally and then principally to review and approve all tax refunds over a certain size. Practically, the real function of the Joint Committee was to provide professional staff support to the two legislative committees, both of which had little professional staff of their own at that time.

The Senate Finance Committee had essentially no professional staff and the House Ways and Means Committee had only one or two professionals in addition to the clerk (Leo Irwin during my time when the Democrats were in the majority, and Gordon Grand when the Republicans were in control, both lawyers). As longtime chief of staff of the Joint Committee, Colin Stam had an unrivaled position as principal advisor on tax policy to both the Finance and Ways and Means Committees. He had an extraordinary memory for the intricacies of the development of tax law and regulations over many years and had a conservative bias that tended to match that of most of the senior legislators with whom he dealt. He was loyal to his principles and unfailingly discreet, seldom, if ever, holding himself available to the press. He worked with individual committee members to perfect amendments to the Internal Revenue Code in which they were interested and was able to deploy his staff of lawyers and economists as needed.

The staff included statisticians as well, capable of estimating the revenue implications of individual amendments, or of estimating overall revenue of the federal government relevant to annual budget consideration. Their estimates tended to be more conservative than those of the Treasury and were generally considered quite reliable.

As influential as he was on tax policy, Stam was a bit of an odd duck. He was very fat. His clothes were usually unkempt, shirttails coming out over his belt, tie askew. Quite bald, he brushed his hair from one side over the bald spot and this lock of hair had a tendency to fall down over his forehead as he spoke. Heading for a committee meeting, he trundled down the hall, clothes awry, masses of papers under his arms. He was a bachelor and lived with a maiden sister somewhere in the Maryland suburbs, along with an old chow dog, and commuted to the New (now the Longworth) House Office Building in an elderly Ford. I have to say that Colin Stam, notwithstanding all his idiosyncrasies, was always extremely friendly and helpful to me, and I certainly owed to him my job with the Joint Committee that was to open for me a whole career.

My first office was in the basement of the Senate Office Building, known simply as the "S.O.B." in the day when there was only one instead of the present three buildings. My early work was pretty tedious, involving the Joint Committee's publication program. One project involved collecting all the Supreme Court cases on taxation and publishing them in one volume. In the process, I learned to prepare an index and to proofread printers' galleys. (I had had some previous experience while working on the *St. Albans News*.) One result of the close application to fine print was that I started to need reading glasses. And I suspect that a second result of the considerable tedium of the job was that I started regularly betting on horse races.

Horse Racing

ORME WILSON was back in Washington—single again after the failure of a wartime marriage although soon to marry an old friend of ours, Mildred Dunn. He had one horse named Astrodome, and we would go to watch him run, usually at Bowie, an old Maryland track that has since shut down. On occasion we went out to watch the early-morning workouts. These were picturesque events—out in the early dawn, mugs of hot coffee around a woodstove in the stable, early-morning mist over the track, leaning on the rails to watch the horses being worked, and trading comments with Orme's trainer, Dabney Harrison. From the track, I would drive straight back to the Senate Office Building in time for work.

Astrodome was what is called a "useful" horse. He was by no means outstanding but was "in the money" sufficiently often to more than pay for himself. On one occasion when he was a winner, I won $1200 in bets and immediately invested the sum with a like amount from Orme to acquire a yearling whose name I now forget. In any event, that horse injured a leg while training as a two-year-old and never did start in a race. So ended my first experience as a racehorse owner.

At the same time, however, Orme introduced me to a bookie, named George, and I soon was making several bets a day on horses running at various tracks around the country. I kept this up for about a year and then realized that I was gradually losing my shirt. So I quit betting except on infrequent visits to a track. There was not a great deal of moral fortitude involved because after about a year of fairly boring work in my basement office at the S.O.B., I moved to the New House Office Building and became fully involved in the legislative activities of the Joint Committee staff.

Joint Committee Work

I SHARED AN office with Larry Woodworth and Gene Oakes, both economists and both with considerable experience in the tax legislative field. We had one secretary, Miss Scheid, for the three of us. (Lawrence N. Woodworth [1918-1978] became chief of the Joint Committee staff on the retirement of Colin Stam in 1964. After distinguished service in that position, he went to the Treasury Department as Assistant Secretary for Tax Policy where he served brilliantly until his untimely death in 1978. He was a wholly dedicated, selfless public servant, devoted to his family, his church, and his community in Cheverly, Maryland. I do not think any thought of self-promotion or private gain ever entered his mind. At a time when public employees are so often the subject of scorn, it is good to know that there are the Larry Woodworths. We can only be grateful to them. I know that I learned a lot from him.) From then on, I had little time for diversions such as playing the horses.

Some of my work was a bit scholarly. Stam asked me to compile a legislative history of the percentage depletion allowance for oil. This turned into an interesting project which was printed as a Joint Committee document. However, the record must have made the rationale for the tax break for oil look pretty questionable because Stam decided to embargo the report, and it was never published. (If I kept a copy for my private files, it has disappeared. When I left the Hill to work at the Treasury in 1955, I left a number of boxes of papers behind. When I returned to retrieve them, they had all been thrown out.) Stam's political antenna doubtless told him that my report spelled nothing but trouble. Oil-producing areas were well represented on the Ways and Means and Finance Committees—as they generally continue to be. Representatives Hale Boggs of Louisiana and Frank Ikard of Texas, both powerful Democrats, were on the Ways and Means Committee. Senators Tom Connally of Texas and Bob Kerr of Oklahoma, also both Democrats, were on the Senate Finance Committee.

More frequently, I was involved in working sessions with the Treasury tax legislative staff, hammering out technical differences on legislation. Then there would be the committee "mark-ups" in executive session, the drafting of the committee report on any bill it reported, action by the full House, and then the shift of the action to the Senate Finance Committee.

The chairman when I first worked with Ways and Means was Representative Robert Doughton of North Carolina, known as "Muley." He was over 80 but was reported to give chase to young female secretaries around the meeting table in his private office in the Capitol.

"Sexual harassment" was not a public issue in those days. Jere Cooper of Tennessee was the next ranking Democrat, followed by Wilbur Mills of Arkansas. Mills probably had the finest mind on the committee and usually took the lead in discussion of technical tax matters or the Social Security Act, which was also in the committee's jurisdiction. Mills, whose legislative abilities I admired, was later chairman of Ways and Means but his career came to a tragic end when he became alcoholic, took up with a stripper named Fanny Fox, and drove the two of them into the Tidal Basin one night. They were pulled out without injury but the notoriety was the end of Mills.

John Dingell of Michigan, whose son, John, now fills his father's seat in Congress, ranked just below Mills. "Young" John is often perceived as anti-environment by the environmental community, but he and I have always gotten along well even though we do not always agree. The fact that we both like to hunt ducks probably has something to do with this. More junior was Thomas J. O'Brien of Illinois, part of the Daley political machine in Chicago. He practically never opened his mouth in the committee unless it was to vote and that was always on strict party lines. He was famous for never having introduced a bill in his entire 20 years in Congress. Rumor had it that he received a percentage on every sewer contract in Cook County. Then there was Hale Boggs of Louisiana who had brains, charm, and great political savvy. It was assumed that he was headed for a position in the Democratic leadership in the House, possibly as Speaker when Sam Rayburn stepped down. Hale died in 1960 in the crash of a small bush plane in Alaska. The site of the crash was never located. His widow, Lindy, served several terms in Congress after his death and still lives in Washington, a good friend. In 1997, she was appointed ambassador to the Vatican. Their son, Tommy, is a prominent Washington lawyer and has a home near us on the Eastern Shore.

Daniel A. Reed of New York was the ranking Republican, and I will have more to say about him. The second ranking Republican was Tom Jenkins of Ohio, third was the able and powerful Dick Simpson of Pennsylvania, followed by Robert Winthrop Kean of New Jersey. Kean was a distant cousin of Aileen's through the Winthrop connection and was the father of Ham Kean and Tom Kean, the latter a popular governor of New Jersey in later years. As I write this, he is president of Drew University and also a director of the World Wildlife Fund. Bob Kean had the best intellect on the Republican side and, particularly on social security matters, tended to lead in discussion along with Wilbur Mills.

The Ways and Means Committee room was and is a rather grand place with room for 25 committee members (15 majority and 10 minority) at the curved, raised dais. There was a large space for interested spectators, and oil portraits of past chairmen, among them James Madison and William McKinley, hung on the walls. During executive sessions, the members sat in the center of the room at tables arranged horseshoe fashion with staff, principally Stam, seated at a table between the two arms of the horseshoe.

The Finance Committee room was much smaller and hence more intimate. However, the room's lack of grandeur was made up for by the stature of the members. During my time, Senator Walter George of Georgia was chairman. To his right sat Senator Harry Byrd of Virginia and to Byrd's right Senator Tom Connally of Texas. Somewhat further to the right was Senator Bob Kerr of Oklahoma, former governor of his state, founder of the Kerr-McGee Oil Company, and teacher of a Sunday School class at his Baptist church every Sunday.

To the chairman's left was Senator Eugene Milliken of Colorado, a Republican power and friend of my parents. When he felt a draft on his bald head from the air-conditioning system, he would open up a clean linen handkerchief and spread it over the top of his head. Thus adorned, he would enter into the proceedings with total lack of self-consciousness, although any witness was probably distracted. To his left sat the redoubtable Senator Robert Taft of Ohio, the GOP conservative leader who was later to be defeated for the Republican nomination for president by Dwight D. Eisenhower.

I remember best the executive sessions of the Finance Committee and relatively small things come to mind. After the committee had dealt with the principal features of a major tax bill—which of course had to originate in the House—the members got a crack at their own pet projects. The occasion was known as "members' day." When Senator Connally spoke up on such occasions and said in his Texas drawl, "Mr. Chairman, I just have a little bitty ol' amendment," we would all shudder in anticipation of a multi-million-dollar tax break for some Texas oil constituent. I recall Taft, whom I always thought of as a pretty cold fish, putting forward an amendment to exclude from federal estate tax the value of works of art belonging to a non-U.S. national which happened to be in a U.S. museum on loan when the owner died. I knew nothing about the matter but doubtless Stam knew all about it and probably had helped draft the amendment. I discovered later that the amendment had been sponsored by David Finley, director of the National Gallery, in order to attract a loan of the Gulbenkian collection. The estate tax exclusion was certainly a reasonable proposition and became known as the "Gulbenkian amendment." It passed in due course but Gulbenkian never did send his collection on loan to the U.S., and it ended up in Portugal.

Occasionally I would find myself in the Senate chamber during debate on a tax bill. Most of the time I would sit in a corner, keeping notes and providing information on request from one of the Finance Committee members. The Senate rules discouraged the presence of staff, and I would make myself as unobtrusive as possible. Nevertheless, on one occasion, I found myself crouched in the aisle next to the desk of Senator Kerr who was responding to questions about a section of the committee bill. Kerr was a large, impressive man with a deep, stentorian voice that carried conviction and credibility. As he finished explaining the provision in question, speaking authoritatively and without hesitation, I looked up at him and said in a hoarse whisper: "That simply is not true, Senator!" Kerr looked down at me and said: "Train, when you are on the floor of the Senate, you have to shoot from the hip!"

Indeed, it was a considerable challenge to ensure that the legislative history of a bill accurately reflected the purpose and intent of its numerous provisions. Once when Senator George, the committee chairman, had explained a lengthy tax bill on the Senate floor, I was given the task of editing the page proofs of the *Congressional Record* carrying his remarks. I found it necessary to rewrite practically his entire statement.

The Ways and Means Committee

THE REPUBLICAN Party swept the 1952 elections, putting Dwight
D. Eisenhower in the White House and capturing control of both
houses of the Congress. Daniel Reed from Jamestown in upstate New
York became chairman of the Ways and Means Committee and my
friend Gordon Grand became clerk. Not long after that, Gordon was
offered the presidency of the Olin-Matthiessen Corporation (now
simply the Olin Corporation) in New York and left the committee
staff after persuading Reed to offer me the position of clerk. I accepted
with alacrity and found myself catapulted into one of the senior staff
positions in the Congress at the astronomical salary of $14,800 per year.

The job was interesting and fun. Reed was an old-timer, first
elected to the Congress during the McKinley administration, and he
boasted—a bit tongue in cheek—that his opinions, particularly on tariff matters, had been formed at that time and that his mind had been
closed ever since. Indeed, he was an old-fashioned protectionist and
proud of it. White-haired, ruddy-faced, and square-jawed, Reed was
an imposing figure. He was by no means a brilliant man but decent,
straightforward, thoughtful, and at times stubborn.

On one unhappy occasion, Reed opposed the Eisenhower administration's insistence on extending the life of certain excise taxes (as best
I can now recall). He succeeded in getting the bill reported out by the
Ways and Means Committee in the form he favored and then went
before the House Rules Committee to request the customary closed
rule. Tax bills were generally considered under a closed rule, as it was
felt that to open such legislation to amendment on the floor would be
disastrous. However, on this occasion, the Rules Committee rejected
Reed's request and granted a modified closed rule which permitted
one amendment. The latter, embodying the administration position,
was introduced on the floor in due course by Representative Dick
Simpson of Pennsylvania, the third-ranking Republican on the committee. The amendment was adopted over Reed's opposition and the
bill, as amended, passed. A majority of the Republicans on his committee voted against him. The defeat was a bitter pill for the old man.

Congressman Daniel A. Reed,
my boss at the Ways and Means Committee

I sat next to him at the table on the House floor throughout the proceedings and felt deeply sorry for him. I had been in an uncomfortable spot and the Treasury, knowing my loyalty to Reed, had avoided me during the whole affair.

I think a word of explanation is due here on the nature of the job of "clerk." For those not familiar with congressional staff terminology, the clerk of a committee is its chief of staff and is now so titled by Ways and Means. Substantive tax work was largely provided by Colin Stam and his Joint Committee staff. However, when it came to tariff and social security issues, Reed and the Republican majority looked to me and the Ways and Means staff, small as it was. Almost my only subordinate professional staffer at the time was Dick Furlaud, a very able young lawyer who had been hired by Grand and who was soon to follow him to the Olin-Matthiessen Corporation as general counsel. (When Olin-Matthiessen spun off the Squibb pharmaceutical business a few years later, Furlaud went with Squibb as CEO.)

In any event, my responsibilities as clerk had less to do with substantive issues and more to do with organizing the work of the committee, scheduling and running hearings, providing liaison with Stam and the Treasury, interfacing with the press, dealing with the countless lobbyists, replying to the voluminous mail, and spending time with the chairman on a daily basis to discuss both near- and long-term plans. In addition, I was responsible for handling all correspondence from Reed's home district dealing with matters within the committee's jurisdiction. The committee had no subcommittees in those days so my office dealt with the full range of its jurisdiction: taxes, tariffs including trade agreements, and social security. The staff totaled ten: assistant clerk Tom Martin, two other professionals, four secretaries, two messengers, and me.

When the Republicans lost the House in the 1954 midterm election (and did not win it again until 1994), I lost the clerkship and moved one door down the hall to become minority advisor. Reed, of course, became the ranking minority member and, thus, continued as my boss. While I no longer had responsibility for the committee agenda or for organizing hearings, much of the work remained about the same. My staff was down to one—a marvelous secretary named Susan Taylor. She had worked with Gordon Grand in the minority office and with me at the full committee. She was efficient, loyal, knowledgeable, warmhearted, and had an excellent manner in dealing with all our many contacts. She and I shared a small one-room office for close to two years and got along beautifully.

Having estimated that the Ways and Means Committee's staff structure, including both majority and minority functions, totaled thirteen, I took a look at a recent congressional directory and counted 65 people on the committee payroll. (Of course, each committee member has his or her own office staff as well.) I cannot help but wonder what all these people do. Granted, the U.S. population and economy have grown substantially over the 40 years since I was on the committee staff. However, the jurisdiction of the committee has not changed. The size of the membership has not changed. The tax laws have always been complicated, and I doubt that added complexity explains added bureaucracy. Indeed, it is probably the other way around—the more bureaucracy, the greater the complexity. The one thing that has changed is the number of lobbyists, which appears to have grown exponentially.

Even if lobbyists have greatly increased in number, there were plenty of them in my years with the committee, and they provided a principal link with the outside world. Lawyers, doctors, retired persons, farmers, labor, truckers, the railroads, airlines, state governments, trade associations, churches, insurance companies, sugar producers, etc., etc.—they were constantly on one's doorstep. I found most of them informative, and they certainly helped me appreciate the diversity of interests involved in almost every legislative issue. So far as I was personally concerned, I never found the lobbying fraternity particularly sinister although I have no doubt some could have been. I do not recall being invited to "expenses-paid" conventions or other get-togethers—perhaps that says more about my perceived influence than the purity of the lobbyists—and I did not attend receptions given by lobbying organizations. In fact, I made a practice of being "busy" for lunch, which often consisted of a sandwich by myself at a drugstore counter several blocks up Pennsylvania Avenue—almost invariably liverwurst with lettuce and tomato and mayonnaise on rye. (Now there's a revelatory nugget to pass on to my posterity!)

I remember one Christmas when I received a very large frozen turkey—I think from the Cowles publishing company. Poor Aileen. I asked her to ship the turkey back to the senders. She finally succeeded but it took about three days of negotiation with Railway Express. (That was before the days of UPS.) I have often wondered what the condition of that turkey was when it got back to where it started.

Gambling Tax

A BIT PRIOR to this, while I was still on the staff of the Joint Committee, I concocted a scheme for the taxation of gambling which was in due course enacted and became part of the Internal Revenue Code. The concept was relatively simple. Many billions of dollars were gambled every year—most of it illegally, as in the "numbers" game or with bookies. Most of it represented cash transactions that totally escaped taxation. I proposed what was essentially an excise tax on slot machines and a flat tax of 10 percent on all other wagers, paid by the receiver of the bet, for example, the bookmaker. I even called up my old bookie, George, for professional advice. Thus, the Ways and Means Committee report on the legislation reflected an expertise on gambling which raised a few eyebrows. My boss, Colin Stam, was delighted with the whole idea and sold it to the Senate Finance Committee as well. It became law and constituted my only completely original contribution to the field of tax legislation.

When the wagering tax was eventually challenged in the courts, it ended up in the Supreme Court. A fellow staffer and I went over to the court to hear oral argument. By pure coincidence, I was wearing a rather loud, checked tweed jacket that day and, as I entered the full courtroom and slid my way down a row to an empty seat, I plainly saw and heard Justice Frankfurter lean over and say in a stage whisper to his neighbor on the bench, nodding in my direction, "There's one now!" Not a few heads turned in my direction, some of them I would suppose being real bookies in unobtrusive dark attire. The law remained on the books for years but was never really enforced.

I Propose a Flat Income Tax

ONE CUMULATIVE impact of my years with the tax committees on the Hill, and later with the Treasury and the U.S. Tax Court, was impatience and frustration with the ever-growing complexity of the Internal Revenue Code. Our income tax law and regulations had become so complicated that it was next to impossible for the average citizen to make out his or her tax return. It took an army of tax lawyers and accountants to shepherd taxpayers through the Byzantine maze of the tax law. And the situation is even worse today. Of course, the principal obstacles to reform are the tax experts who have a vested interest in complexity and the members of Congress who may benefit from the campaign contributions of special interests who seek yet more changes in the law.

In any event, in the fall of 1976 when I was EPA administrator and should have had other things on my mind, I read in the press of the progress of that year's principal revenue bill through the Congress— doubtless named something like the "Tax Reform and Simplification Act of 1976." I happened to read that the House of Representatives had adopted an amendment to the bill providing an income tax credit for the cost of purchasing home garden tools. I could hardly believe my eyes. I was outraged that anyone should even suggest, let alone the House approve, an amendment providing that the federal government should bear the entire expense of an individual's purchase of garden tools.

It was the proverbial straw that broke the camel's back. I sat down and wrote an article entitled "Real Tax Reform" which proposed scrapping much of the existing tax code—as being beyond fixing—and substituting a relatively simple flat income tax with essentially no deductions. The article was lengthy for an "op-ed" piece but the *Washington Post* carried it in its entirety in its Outlook section on Sunday, October 24, 1976. My friend Senator Claiborne Pell inserted the article in the *Congressional Record* of Friday, January 14, 1977.

While the flat tax is a relatively familiar concept today, it was a pretty novel idea in 1976, and I, at least, had never seen it seriously proposed before then. Be that as it may, the idea did not generate much excitement at the time. Since then, Congressman Bill Archer of Texas, chairman of the House Ways and Means Committee, has proposed such a reform and, in 1996, Steven Forbes made a flat tax the centerpiece of his campaign for the Republican nomination for president.

This is not the place to argue the merits of a flat tax, and I simply wish to place on the record my proposal of the idea in 1976.

Engagement and Marriage

IT WAS SHORTLY before I became clerk of the committee that I met Aileen and my life was transformed. She had just gotten her divorce from Edward Travers and had rented a house at 1529 29th Street in Georgetown. It was Aileen's first night in Washington and the Foleys had asked her and some appropriate young man to dine with them and then go to a dance being given by Morris and Gwendolyn Cafritz at their large place on Foxhall Road. As luck would have it, Aileen's sister Helen had recently married a classmate of mine at Columbia Law School, Josiah A. Spaulding (Si), and Si made the fateful suggestion that I be invited as Aileen's date.

While, so far as I know, Emily (Aileen's mother) did not know my parents, who were almost a generation older, they had numerous mutual friends so I passed muster on that score. Then at dinner, Ed (Aileen's stepfather) and I had a lot to talk about on tax matters and the Hill, as he had been general counsel and later Under Secretary of the Treasury during the Truman administration. He loved talking politics and political personalities so we hit it off in fine shape. Finally, and most to the point, Aileen was an absolute knockout. I remember little or nothing of the Cafritz party other than the fact that Aileen and I sat together at the bottom of the garden and talked until the small hours. I was smitten and from then on there was no one else. For Aileen it was a bit more complicated, as she had just succeeded in disentangling herself from one marriage and did not want to rush into another. Needless to say, we saw a lot of each other from then on. The fact that Aileen had two very small children, Nancy and Emily, must have given me some pause, but I do not recall being worried by the fact. Anyway, they were two delightful little girls and there was always a nurse to spirit them away at appropriate moments. It was a year and a half before we became engaged and just short of two years before we married on May 27, 1954.

An exciting adventure for Aileen during that period was to attend the coronation of Queen Elizabeth II on June 2, 1953, together with Jacqueline Bouvier, soon to be married to John F. Kennedy. On very short notice, the two sailed on the *United States*, spent about a week in London, taking in the coronation as well as some of the more glamorous parties, and spent a week in Paris. When they returned, I went to Idlewild Airport to meet their plane. Also pacing impatiently up and down awaiting the plane was Jack Kennedy (for whom the airport would later be renamed). When he married Jackie not long after, both Aileen and her sister Helen Spaulding were bridesmaids.

Aileen Bowdoin Travers and Jacqueline
Bouvier (soon to marry John F. Kennedy)
on board S.S. *United States* en route to
the coronation of Queen Elizabeth II, 1953

The circumstances of our engagement were a bit unusual. It had
snowed hard the night before in Washington, and I hired a horse and
sleigh with driver from the stable that then existed where the Watergate now stands. Ed Foley and Aileen's little girls came along for the
ride and sat up front beside the driver. Aileen and I were in back snug-
gled under a large carriage blanket. The streets were practically deserted and, of course, had not been plowed or had sand or salt applied
to them. Conditions were ideal for sleighing—and, as it turned out,
for romance. Sometime during that two-hour sleigh ride along Pennsylvania Avenue and around Washington Circle and neighboring
streets, Aileen's defenses finally gave way, and we became engaged.

We were married at St. John's Church by its longtime rector, Leslie
Glenn. It was a small wedding with principally our immediate families
in attendance. Middy was my best man and Aileen was given away by
her father, George Bowdoin. The wedding was followed by a large
reception at the Foley house on Wyoming Avenue. We spent our wedding night at the Tuleyries, the Wilson place near Berryville, Virginia,

Father, Cuth, the author (who apparently forgot his waistcoat), and Mid at bridal dinner, the Alibi Club, May 1954

With my mother at bridal dinner

Newly married, at wedding reception. Ed and Emily Foley, Aileen and the author, my mother and father, and Nancy and Emily (in front)

The Tuleyries, White Post, Virginia, where Aileen and I spent our wedding night. This photo by J. C. Giordano was taken 45 years later on the occasion of an anniversary dinner for family and friends.

The author on the porch of our
honeymoon cottage at the Greenbrier,
White Sulfur Springs, West Virginia

where I had visited so often as a boy. We had the wonderful old house all to ourselves, except for Helen Taylor, Orme's nurse as a child, who served us supper in front of the fire in the living room. A pair of mourning doves was nesting on a windowsill of our bedroom and someone had put a small sign inside the window: "CAUTION. TURTLE DOVES NESTING." The next morning we drove on to the Greenbrier Hotel at White Sulfur Springs, West Virginia, where I had rented "Carolina A," a large cottage, and where we spent the rest of the Memorial Day weekend. That was all the time I could spare from my duties on the Hill.

Woodland Drive

EARLIER THAT spring, we had bought 3101 Woodland Drive and it was all ready for us to move into on our return from our short honeymoon. The house was rough stone, with leaded diamond-paned win-

Aileen on the porch of our
honeymoon cottage

dows, steep roof angles, and a very long, steep flight of stone steps to
the front door. Aileen knew the house by sight because the Foleys had
rented a house for a time right opposite on Thompson Circle and,
when I called her in March while she was in Florida staying with her
father and told her about the house, she said, "Not that God-awful-
looking house with leaded windows!" Anyway, when she had a chance
to inspect the house, the interior was bathed in sunshine, and the garden rose up the hill behind the house with great ancient oaks from the
original forest shading a brilliant green lawn, all bordered by masses of
azaleas in full bloom. It was an enchanting spectacle, and we both
knew we had found our home. We bought the house from Bill and
Florence Willard for $80,000. (A stone walk in the garden was paved
with very large bathroom tiles from the old Willard Hotel.)

Throughout our life together Aileen and I have tried to share
expenses on as even a basis as possible given the realities of our individual circumstances at any given time. I do not recall our ever having
an argument over money. In the case of the Woodland Drive house,

Emily and Nancy,
Oyster Bay, 1954

she put up the $30,000 cash required and I took over the monthly payments on the $50,000 mortgage. The house was to be our home for the next 25 years and all our children grew up there. Nancy and Emily were adopted by me shortly after our marriage and grew up in every respect as my own offspring. Adopting them was one of the best decisions I ever made.

We put in a swimming pool at the top of the garden—marvelous for a hot summer's night "skinny dip"—and later a cabin. We enlarged the terrace behind the house and it was the center of our life in the warm months. Aided by a tent, Emily's coming-out party—a dance—was held there in June 1968, followed a few days later by Nancy's wedding reception. For Nancy's wedding, the tent was decorated in part by cages of white sulphur-crested cockatoos.

Caribbean Cruise

IN NOVEMBER 1954, six months after our wedding, Aileen and I found time to take a more extended honeymoon trip. Our friends Phyzzie and Bob Lee (usually called "General") had just gotten married and we chartered a boat with them for a cruise in the Caribbean.

3101 Woodland Drive, N.W., where we lived from 1954 to 1977

Mollihawk

Our craft was a 70-foot schooner named *Mollihawk,* a beautiful wooden "character" boat and already over 50 years old. We chartered her from the Nicholson Yacht Company in St. John, Antigua, and the Nicholson family had sailed aboard her from England to Antigua a number of years before. Our skipper was young Rodney Nicholson and his recent bride, Julie, who cooked. Thus, for all six of us, it was truly a honeymoon cruise.

With Phyzzie and General, we flew to Antigua, spent a night at the Mill Reef Club (of which Aileen and I have now been members about 40 years), and boarded *Mollihawk* at English Harbor. Nelson kept his fleet at English Harbor but *Mollihawk* was the only craft there when we went aboard. (The last time I was at English Harbor, perhaps in 1987, there were at least 100 good-sized craft at anchor or moored there.) We sailed south in the stiff trade wind, visiting Guadeloupe, Dominica, Martinique, St. Vincent, the Îles des Saintes, St. Lucia, and on down into the Grenadines as far as the Tobago Cays. We stopped at both Bequia and Mustique, the latter for sale in toto for £50,000. It was a glorious trip, and we barely saw another yacht the entire three weeks.[1] How times have changed!

Arrival of Bowdy and Errol

A YEAR LATER in October 1955, our son, Charles Bowdoin Train, was born. (He has always gone by his second name and usually by the nickname Bowdy.) I was a nervous first-time father and insisted on our going to the hospital at the first sign of a cramp and hours before the final event. Our daughter Errol Cuthbert Train, named for my mother, was born in May 1959. Aileen remembers my mother arriving at the hospital to see her newborn namesake, wearing her most festive yellow suit and hat. With Errol, our family and house were full. Both Bowdy and Errol were born at George Washington University Hospital. Both were healthy babies and Aileen had no complications.

All three of our daughters went to Potomac School in Virginia, transported by school bus, until they went away to boarding school— Nancy and Emily to Foxcroft in Middleburg, Virginia, and Errol to St. George's, at Newport, Rhode Island. Bowdy went first to Beauvoir and then to St. Albans. Both those schools were situated on the Cathedral Close, only a few blocks from our house, so that, as he grew older, he generally walked to and from school.

1. An account of the trip, entitled "A Really Good Time!" by Julie Pyle Nicholson, was published by *Motor Boating,* in two parts, March and April 1956.

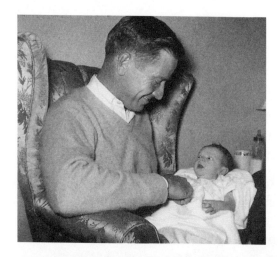

With Bowdoin (Bowdy),
aged 12 days

Bowdy visits with his
grandmother Train,
1957

Errol, c. 1960

African Safaris and Other Events

BETWEEN THOSE two happy events, Aileen and I made our first safari in East Africa. Indeed, a lot had happened in the intervening three-plus years. We went on our first safari in 1956; later that year I went to the Treasury as head of the Legal Advisory Staff and Assistant to the Secretary; in 1957 President Eisenhower nominated me and the Senate confirmed me as a judge of the United States Tax Court; that same year we took Nancy and Emily on a sailing cruise in the Aegean, followed by a tour of northern Italy and ending in Rome; and then in 1958 we went on our second safari in Africa. (Our African trips are detailed in a later chapter.)

Somewhere in that period, but perhaps not until the fall of 1959, we packed into the Bob Marshall Wilderness of western Montana for a ten-day hunt for deer, elk, and goat. That was a great trip into spectacularly beautiful, wild country. It was tough going at times, with snow up to my horse's belly. It got still tougher when I came down with an attack of kidney stones and had to ride out of the backcountry all one day in great pain. How Aileen and I squeezed so much into such a short time period is amazing as I look back on it. I was employed full time and, as Aileen points out, she "was busy having babies."

The Treasury and the Tax Court

WHEN I HAD first become minority advisor to the Ways and Means Committee in 1955, I set my sights on appointment as a judge of the U.S. Tax Court. At age 36, a judicial appointment seemed an extraordinarily attractive prospect. I doubt that it ever occurred to me to ask myself whether that was what I wanted to do the rest of my life. Indeed, for most relatively young people, the concept of "the rest of your life" has little reality or meaning. In any event, I went to work on the matter and enlisted the support of just about every member of the Ways and Means Committee, both Republican and Democratic, as well as various others with political influence. Finally, Chappie Rose (H. Chapman Rose), Under Secretary of the Treasury and a friend of mine and of my family, came to see me and offered a suggestion. He said that the feeling was that I was not quite ready for a judgeship but that, if I were willing to come to the Treasury as head of the Legal Advisory Staff, I could have a judgeship the next time a vacancy on the Tax Court arose. It was a good deal and I took it.

The Legal Advisory Staff reviewed all Treasury regulations proposed by the Internal Revenue Service, worked on tax legislation, and represented the department before the congressional committees on tax matters. (Under Democratic administrations, my post was titled "Tax Legislative Counsel.") Over the years, the position had been filled by a number of distinguished tax lawyers, including such a luminary of the tax bar and academia as Stanley Surrey. I had a top-notch professional staff at the Treasury, all lawyers, several of whom, such as Leonard Silverstein, have gone on to be illustrious members of the bar. Tax policy matters, particularly as they involved economic issues, were handled by the Office of Tax Analysis, headed by Dan Throop Smith, while I was there. Later, the legal and economic functions were consolidated under an Assistant Secretary for Tax Policy, and Dan became the first to fill the position.

My office was on the west side of the Treasury Building, looking out toward the White House, and on the third floor, the same as that of the Secretary and other high-ranking officials of the department—not that I considered myself in that category. However, I did park my car at the Secretary's entrance at the southwest corner of the building and used the small elevator there to reach my floor. My car was a modest convertible Chevrolet Belair. The official cars parked in the same small enclosure were mostly high-powered sedans confiscated from drug dealers by the Alcohol and Tobacco Tax Unit of the Treasury.

The Secretary of the Treasury at the time was the redoubtable George Humphrey, former head of the Hanna Company of Cleveland, and generally considered the most powerful person in the Eisenhower Cabinet insofar as domestic matters were concerned. I recall one morning arriving on crutches with my left foot in a cast. As luck would have it, I shared the small elevator with the Secretary who naturally inquired as to what had happened to me. "I broke a bone in my foot while demonstrating how to dance the Charleston on the carpet in my living room," I explained. From the expression on his face, I was certain that the ultra-conservative Humphrey was saying to himself something like "And this is my top tax lawyer?" However, he was friendly about it and held the door open for me to get out.

Most of the time, I only saw the Secretary when I was asked to lunch in his dining room, which was reasonably often. One day, Aileen and I were at the Humphrey residence, a large house on Foxhall Road which is now part of the German Embassy. Humphrey had recently given up smoking and I think we both were sharing experiences in that regard. "I was here at home by myself one day," said Humphrey, "and I wanted a cigarette. I started looking for a light and got more and more frantic as I couldn't find a match in the entire house. Finally, I stopped and said to myself, 'George, you damn fool, here you are one of the most powerful men in America and you have just spent a good half hour looking for a match. How stupid can you get!' So I threw away the cigarette and have never had another!"

At the beginning of the Eisenhower administration the Under Secretary of the Treasury was Randolph Burgess, a tall, courtly New York banker, whose wife, Helen, was a Hamilton cousin of Aileen's. His place was taken by Chapman Rose with whom I had worked when I was on the Hill and whom I have already mentioned. My direct boss was the general counsel, Fred Scribner, who eventually became Under Secretary when Chappie left. About 15 years later when I received an honorary doctor of laws degree at Princeton, Chappie was a trustee and acted as my escort for the occasion.

A key person in my operation was my secretary, Marian O'Connell. She had worked for several of my predecessors and was a top-flight, professional executive assistant. She knew all the bureaucratic ropes, handled the enormous flow of communications with great efficiency, and terrorized my subordinates and others who needed to be kept in their proper place. When I finally went to the Tax Court, she came with me to get my office organized but had to return to the Treasury for long-term job considerations. In 1969, when I became Under Secretary of the Interior, she joined me again and then went with me to the newly formed Council on Environmental Quality when I became chairman in 1970. From there, the O'Connell-Train team moved to EPA where we ran the agency until 1977 and then to the World Wildlife Fund until she retired in 1981. Marian was a highly competent assistant and a warm and loyal friend. She even baby-sat for Errol on a few weekends when we were away. I owe her a large debt of gratitude.

The U.S. Tax Court

I HAD BEEN at the Treasury little more than a year when the Secretary asked me to come and see him. He told me that Tax Court Judge Van Auken was retiring and that, true to our understanding, the vacancy was mine if I wanted it. I started to answer in an enthusiastic affirmative but he broke in and said more or less: "Before you make a decision, Russ, let me say that I think it would be a mistake for you to go to the court." He proceeded to give me his reasons which I think boiled down to my being awfully young (37) for a judgeship and that I would have a lot of other opportunities. I think he saw the court as something of a dead end where I would lose the opportunity to parlay my experience on the Hill and at the Treasury into a successful career in law or in business. Humphrey was an entrepreneur and a successful one and I think he just could not understand why a young man such as myself would want to bury himself on the Tax Court—or any court, for that matter. I agreed to take 48 hours to think it over before I made a decision but at the end of that time I told him I wanted the job. He said "Fine" and that was that. Following my nomination and Senate confirmation, President Eisenhower appointed me a judge of the United States Tax Court on May 13, 1957.

It was personally gratifying that the full Ways and Means Committee membership (25) addressed a letter to Senator Harry Byrd, chairman of the Senate Finance Committee, unanimously endorsing my nomination and urging my speedy confirmation. The letter was signed by my old boss Daniel Reed and by his Democrat successor as chairman, Jere Cooper of Tennessee. Secretary Humphrey wrote me a warm letter after I was sworn in: "Dear Judge: I am delighted to so address you and to know that you have been duly sworn into that office. You'll do a grand job and be a great credit to the Court . . ."

The U.S. Tax Court had been created by the Congress in 1926 to help ease the tax litigation burden on the district courts and also to provide taxpayers with a less burdensome process of adjudicating tax issues—and, presumably, a more expert forum for considering such issues. Under the old English common law, a subject (citizen) could never sue the sovereign. Therefore, when a citizen claimed that he had been wrongfully taxed, he was only permitted to bring a personal action against the tax collector for "monies wrongfully had and received." He was entitled to trial by jury if he wanted it. This is essentially the nature of a taxpayer's case in the Federal District Court today. The hitch is that, in order to avail himself or herself of that potential remedy, the taxpayer must pay the tax in question and then sue to get it back. Under the alternative Tax Court process, the taxpayer need not pay the tax in advance but simply must file a claim within 90 days of the receipt

U.S. Tax Court judge

of a deficiency notice from the Internal Revenue Service. There is no jury trial in the Tax Court.

During my years on the Tax Court, it was situated in the Internal Revenue Service building at 12th and Constitution. The location was a somewhat unhappy one in that it could give the impression that the court was part of the I.R.S. rather than an impartial judicial body. Several years after I left the court in 1965, it got its own very modern facility at 400 2nd Street, N.W. The Tax Court had 16 judges when I was a member, now 19, all appointed for 12-year terms unless they were filling an unexpired term, as in my case. The chief judge arranged the trial calendars, assigned judges to the various calendars, took such calendars himself as he wanted, presided at the regular Friday court conferences, and was responsible for the overall administration of the court. During my time on the court, the chief judge was Edward Murdock.

Considerably older than I—which was true of all the other judges as well—Ned Murdock was a fellow Princetonian and we were good friends. He had been even younger than I when first appointed. We went together on several quail hunting expeditions to South Carolina with a couple of other friends, Bob Myers and Phil Bowie. Ned had a quick mind and a fine sense of humor. During a court session in Washington, D.C., one day, a taxpayer representing himself—as was permitted under Tax Court rules but very seldom availed of—closed his case by declaring: "Your honor, as God is my judge, I do not owe this tax." Judge Murdock, who was presiding, responded without a moment's pause: "He's not. I am. You do." *The Washington Post* wrote a lead editorial on the decision, praising it as a model of judicial brevity and clarity.[1]

Since one of the purposes of the Tax Court is to provide greater convenience to taxpayers who want to dispute a tax assessment, the court conducted trial calendars throughout the country. In some major population centers, such as New York, Chicago, and Los Angeles, court sessions were almost continuous. In other places, such as Boise, Idaho, or Helena, Montana, or Huntington, West Virginia, a calendar might be an annual occurrence, at best. Each calendar was assigned to an individual judge. Thus, we "rode circuit" in the traditional sense, presiding over the calendars, assisted by an experienced court clerk. The calendars were normally organized to last either a week or two weeks but could vary radically from that schedule. I once had a one-week calendar in Galveston which was moved after a week to Houston where it ran for another two weeks—almost all taken up by a case brought by the Diamond Shamrock Corporation.

About six calendars a year were normal for each judge. The rest of

1. Walter Cronkite in his excellent memoir, *A Reporter's Life* (Alfred A. Knopf, New York [1996], p. 127), tells the exact same story but attributes it to an English judge.

the time was spent in my chambers at the court's Washington headquarters, working on the cases I had heard, deciding them, and writing
my opinions. In this regard, I had the invaluable help of two law clerks
who studied the word-for-word transcripts of the trials, reviewed the
briefs filed by the parties, and researched the law involved. Several
came with graduate degrees in both accounting and law, a valuable
combination for a tax attorney. My law clerks were a fine group, fresh
out of law school, and they stayed with me about two years on the
average. Several were graduates of the New York University (NYU)
Law School. One, Herb Chabot, went on to be a member of the staff
of the Joint Committee on Internal Revenue Taxation and has now
been a judge of the Tax Court for about 20 years.

Opinions that did not cover new ground and essentially followed
established precedent were usually issued as Memorandum Opinions.
The opinions in cases that involved new issues or that departed from
precedent were assigned by the chief judge to be reviewed by the entire
court. Those judges who were not away from Washington met on Friday morning in the court's conference room. There you had to present
and defend any of your opinions that had been assigned for review. If
the court supported your decision and opinion, the latter was issued
and published as a Tax Court Opinion. If the court rejected your decision and opinion, the latter was assigned to another judge to rewrite to
reflect the court's view. I only recall one case of mine that was rejected
by the court and that was by a 13-1 vote which left little room for doubt
as to the court's view of my effort. The case involved my conclusion
that the application of a particular tax was unconstitutional.[2]

Given the fact that I had never practiced law in any conventional
sense and certainly had had no courtroom experience whatsoever, joining a trial court as a judge was not only a bit unusual but also a bit
scary. I recall presiding on the first morning of my first calendar in
Philadelphia in 1957. Everything had gone fine and in midmorning, I
decided to call a short recess which was customary and would give me
a chance for a much-needed cigarette. (Those were the days when I

2. My Memorandum Opinions fill seven volumes and the published Tax Court Opinions of my cases fill another four volumes. My last opinion was filed July 31, 1965.

was still smoking between one and two packs a day.) I banged the gavel and announced the recess. The clerk intoned, "All rise." All in the courtroom rose to their feet. The door to my chambers was directly behind the bench. I turned and grasped the doorknob. I was unable to turn it. I later speculated that my hand was so sweaty from nervousness that I could not get a grip on the knob. The people in the courtroom continued to stand awaiting my departure as I struggled with the door. Finally, in something of a panic, I addressed the courtroom over my shoulder: "The damn thing won't open!" With this breach of judicial decorum, the door suddenly opened, and I fled the room.

I found that I enjoyed the trials and that, despite my lack of courtroom experience, I handled most evidentiary and procedural issues with confidence. I brushed up on the law of evidence and learned that, when in doubt, plain old common sense usually provided a pretty good guide. In any event, I was never criticized on appeal for rulings on evidence.

While I enjoyed the courtroom experience, life outside the courtroom while on the road was usually boring. If I had friends in the city where the court was sitting, that helped. However, I had to avoid social contact with the tax bar in the city and often found myself either dining with my court clerk or dining alone. Once, when conducting a two-week court session in New Orleans, I took advantage of the locale to carry on a sort of gastronomical tour of the town, keeping notes on restaurants and menus which I then reproduced for the edification of the other judges. I walked a lot, both for the exercise and to break the monotony. It was a good way to get to know the particular town.

There were some amusing incidents. Once, when I went to Huntington, West Virginia, I understood that one of the cases on the docket involved the alleged underpayment of taxes by the operator of a brothel and that one of the main foundations of the government's case involved a count of the towels that the brothel sent to the laundry. Naturally, I was looking forward to what promised to be a somewhat colorful trial.

I checked into my hotel and had no sooner settled into my room shortly before dinner than there was a knock on the door. I opened the door and was confronted by a rather gaudy blonde. "Hello!" she said archly, batting her eyes at me. "I heard that you were looking for company." "No thanks!" I said hastily and quickly shut the door. She said something unprintable and let fly a kick at the door panel. The next day, when the brothel case was called, it settled without a trial. It was pretty hard not to conclude that I had been targeted for a setup.

We did not set calendars during July and August and that period was open for vacations subject, of course, to the backlog of cases each of us had in the office—usually quite large. On the whole, however, judges were free to set their own work schedules (aside from trial calendars—and the individual judge's preferences were always considered in that regard).

CHAPTER 12

Nonquitt, the Church, and Other Non-Judicial Activities

IN ABOUT 1959, Aileen and I started going in the summers to Nonquitt, Massachusetts, on Buzzards Bay near New Bedford, renting for a couple of summers and then buying a large frame house facing onto the North Beach and the bay. Nonquitt was an old summer community close to Padanaram Harbor, dating back to the late nineteenth century. General Philip Sheridan of Civil War fame had summered in Nonquitt and was instrumental in having a U.S. post office located there. Two unmarried Sheridan daughters lived in the house next to ours but one. Every Fourth of July, the summer residents and their children gathered in front of the Sheridan cottage, small children on their parents' shoulders. The general's well-polished boots were stood up at the top of the front steps, the two old ladies came out and waved, and we all recited the Oath of Allegiance. Tradition died hard at Nonquitt!

Nonquitt had long had Washington ties. Our friends Charlie and Ginny Glover and Mike and Margot McConihe had gone there for years. Among my parents' friends were Fred and Texie Brooke and the Fays. The atmosphere was relaxed and informal, perfect for vacations. For children, it was near paradise. The swimming was wonderful in the relatively warm water of Buzzards Bay. Sailing classes were offered in the fleet of "Beetlecats." There were four tennis courts and a nine-hole golf course. There was a children's camp and, best of all, the kids could bike or otherwise wander at will about the large Nonquitt property. Emily starred at the camp and became known for her nurturing ways with the younger children. By the time she was 9 she was known as "camp mother." Aileen and I played tennis, swam, and sailed on

At Nonquitt, Massachusetts, 1961. Left to right: Aileen with Errol, Bowdy, Nancy (in back), Emily, the author. Dogs from left: Razz, Toby, and Swift

Mother and Aileen, Christmas 1958

friends' boats. We cruised with the Glovers on their Concordia yawl built at the Concordia yard in Padanaram and sailed to Cutty Hunk and Naushon in the Elizabeth Islands across Buzzards Bay. Naturally, we went to New Bedford to see the Whaling Museum and the Grinnell mansion. (See *The Bowdoin Family* for Aileen's relationship with the Grinnell family.)

Except for a vacation in August, I commuted regularly to Nonquitt by train, taking the Federal Friday evening from Union Station and

Nancy, 1961

getting off at Providence early the next morning. Aileen usually came
to get me but sometimes I took a taxi. I would reverse the process and
return to Washington by train late Sunday evening. It was not a very
relaxing schedule, particularly as Nonquitt social life tended to get
compressed into the weekends. But we had many good friends there
and felt sad when we sold our house in 1967. However, that was when
we bought Grace Creek Farm on the Eastern Shore, and we were
ready to move on to other things. By that time, our children had pretty
much outgrown Nonquitt, and the farm within easy reach of Washington made much more sense.

Years later, in August of 1979 and 1980, we rented a small frame cottage on Edgartown Harbor at Martha's Vineyard. Walter and Betsy
Cronkite had a much larger house on the same property and we shared
a dock, where they kept their yacht, *Wyntje,* and we swam. We became
good friends of the Cronkites and had many other friends on the
Vineyard. They were two pleasant summers, and we might well have
continued to go to the Vineyard. However, when we suggested to our
landlord that the 50-year-old horsehair mattresses should be replaced
with something more modern and less allergenic, our tenancy was ter-
minated.

Emily, 1961

Non-Judicial Activities

UNLIKE MOST of my fellow judges who were not Washington natives, I was involved in a variety of civic activities. I was a member of the board of governors of the Metropolitan Club. I also became a member of the St. Albans School board and served as chairman for several years. Among those on the board when I was chairman were Phil Graham, publisher of the *Washington Post*, who tragically committed suicide during that time, and John Warner, then married to Paul Mellon's daughter Cathy, and later married to the actress Elizabeth Taylor. After his fairly short-lived marriage to the latter, he became (and still is) U.S. senator from Virginia.[1]

1. The only time I met Elizabeth Taylor, certainly one of the most famous film personalities of my time, was at a large dinner dance at the Chevy Chase Club. She was the date of Ardeshir Zahedi, the charismatic ambassador of Iran and close friend of the Shah. He and she danced together several times but I noticed that no one else danced with her. It seemed to me a wasted opportunity so I took a deep breath and cut in on them. They both seemed a bit surprised but Ardeshir introduced me and off we

The headmaster of St. Albans at the time was the much-beloved Charles Martin, who had replaced Albert Lucas, the headmaster when I was a student. Our board usually met in the headmaster's study, a place I viewed with some awe. Charlie had an English bulldog who slept noisily in our meetings and whose physiognomy is immortalized in one of the stone gargoyles of the cathedral. Charlie was headmaster throughout Bowdy's eight years at St. Albans, and I will always be grateful to him for his caring and helpfulness. (Martin retired in 1977 after being headmaster for 28 years and he died in 1997 at the age of 91. Aileen and I attended his memorial service at the cathedral.)

St. John's Church

AFTER OUR marriage, I became increasingly involved with St. John's Church on Lafayette Square, across from the White House. James Madison, who was president in 1815, was a communicant, and every chief executive since has attended regular or occasional services. Thus, it is sometimes called the "Church of the Presidents." The parish house adjoining the church at 1525 H Street was once the British legation where Lord Ashburton and Daniel Webster signed the treaty fixing the border between the New England states and the Canadian Maritime Provinces. (The present Lord Ashburton had been a guest at Long Point when I was there.)

St. John's was, of course, the "Train church," and my grandparents had joined the church in 1884. As a boy, my father sang in the choir and many years later served as a vestryman. The American flag hanging toward the front of the church had been given by the family. While I had not been much of a churchgoer during my bachelor days, Aileen liked to go and we became quite regular attenders. As soon as they were old enough, our children all went to the Sunday school.

danced. Groping for conversation, I asked her where she had just come from. "From the moon," she breathed huskily. I am afraid our conversation became even more desultory. She was quite overweight at the time so dancing was not exactly her thing. Her eyes were astonishingly beautiful, and I remember describing them to Aileen afterwards as "limpid, violet pools in which one loses oneself."

St. John's Church (Lafayette
Square) with the Washington
Monument and White House
in the right background

I was first asked to be an usher at the regular 11 o'clock Sunday services. In 1957, I was elected to the vestry and I recall that at my first
vestry meeting our longtime rector, Leslie Glenn, who had married
Aileen and me three years before, announced his retirement. His place
was taken by Donald Mayberry, a fine person, who eventually decided
that he was not the right fit for St. John's, and he too left. By that time,
I had become junior warden (1961) and headed the search committee
for Mayberry's successor.

"Head-hunting" it would be called in most other contexts and it
was a new experience for me. We made a list of potential candidates and
then members of my committee fanned out over the Middle Atlantic
states on Sundays to visit churches and listen to sermons. Out of this
process emerged one outstanding candidate, John C. Harper, rector of
St. Matthew's Church, Bedford, New York. He was young, person-
able, with an attractive wife and small children. He preached a fine
sermon that was not too long. The music and choir were splendid and
the service was exactly as we liked it. Finally, he was extremely popular
with his parishioners.

Our vestry authorized a "call" to Harper and we duly sent off the
appropriate letter. To our surprise his reply came back quickly and in
the negative. It was hard for us to believe that anyone would turn down
St. John's! After a telephone conversation, he and I agreed to meet in

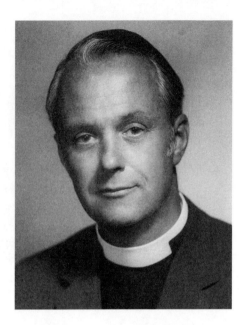

Reverend John C. Harper, D.D.

New York City for further discussion. So on the Wednesday evening before Thanksgiving, we met at the Harvard Club on West 44th Street. Over drinks and dinner, we talked for several hours. We hit it off personally, and I was able to reassure Harper on a number of matters on which he had concerns.

In due course, John Harper accepted our call and became the thirteenth rector of St. John's, serving as rector from 1963 to 1993. It was a happy choice all around. John was a very popular pastor, and the church grew and strengthened in every respect. I have always felt pleased at having played a major role in bringing him to St. John's. John and Barbara were and are good personal friends of Aileen and myself. I became senior warden in 1965 and served in that capacity until 1969 when I became Under Secretary of the Interior and felt that I should withdraw from such outside obligations.

National Cathedral

AT SOME POINT, while serving on the vestry of St. John's, I had been elected a member of the chapter of the Washington Cathedral and for a short time served on the chapter's executive committee. I probably resigned from the chapter at the same time as I resigned from St. John's vestry.

Among the "perks" that went with chapter membership were reserved seats in the Cathedral Choir on Christmas Eve and on Easter. We took advantage of these on at least two Christmas Eves and these were magical times, with the marvelous boys' choir (all scholarship students at St. Albans) and their clear, pure voices and with masses of candles lighting the great columns and vaulted ceiling. The cathedral is a place of great beauty, of soaring spaces and timeless strength—all totally different from the more intimate scale of a parish church. My associations with it go back to my school days and usually relate to ceremonial occasions such as my confirmation in the Bethlehem Chapel, giving the commencement address from the pulpit at the time of Bowdy's graduation from St. Albans in 1972, and reading the Lesson on Environmental Sunday in 1993.

Audience with Emperor Haile Selassie

MY ASSOCIATION with the cathedral provided an unexpected bonus in 1966, when I was in Addis Ababa, Ethiopia, on African Wildlife Leadership Foundation business, and had a private audience with His Imperial Majesty Haile Selassie, the Lion of Judah. I had arrived at the palace by myself and been ushered into a waiting room on the ground floor. Finally, I was led up a broad central staircase with one of the emperor's pet Chihuahuas yapping at my heels. I entered a very large room and the emperor was at his desk on a raised platform on the far side. He rose to greet me as I approached. He was a diminutive figure but the raised platform elevated him sufficiently that we were on the same eye level. Aside from his court chamberlain who translated, we were alone.

After the exchange of the usual pleasantries and after I had told the emperor where I had been in his country, I went on to congratulate him on his recent establishment of a Wildlife Service. He nodded and smiled. Then some sort of madness overcame me and I went on to say something to the effect that I had observed that of the 28-member staff of the Wildlife Service, 25 were his relatives and that struck me as a potential problem. His face froze. The emperor was not amused. The audience was clearly not a success and would doubtless be ended abruptly at any moment. Suddenly, I had an inspiration. "Sir," I said, "when I was a boy, I went to St. Albans School on the Cathedral Close in Washington. I recall your visiting Washington at that time and coming to the cathedral. On that occasion, you gave the cathedral a very beautiful, jeweled Coptic cross. That cross is still treasured by the cathedral and is carried in the ceremonial procession on all great feast days such as Easter."

Haile Selassie watched me without expression in his dark, intelligent eyes as he listened to the translation. Suddenly, his face was wreathed with smiles and he said he remembered the occasion very well. The audience was saved and the emperor became friendly and responsive. The occasion had been rescued by my miraculous memory of that event in the cathedral at least 30 years before.

Pillar of the Church

AS CAN BE seen from all this, I became a veritable pillar of the church—and I enjoyed the role. On Sundays, Aileen and I occupied the old Train pew at St. John's although pew rents had been abolished soon after John Harper became rector. The American flag given by my father in memory of my grandfather hung over the south door (now moved to the north). I wore my best dark, pin-striped suit and passed the plate as my father had before me. Following the collection, I led the parade of plate-passers up the aisles to the chancel where we handed the plates to the rector and then joined in singing the doxology.

After the service and after picking up our children from Sunday school, Aileen and I would spend some time being sociable in front of the church. Many of the congregation were personal friends. While in about 1958 I had led the Every-Member Canvass—the church's annual-giving campaign—most of my church activities were limited to the regular monthly vestry meetings and the Sunday services. I seldom became involved in the various other church activities. The junior warden, Phil Watts, and I lunched regularly with John Harper at the Metropolitan Club. As lay officials of the church, our responsibility was for the physical and, most importantly, the financial well-being of the parish, and on these aspects of its life we tried to keep a pretty close eye.

Aileen was by far the more devout of the two of us, and to this day she welcomes opportunities to go to church. I was always "comfortable" in the church and felt at home with its hymns, its prayers, its liturgy. My forebears were men and women of faith and piety and I think I enjoyed following in that tradition while at the same time avoiding too close an examination of the niceties involved. I have never paid much attention to doctrine and have found it easier so. I am impatient with the proliferation of denominations and, indeed, of separate religions and their animosity toward one another.

I remember once as a boy walking up Que Street in the evening with my father—probably we were walking the dog—and he spoke to me very briefly about his belief in God. What brought about this unaccustomed subject I do not know, but what has stuck in my mind was his saying that "you can't weather a winter storm in the North Atlantic on board a destroyer without believing in God!" That was perhaps a simplistic, sailorman's approach but it carried conviction. A belief in God can be a great strength, and it certainly provides an important counterweight to the self-centeredness of most human beings.

Churches are important transmitters of values in our society along with our families and schools. At the same time, I am quickly turned off by religious dogma, and I think that one reason I find the Episcopal Church more comfortable than others is that it tends to be tolerant of divergent views. Finally, I strongly support the insistence of my Baptist-clergy ancestors on an absolute separation of church and state. Theocratic government and theocratic political parties are a disaster wherever they crop up in the world. It is sad that the Southern Baptist Convention has abandoned its roots in this regard and, like other fundamentalist religious groups around the world, now promotes religious involvement in politics.

I seem to have dwelt on my church-related activities and religious attitudes more than I meant to. However, those activities played an important part in my life for many years and I do not want to present myself either as a deeply religious person on the one hand, or as a sanctimonious hypocrite on the other. With the purchase of Grace Creek Farm in 1967, our Sundays were almost always spent on the Eastern Shore and our churchgoing pretty much came to an end except for Christmas and Easter, christenings, weddings, funerals, and the like.

I have to say, however, that to be part of the world of nature, with all of its incredible beauty, diversity, and complexity, and to feel the interdependence of all its parts, including most importantly ourselves, is in itself an overwhelmingly spiritual experience. While at the World Wildlife Fund, I gave several speeches on the general subject of ecology and religion.

CHAPTER 13

Introduction to Africa

THE EXTRACURRICULAR activity that undoubtedly attracted the greatest amount of time and interest on my part was the conservation of African wildlife. As already mentioned briefly, Aileen and I had been on safaris in East Africa in 1956 and 1958, the latter having been about a year after I joined the Tax Court. Those trips to Africa played such a central role in the future course of my life that I must give some account of how this all came about.

In a profile on me in 1969, the *New York Times* put it this way: "Russell Errol Train shot an elephant and was chased by a rhinoceros. Life was never the same after that. For the safari that took Mr. Train to Africa turned him into a conservationist."

Aileen is fond of recounting that, when we married and I moved to Woodland Drive from my house in Georgetown, I came with a cook named Gloria, two suitcases of clothes, my black Labrador, Swift, and about two hundred books about hunting in Africa. With due allowance for some embellishment on her part, she had it essentially right. Apparently, I talked of Africa from time to time because about six months after our marriage Aileen said to me, "Why don't we stop talking about it and go!" A friend in Washington, Charles Hook, who was just leaving the government as Deputy Postmaster General, told me that I ought to talk to his successor, Maurice Stans, about an African safari. I spent a couple of hours with Stans, who with his wife, Kathleen, later became great friends of ours.[1] The upshot was that we arranged a one-month, tented, hunting safari in Kenya with the premier outfitting firm, Ker & Downey.

And so in the late summer of 1956, Aileen and I flew to Rome and

1. Stans became director of the Office of Management and Budget (OMB) and Secretary of Commerce in the Nixon administration.

On safari, Kenya, 1956

On safari,
Northern Frontier District,
Kenya, 1956

then on to Nairobi where we were met by our professional hunter, George Barrington. We camped and hunted along the Athi River, then near Lake Magadi, and in the Northern Frontier District (NFD) northwest of Iseolo. I secured elephant, greater kudu, lesser kudu, buffalo, Grant gazelle, and leopard trophies plus a few animals for camp meat.

The experience was everything I had dreamt of. It was a wonderful adventure in which we were in wild, remote country, spending most of our time hunting on foot using a local tribesman as a tracker. Aileen

Aileen on safari,
Kenya, 1956

only hunted once herself and did not enjoy the experience. However, she thoroughly enjoyed going along on the hunts and was always right with me as we followed up our quarry. At the request of the Smithsonian, we collected insects on that trip—*dudus* in Swahili.

Two years later we were back again in Kenya on another one-month hunting safari, again with Ker & Downey and our hunter, George Barrington. We traveled there that time via Athens, Stanleyville (now Lumumbashe) in the Belgian Congo, Lake Kivu, the Virunga Volcanos in Ruanda, and the Queen Elizabeth National Park in Uganda. In the Virunga Volcanos we tracked and came up with small bands of mountain gorillas, a marvelous experience and long before the gorillas became "habituated" to visiting tourists. We were unarmed and the encounters with the gorillas were heart-stopping events.

In Kenya, we hunted first near the Tana River and I secured a magnificent elephant with each tusk over 100 pounds—a rare trophy even in 1958. We then spent two weeks in the forests on Mount Kenya hunting the elusive bongo, the second-largest African antelope after the eland. I failed to get one. This second safari, although we considered ourselves old Africa hands by then, was every bit as rewarding and exciting as the first.[2] We continued our collecting for the Smithson-

2. The complete story of those two safaris is told in two mimeographed books, both unpublished: *African Safari* (1956) and *Back to Africa* (1958), which we distributed to family and friends at Christmastime those years. Each was written by me with suggestions from Aileen and was based on a daily journal that I kept. The keeping of such a journal became a habit followed on most trips after that.

Elephant tusks
weighing 101 and
102 pounds.
Tana River District,
Kenya, 1958

ian, concentrating this time on small mammals such as rats, squirrels,
bats, etc.

We loved every moment of those safaris—the cold early mornings,
the heat of midday spent in the shade of an acacia, the incessant calling of the doves, the hot, dry smell of the African earth, the spoor of
the passing game, the sight of the game itself, the tension and concentration of the hunt, the beauty and incredible variety of the birds, the
sundowner beside the fire and the tales told at such a time, the camp
itself and the soft sound of African voices, the nights full of stars, the
occasional roar of the distant lion, the call of a hyena. It was heady,
romantic stuff and we ate it up. Of course, there was a good deal of
naiveté in all this, and we obviously were exposed to very little of the
reality of modern Africa. Never mind, I was in love with Africa and
still am—the old Africa of the early hunters, explorers, and settlers, of
golden landscapes and immense skies, of teeming wildlife, of Isak
Dinesen, Ernest Hemingway, and Elspeth Huxley. Truly, in the phrase
of my friend Ian Player, Africa is the "land of the soul."

I have returned to Africa again and again over the years—about 20
times, I would guess—and hope to go back again, God willing. I never
hunted there again after those first two safaris, not because I am

Hunting on Mount Kenya, 1958

opposed to hunting, but because my interest waned; I had done that. And I had other things to do. Important in that respect was the formation of the African Wildlife Leadership Foundation (AWLF), now simply the African Wildlife Foundation (AWF).

African Wildlife Leadership Foundation

SOMETIME AFTER our return from the second safari in the fall of 1958, my friend and safari mentor, Maury Stans, invited us to join the African Safari Club of Washington, an organization newly formed by a small group of Washington businessmen who had gone on a hunt together in Mozambique. The group met at the Roma Restaurant on Connecticut Avenue opposite the Uptown movie theater, and its main purpose was to provide a venue for the exchange of African hunting experiences.

After Aileen and I had attended several evenings of that sort, I suggested that the group develop a conservation mission. The suggestion received a reasonably warm response, and, as so often happens in such cases, I was asked to head a committee to develop some ideas as to what might be done. My committee consisted of Arthur (Nick) Arundel, Jim Bugg, Kermit (Kim) Roosevelt, Maury Stans, and Ed Sweeney. Kim was a grandson of Theodore Roosevelt. His own father, also named

Kermit, had accompanied T.R. on his famous African safari in 1910-1911. The committee met only once and at my Tax Court chambers.

We quickly decided that the most important wildlife conservation task in Africa was to equip Africans themselves with the skills that would enable them to manage their own wildlife resources, to run game departments and national parks. That priority emerged very quickly in our discussion. The forces of independence were sweeping through Africa and the colonial powers were rapidly turning over control of their colonies to their African inhabitants. While the Europeans had done a fair job of training Africans in a variety of administrative areas, they had done little or nothing to train them as natural resource managers. In the British colonies in particular, the management of game and parks had mostly been the bailiwick of gifted and dedicated amateurs, often retired British and Indian army officers. What these men lacked in professional training they made up for with their passionate love of nature—birds, animals, and plants. It seemed unlikely that many Africans, with different priorities, would be similarly motivated. Thus, professional training at a variety of levels seemed a clear priority. Second, we decided that the focus, initially at least, should be on British East Africa, in large part because we had more familiarity with that area.

Obviously, such a mission would require raising money in significant amounts if it was to be effective at all. Equally obvious was the fact that to raise funds of that sort would require not only an organization which was tax exempt but also one to which contributions would be tax deductible. That ruled out the African Safari Club of Washington as the vehicle since it was a social, not a charitable, organization. Finally, we decided on a name: the African Wildlife Leadership Foundation, the "Leadership" being intended to convey the sense of Africans developing the capacity to manage their own wildlife resources.

We informed the Safari Club group of what we were doing but any real association between the organizations soon evaporated. One of my law clerks, Lee Rogers,[3] drew up incorporation papers under the

3. Edward Lee Rogers, one of my first law clerks, who went on to a distinguished career in the law, including environmental law. He died tragically in an auto accident in 1998.

laws of the District of Columbia; I gave him the $15 filing fee; he filed the papers at the District Building; and AWLF was in business. That was early 1961. It is not my intent here to recount a history of the organization, which continues to be a major force in African conservation, but rather to touch on those aspects of its history that had a significant relevance to the direction of my own life.[4]

We established a board, elected members and myself as chairman and CEO, positions I held until 1969. At the outset, the AWLF headquarters was essentially my office although I rented a postal box at the Benjamin Franklin Station across the street and that is where all mail, including donations, was addressed. Subsequently, I rented a small office in the National Press building with a secretary. In any event, judge or not, I was the chief cook, bottle-washer, whatever, of AWLF in those early days. I raised essentially all the money, designed our program and projects, kept in touch with those involved with conservation on the ground in Africa, and did what communication we had with the public at home. Later on, others came on board to share the responsibilities. John George became executive director for a time.

We soon had several young Africans at U.S. universities studying wildlife management. The first of these, Perez Olindo, went on to become the first African director of national parks in Kenya. He continues to be a loyal friend and often signs himself in letters to me as "Your African son"! Thanks to Paul Mellon and his Old Dominion Foundation, we provided the initial funding for the College of African Wildlife Management at Mweka, Tanzania. Later, we did the same for a similar institution for French-speaking Africa at Garoua, Cameroon, thanks in that instance to Laurance Rockefeller and the Rockefeller Brothers Fund. Jim Hyde, consultant to RBF, became a good friend and advocate for our African initiatives. We established education programs at Nairobi National Park in Kenya and at Murchison Falls National Park in Uganda. Those were some highlights of our early days.

When I had a court calendar in some city such as Dallas, I would

---

4. The history of the African Wildlife Foundation (AWF) is told in *Thirty-Five Years of Conservation in Africa: A History of African Wildlife Foundation* by Jacqueline Russell; foreword by Russell E. Train. Published by AWF, 1997.

Ian Grimwood

try to develop a list of people who had been on safari in Africa and get in touch with them. Usually, I would contact them in advance and try to have a meal with them. Occasionally, I would be invited to give a talk on African conservation by some like-minded group. On one occasion in Pittsburgh, I did a program on WQED, the local public broadcasting TV station.

A major effort turned out to be the institution of the *African Wildlife News,* whose format was tabloid in form and modeled after the old *St. Albans News* of which I had been managing editor. I even went to the same printer, the McArdle Press, which was then located at 22nd and M Streets in a building now occupied by the Nigerian Embassy. I wrote the copy, including the editorials, even took some of the photos, wrote the heads, corrected the galleys, and did the cutting and pasting and the final layout of the paper. The *News* went out free to all donors as well as to others who had been on safari or otherwise were believed to have an interest in African wildlife. My good friend Jack Block, managing director of Ker & Downey in Nairobi, had been generous in his help in providing a list of safari clients—an action K & D never did before or has since.

Hugh Lamprey

John Owen

My excellent judicial secretary, Evangeline Jensen, typed the copy until AWLF was able to hire its own secretary. Chores such as laying out the paper were done by me at the printer and in the evenings. I don't believe the entire operation really impinged on my official duties but it certainly did on my personal life. Aileen was understanding and, in fact, shared my enthusiasm for AWLF. Friends and collaborators from Africa, such as Major Bruce Kinloch, chief game warden of Tanzania, Major Ian Grimwood, chief game warden of Kenya, and John Owen, director of the Tanzania national parks, visited us in Washington. A particularly valued associate from Africa was Hugh Lamprey, distinguished wildlife scientist, who became the first principal of the College of African Wildlife Management, then director of the Serengeti Research Institute, and finally head of the World Wildlife Fund office in Nairobi. All of these men and their wives became close friends of Aileen and myself, friends with whom we shared a deep commitment to conservation in Africa as well as many experiences in the African wilds.

I made several trips to Africa on AWLF business, sometimes on my own and sometimes accompanied by Aileen. I felt we were really

Bowdy on safari, 1966

accomplishing things in Africa, and I was having great fun. A small
organization in which you personally do almost all the work—and
AWLF could not have been much smaller—can be enormously satisfying. There is little question that larger organizations with larger
bureaucracies may have the potential for greater accomplishment but
the personal satisfaction factor tends to decrease with size. Of course,
the principal factor in my enjoyment of the AWLF involvement was a
passionate belief in our mission to save African wildlife for the future.
My associates and I were deeply committed to that goal. It is gratifying that AWF (as it is now known) continues stronger than ever today.
My old friend ambassador Robinson McIlvaine was an outstanding
president for several years. Today, Michael Wright, formerly of WWF,
is the CEO and is doing a fine job.

There were further safaris (non-hunting) in those years. On one
memorable occasion in 1966 we were accompanied by Nancy, Emily,
Bowdy, and Bowdy's friend Will Bundy, son of McGeorge and Mary
Bundy. Bowdy was 10 and he and I traveled to Africa together, spending several days in London—visiting the Tower, watching the changing of the guard at Buckingham Palace, seeing Madame Tussaud's
Waxworks, etc. He had his first taste of Haut Brion and altogether we
had a great time together. We flew to Uganda and then up to Murchi-

Bill Eddy

son Falls National Park and on to Kidepo National Park on the border with Sudan.

Bowdy and I caught up with Aileen and the rest of our entourage at Amboseli National Park on the border of Kenya and Tanzania. The College of African Wildlife Management, which AWLF had helped found, lent us some vehicles and staff and we did a ten-day safari, much of which we spent in the Tarangire Game Reserve (now a national park, thanks to funds provided by Charles Engelhard through AWLF). Our guide was Patrick Hemingway, a son of Ernest and a valued teacher at the college. It was a wonderful time, complete with a full-bore elephant charge which left everyone unscathed but limp with excitement.

A special friend in those years was Bill Eddy, an inspired and gifted teacher, who had received a Ford Foundation grant to initiate a program in Tanzania to introduce African school students to their wildlife and national parks. Although I could never persuade Bill to become a regular member of the AWLF staff, we worked together on a number of enterprises in Africa. He and his wife, Beryl, became and remain treasured friends. Then there was Frank Minot who headed our

AWLF office in Nairobi and Rob Milne who ran our education project at Nairobi and later became the distinguished director of the International Affairs Office of the U.S. National Park Service. These are but
some of the personal relationships that made my work with AWLF so
satisfying and such a joy.

I had many more associations with Africa in later years, particularly
with the World Wildlife Fund, but the above is how it all started.

CHAPTER 14

Sailing

ANOTHER OUTSIDE interest that loomed large in our lives during those years was sailing. Our next-door neighbors on Woodland Drive were Henry and Mary Porter, wonderful people who became dear friends. Henry was a sailor and, being an engineer and physicist by training, was an expert on all the technical aspects of the design and operation of a boat. Aileen had grown up at Oyster Bay, Long Island, had been active in the Seawanaka Yacht Club, and was an accomplished sailor.

Together with the Porters, we bought a 40-foot, Adkins-designed, wooden ketch, named *Traveller*. She had been in the charter business and had been built at Abaco in the Bahamas by her captain-owner. I think she only cost us about $15,000 but we put in a new engine after we brought her up from Miami and gave her a thorough overhaul. We kept her at Hartge's boatyard at Galesville on the West River on the Western Shore of Chesapeake Bay. During the sailing season, which was from April to November, we normally alternated weekends with the Porters but always arranged to be together at least a couple of times a season. *Traveller* accommodated four easily and six with a bit more effort. Aileen and I would handle her by ourselves on occasion, which was a delight, but usually we had friends aboard or our children, particularly Bowdy and Errol or one of them with a friend.

Typically, we would go aboard *Traveller* Friday afternoon and make the short run from the West River to the Rhode River for the night. The next day would be an all-day sail, usually to a destination on the Eastern Shore. We would drop anchor in a protected spot such as Dividing Creek off the Wye River. We seldom had to share an anchorage with other craft although today most choice anchorages are crowded.

Traveller

I can think of few times as happy as those cruises, particularly after the anchor was down, sails furled, and it was time for a drink—usually bourbon on the rocks with a lemon twist for me at the time—sitting in the cockpit enjoying the sunset. Of course, Aileen had to cope with supper and the galley. Overall, however, sailing was very much a shared activity. Aileen was the expert but I learned reasonably fast. She was always much better than I at trimming the sails to take maximum advantage of the wind and at timing our coming about so as not to lose way. In other words, she was a much better sailor. However, she always let me feel that I was the skipper.

After we bought Grace Creek Farm in 1967, we tried to keep *Traveller* moored off our dock, but it did not really work. Moreover, the farm came to occupy more and more of our weekend attention, and it became obvious that the boat was more than we could really enjoy. The Porters also were using the boat less so in about 1969 we sold *Traveller*. We had had ten wonderful years sailing the bay aboard her and she had been very much part of our lives and that of our children's during

Mary and Henry Porter, next-door
neighbors, co-owners of *Traveller,*
and dear friends

With Bowdy aboard *Traveller*

that period. And it was she that introduced us to the Eastern Shore
and its unspoiled shorelines, leading in due course to the purchase of
our farm.

Nancy finished Potomac in 1960 and went away to Foxcroft that
year, graduating in 1964 when she went to Wellesley. Emily followed
her to Foxcroft that same year, graduating in 1968 when I was honored
by being the commencement speaker. Emily spent one year at Wheaton
College and then transferred to the University of Pennsylvania where
she graduated in 1972. Those were restless years for her generation and
she moved on to San Francisco where she got a master's degree in education at the University of San Francisco and became head teacher in

a church school. As a result, neither Nancy nor Emily shared as much
of our boat life or, later, of our farm life, as did Bowdy and Errol. However, we did have some wonderful times together.

Aegean Cruise

IN 1957, between our East African safaris, we took Nancy and Emily
on a cruise in the Aegean and then on a tour of northern Italy. We
chartered a sailing yacht named *Stormie Seas* modeled on a Greek
caïque. The owner and skipper was Sam Barclay, a tall, rangy Englishman with blond hair to his shoulders. He had smuggled arms, communications equipment, and other contraband to the Greek underground during the German occupation in World War II. He was a
legendary figure around the islands and was looked upon with both
awe and affection wherever we put ashore. After the war, Sam had sal-
vaged timber and other materials from boats sunk in Tobruk harbor
and had built the *Stormie Seas* from these. She was a "character" boat
with ratlines and fife rail, stays that Sam set by heaving against them,
sails dyed a reddish ochre using the raw earth from cliffs near Athens,
and a massive tiller carved in the shape of a woman's arm and hand.
You held her hand as you steered.

We did the sights of Athens and then sailed to Delos, Naxos, Mi-
konos, Skopelos, Skiathos, Skiros, and other islands that I forget. On
Delos, Aileen and I and the two girls spent the night alone ashore
among the ruins—against all the rules. As the full moon rose, the shadows shifted and the girls were convinced they saw lions, centaurs, and
other stone sculptures come to life and move. In the dawn, we climbed
Mount Cynthos to the cave near the top where legend has it that
Apollo was born. As we entered the cave, a shaft of light from the rising sun lit the exact spot on the cave floor. There was a small sprig of
wildflowers left there as an offering.

A highlight of our visit to Skopelos was riding donkeys up a mountain to a monastery on top. There we poked around and in a little room
Emily took the lid off what looked like a shoe box. She stared for a

Nancy, Ed Foley, Emily, Emily Foley, and Aileen on a barge on the Seine, Paris, following our 1958 safari

moment at the contents and then declared: "Look! Melons." "Skulls," explained our guide, a nun. Skiros was the site of the grave of Rupert Brooke, whose poetry my father so loved.

From Athens, we flew to Milan. There we climbed to the cathedral roof where nuns sold us Coca-Colas. We stayed at Bellagio on Lake Como and there Nancy and Emily walked down to the hotel's swimming area on the lakeshore and Emily recorded in her diary: "The men wore white bikinis and we saw all the sights." We drove across northern Italy, staying briefly at Bressanone and Cortina; then we spent several days in glorious Venice at the Gritti Palace and on to Siena, Florence, and Rome.

The next summer, while we were on safari in East Africa, the two girls went to a well-known and highly recommended camp in the south of France. We saw it as a great opportunity for them to learn French. The reality was that the poor kids froze and starved for the month that they were there and hated every moment. Emily Foley gave us hell for "abandoning" them while we enjoyed ourselves in Africa. At the end of our safari, I flew straight home to resume my judicial duties while Aileen went to Europe, rescued Nancy and Emily, and joined the Foleys in Brussels for the World's Fair. They sailed home on the *United States,* and I met them on the dock in New York.

CHAPTER 15

From Judge to Conservationist

BY 1961, I was 40, a federal judge, and becoming known in the international conservation world. Not long after the establishment of the African Wildlife Leadership Foundation, a group of international conservationists, mostly European and including such luminaries as Sir Julian Huxley, organized the World Wildlife Fund (WWF), with international headquarters in Switzerland, designed to raise funds in support of international conservation efforts, woefully underfunded at the time. H.R.H. Prince Bernhard of the Netherlands was named international president. In September, WWF-U.K. was established with H.R.H. the Duke of Edinburgh as president and in December WWF-U.S. was launched.

I was asked to be one of the founding directors of WWF-U.S. and also vice president and I accepted with enthusiasm, thus beginning an association which continues to the present. The WWF-U.S. president was Ira Gabrielson, who had been an outstanding director of the U.S. Fish and Wildlife Service. John I. Snyder was chairman but was soon replaced by John D. Murchison of Dallas, heir to an oil fortune. There were five of us in that group of founding directors, including Kermit Roosevelt and Harold J. Coolidge. The latter was probably the leading U.S. proponent of international conservation. He lived in Washington and was a valued mentor to me on conservation matters. He was an early AWLF trustee and always highly supportive of our African enterprises. On the WWF board, he saw to it that some WWF funds—as modest as they were at the time—were directed to AWLF projects. A fund-raising dinner at the Waldorf Astoria in New York in June 1962, with Prince Bernhard and Prince Philip as the guests of honor, helped promote WWF to the public. Over lunch in Washington in April 1999,

Fairfield Osborn

Prince Bernhard ("PB") reminisced about Prince Philip's preemptory manner with the press on that occasion. The principal office of WWF-U.S. was in Washington, where it has remained over the years.

The Conservation Foundation

ANOTHER EARLY member of the WWF board was Fairfield Osborn, president of the New York Zoological Society (NYZS), which included the Bronx Zoo, and chairman of the board of The Conservation Foundation (CF). He had started CF to provide an outlet for his environmental interests, such as controlling human population growth and regulating pesticides, that extended beyond the normal interests of the zoo.

Fair, as he was known by his friends, was a good deal older than I and probably at least 70 when we first met. He was a strong personality and a power in his field. The Osborns were an old New York/Hudson River Valley family, and his father, Henry Fairfield Osborn, had been head for many years of the American Museum of Natural History. Fair had established a small African program under the auspices of NYZS, and he began to look with a somewhat jaundiced eye on the growing success and visibility of AWLF. Part of his concern doubtless arose from the fact that I was raising funds from some of his longtime supporters in the New York area, and he was definitely not used to being challenged on his own turf.

One day, Fair called me at my Tax Court office. He opened the conversation by complimenting me on the growing success of AWLF. Then he emphasized that it was wasteful to have several organizations doing the same thing, that NYZS already had an African program and planned to expand it. The plain message was that we should either fold up and quit or join up with NYZS in some way. I retorted that the reason NYZS was planning an expanded African program was that "we have lit a fire under you!" There was a pause at the other end of the line and then: "Train, you son-of-a-bitch!" I took that to have been said not as an insult but as an expression of admiration, which became mutual. Fair was a great man. He was an effective and articulate spokesman for conservation and had done a splendid job in building NYZS and creating the Conservation Foundation.

Not long after, Fair suggested to me that I leave the Tax Court and become president of The Conservation Foundation (CF), taking the place of Sam Ordway who wanted to retire. I had been on the court about six years and was undoubtedly restless. I remember that, shortly after I had gone on the court, a friend from my earlier life had asked me how I liked my judicial role. "It's fine," I said, "except that the phone never rings!" That was a bit of an exaggeration but the fact was that life on the court was fairly secluded, certainly as compared to my jobs on the Hill where one worked in a constant turmoil of lobbyists and politicians. That may have been one reason I had gravitated into so many non-judicial activities, particularly conservation. Perhaps Secretary of the Treasury George Humphrey had been right in the first place. Aileen, always one to face reality, finally said to me on one occasion, "Russ, it seems to me that you are going to have to decide to be either a judge or a conservationist." I knew she was right but had

With Laurance and Mary Rockefeller
at the JY Ranch, Jackson, Wyoming

avoided coming to grips with the issue. Now I had to. I lunched with
Fair in New York at the University Club to discuss the possibility of
my resigning from the court and becoming president of CF.

I indicated that I would need a salary at least equal to what I was
receiving as a judge, namely, $50,000 per year. He was somewhat taken
aback, as the CF tradition was to have gentlemen of wealth at the top.
A more difficult issue was the future location of CF. I had no intention
of moving my life to New York. Not long after, Laurance S. Rockefeller and I had lunch at the Metropolitan Club in Washington and
pursued these issues as well as his own perspectives on CF. Laurance
was vice-chairman of the board and had been a generous supporter
since its inception. He was also a devoted admirer of Fair's. He was less
interested in ecological research and more interested in linking environmental policy to human needs. Thus, he was a strong supporter of
open space protection, not just for the sake of preservation but because
of the opportunities provided for outdoor recreation. That is a somewhat simplistic example of his thinking but it conveys the general
idea. In any event, he wanted to be assured that, if I became head of
CF, I would not devote all my efforts to esoteric studies and would
give appropriate priority to his more pragmatic approach. This created

no problems for me and Laurance and I became good friends over the years.[1] He has been and remains a major force in conservation, particularly in the United States, but also internationally.

In due course, Fair and I reached agreement on all issues and I agreed in principle that I would leave the bench and take on the presidency of CF. A difficult problem for me was the timing of the move. I had presided over a number of trials where the cases had not yet been decided, and it was a point of honor with me to decide all the cases I had heard. In the event, this took about a year. To this day, I am amazed how understanding Fair and his associates on the CF board were on the matter. President Johnson accepted my resignation by a letter, dated July 29, 1965, arranged by my friend McGeorge Bundy, then national security advisor. The president expressed regret at my resignation but then went on to say: "I am gratified to learn, Russell, that you will be applying your great gifts to the conservation effort—an endeavor which, more than ever before, is crucial to the future of our nation." Aileen and I spent that August with our children at "Barney's Joy," South Dartmouth, Massachusetts, rented from Angelica Russell. Effective after Labor Day 1965, I became president of The Conservation Foundation.

My first public exposure in the new job was a speech at the Jackson Lake Lodge in the Grand Teton National Park before a joint conference of the American Forestry Association and the Council of State Garden Clubs. It was quite a high profile affair with both Laurance Rockefeller and Lady Bird Johnson present. The theme of the conference was "Natural Beauty," a follow-up on the recently completed White House Conference on Natural Beauty which they had co-chaired.

I was introduced by the Wyoming governor, Cliff Hanson. I had spent days composing the speech while at "Barney's Joy." I emphasized that "natural beauty" was not a simplistic, cosmetic approach to con-

1. An excellent biography of Rockefeller is *Laurance S. Rockefeller, Catalyst for Conservation*, by Robin W. Winks. Island Press, Washington, D.C. (1997). Winks describes not only the many contributions of LSR to conservation but also his philosophy of conservation and its evolution over time.

Giving a press
interview as president
of The Conservation
Foundation, 1966

servation but one which put the issues into a context that could be
understood by a wide public. I covered many aspects of conservation,
and it was a long speech. When I lunched with Laurance Rockefeller
at his New York apartment in February 1998, he recalled that, when he
had commented to me about the speech's length and the number of
matters it covered, I had replied that I wanted to include everything
on my mind because the speech might turn out to be my last. Actually,
the speech was a great success and got good press coverage around the
country. It got me off to a good start as a full-time environmentalist.

At about the same time, I went on the board of the American Conservation Association (ACA), chaired by Laurance and funded by him
through Jackson Hole Preserve, Inc., another nonprofit, philanthropic
entity founded and chaired by him. With the exception of my time in
government, I served on the ACA board until 1996, by which time
Laurance's son, Larry, had taken on its chairmanship. Through relatively small grants, ACA has been a powerful conservation influence,
particularly in providing seed money for young organizations and new
initiatives.

CF was a small organization that had been housed for years on an
upper floor of an old building on 43rd Street in New York, reached by

Family group in
the garden of our
Woodland Drive
house, 1963

a rickety cage elevator. I doubt that its budget exceeded a few hundred
thousand dollars. However, it had considerable prestige in the ecological world, in great part derived from Fairfield Osborn, who had written two well-received books that warned of environmental disaster
unless such problems as human population growth were addressed.[2]

However, whatever the stature of CF, my family and Aileen's were
totally nonplussed by my leaving the bench and entering an environmental career. To give up the prestige of a federal judgeship was bad
enough. To do so to head an environmental organization was inexpli-

2. Osborn, Fairfield. *Our Plundered Planet.* Little, Brown and Company, Boston
(1948). *The Limits of the Earth.* Faber & Faber Limited, London (1954).

cable. None of them had a clue about environmental issues. When I tried to explain, they listened politely but it was plain that they simply did not understand what I was doing or why. Sadly, they really never did. I will have to say, however, that most of our friends didn't either. Times have changed in that regard.

National Water Commission

IN 1966, I was appointed by President Johnson a member of the National Water Commission, charged by Congress with reviewing national water policy such as the criteria for establishing the economic viability of dams and other water projects, mostly in the West. It was a small group, chaired by Charles Luce, the Under Secretary of Interior. (I would later become his successor as Under Secretary.) I was expected to represent the environmental side of the water policy equation, not a field with which I had much familiarity. We filed a strong report which pointed out such facts as that the interest rate assumptions used in the economic analysis of federal water projects were wildly unrealistic. Unfortunately, reform of such matters would have drastically reduced the number of water projects so dear to congressional hearts, and Congress did not act on our report, although some of our recommendations did get incorporated in legislation over the years. It was an interesting endeavor, and I gained a a high regard for Chuck Luce.

I was with CF until the end of 1968. They were interesting years that deserve relating in more detail than is possible here. We had a small but able staff. Frank Fraser Darling was a world-renowned British ecologist. He kept his base in England but spent extended periods with us in Washington. On his retirement, a distinguished American ecologist, Raymond Dasmann, took his place on a full-time basis. Frank Gregg was vice president, as was Sidney Howe, who later became CF president.

Once CF was established in Washington in a modern office building at 1250 Connecticut Avenue, I moved AWLF in with us. At first, I continued to operate the latter as I had before but this soon became

Promoting the African
Wildlife Leadership
Foundation at the
White House
with Alice Roosevelt
Longworth and
Lady Bird Johnson

impractical. Janet Bohlen joined us and took responsibility for the
African Wildlife News, which was a demanding job. Gordon Wilson
became executive director. CF itself made its principal focus the bringing of environmental values into decision-making generally but particularly into developmental decision-making.

In this connection, we undertook a project south of Naples on the
west coast of Florida to demonstrate how real estate development
could be designed to protect heron rookeries and mangroves along the
shoreline, vital to fish populations. With CF financial support, Ian
McHarg, professor of landscape architecture at the University of
Pennsylvania, wrote a seminal book on ecologically sensitive landscape planning, entitled *Design With Nature.*[3] (Several years later, my
daughter Nancy worked as McHarg's secretary while her husband, St.
John Smith, attended the School of Architecture.)

We worked closely with like-minded congressional staff and played
an important role in developing what became the National Environmental Policy Act (NEPA). Indeed, when the Senate Interior Com-

3. McHarg, Ian L. *Design With Nature.* Natural History Press, Garden City, NY
(1969). Republished by John Wiley & Sons, Inc., New York (1992).

mittee which developed the legislation wished to employ Lynton (Keith) Caldwell, professor of political science at the University of Indiana, as consultant, the committee asked CF to pay his compensation. We knew Caldwell well, as he had been a member of CF's Advisory Council for some years, and were happy to cooperate in that fashion. As it turned out, Caldwell was responsible for developing the environmental impact statement process which became central to the NEPA legislation.

Chairing Nixon Task Force

IN THE FALL of 1968, soon after Richard Nixon was elected president, I was asked by his transition team to chair a Task Force on the Environment to advise the incoming president on environmental issues. Dr. Paul McCracken, later to be Nixon's chairman of the Council of Economic Advisors, headed the whole task force enterprise which covered the entire scope of government from tax policy to national security to agriculture to space exploration, etc. I did not know McCracken then but his deputy was Henry Loomis, a distinguished public servant and old friend who had become a member of the CF board at my suggestion.

It was at Henry's initiative that the environment was added to the scope of the task force operation and that I was asked to head it—circumstances fateful for the future course of my career. In any event, I put together an outstanding bipartisan group, and we wrote a brief but succinct report recommending that the new administration give a high priority to environmental matters and that it create a focal point for environmental policy-making in the White House.

Nixon's transition headquarters were at the Hotel Pierre in New York and shortly before his inauguration he gave a large dinner in the hotel ballroom for all the members of his various task forces. There must have been at least 500 people there. The task force chairmen sat on the dais with Nixon. I sat on his immediate left and, once I had been able to disengage him from conversation with the man on his right who chaired the task force on space programs, we had a discussion on "politics and the environment." Having been informed in advance of the dinner that I would be seated next to the president-elect, I had decided that the best way to engage his interest was to discuss the political aspects of environmental issues. I emphasized that concern for the environment cut across geographic boundaries and across economic groups and suggested that an environmental agenda could be a unifying political force. Nixon listened with interest and then said: "But what of the poor and the blacks in our cities? What is their interest in the environment?" Thus, he instantly put his finger on a key weakness in my thesis. Earlier there had been a crowded reception and I recall that, as I shook hands with the president-elect, he had said somewhat enigmatically: "I think we have plans for you!"

CHAPTER 16

Return to Government

Under Secretary of Interior

ALMOST IMMEDIATELY after Nixon took office, I was asked to join
the new administration as Under Secretary of Interior. The offer had
been triggered, I feel sure, by the opposition in the Senate to the nominee for Secretary of Interior, Walter Hickel. Hickel had been governor of Alaska and before that had been involved in a variety of development projects in the state. Given the environmental responsibilities
of Interior—national parks, fish and wildlife, outdoor recreation, and,
in those days, water pollution—his record as a developer gave the
Democratic majority an issue to rally around. Thus, I was proposed as
an environmentalist to balance the Hickel nomination. At least, that's
the way it seemed and the way the media treated it at the time of my
nomination.

I promised an answer within 48 hours. Aileen and I talked late into
the night but I think from the beginning we knew there was no walking away from the opportunity. After all, I had been talking for some
while of the importance of building environmental/ecological values
into decision-making and here was an opportunity to practice what I
had been preaching and to do so where it would really count. I went to
New York and spent the night with Laurance and Mary Rockefeller.
He was totally supportive and, indeed, enthusiastic about my taking
the job.

The next day I lunched with Fair Osborn at the Mayfair House on
Park Avenue. We had a martini first—straight up and very cold, as he
liked them. I felt saddened by the situation; he was over 80 and all of a

Being sworn in as
Under Secretary of
Interior by Supreme
Court Justice
Potter Stewart,
with Secretary Hickel
at left and Aileen
holding the Bible

sudden his carefully crafted plan for CF was being knocked into a cocked hat. However, he rose to the situation with spirit. Convinced that I was doing the right thing, he raised his glass and fixed me with his bright eyes and said: "That's great! Here's to the future!" He was quite a guy.

My term as Under Secretary was a short one, lasting just a year, and it did not begin propitiously. When Hickel had been making his courtesy calls on the members of his confirmation committee, he had made the mistake of being accompanied on his call on Senator Ed Muskie by James Watt, an anti-clean water quality lobbyist for the U.S. Chamber of Commerce. Since Muskie was the leading proponent in the Senate of clean water legislation, he went through the roof and issued a blast against Hickel that made all the papers. (Of course, in those pre-EPA days, the Federal Water Pollution Control Administration was part of Interior.)

In any event, with that background and after I had moved to Interior but before the Senate had acted on my nomination as Under Secretary, I had a call from Hickel's immediate assistant, Carl McMurray, who said more or less the following: "The Secretary wants you to appoint Jim Watt as your Deputy Under Secretary." I replied that the Secretary had hundreds of positions that he could fill but I only had about three or four in my immediate office and believed that he should leave those to me to choose. McMurray took that message to the Secretary and soon called me back: "The Secretary orders you to appoint Watt!" "In that case," I said, "I will carry out the Secretary's order but ask that the White House immediately withdraw my nomination from the Senate." A few moments later, McMurray again called back: "The Secretary says to forget all about it!" I really had no choice but to take the position I did because my credibility and usefulness as Under Secretary would have been fatally compromised had I acceded to Hickel's wishes. Hickel later found a spot in the department for Watt but we never had any contact. Watt became almost a household word when President Reagan made him his Secretary of Interior and he became famed for his anti-environment positions.

I heard no more of the matter. Hickel may even have respected me for hanging tough. It turned out to be a year full of exciting challenges. The Secretary gave me responsibility for the departmental budget and for all legislative matters. My office developed the Coastal Zone Management Act which remains law today. Deputy Under Secretary Boyd Gibbons, whom I had selected following the Watt affair, was responsible for that achievement. With Buff Bohlen, my administrative assistant, taking the lead, we developed for the Stratton Commission a comprehensive plan for reorganizing federal civil functions relating to the oceans. Naturally, our plan involved centralizing these functions in the Department of Interior. We lost that one when Hickel lost favor in the White House, and the functions were consolidated in the Department of Commerce as the National Oceanic and Atmospheric Administration.

In addition, with the great help of Jack Horton, we coordinated the department's and later the administration's response to the proposal to build the trans-Alaskan oil pipeline. This responsibility required several trips to Alaska, including the North Slope oil fields and Point

As Under Secretary, inspecting an oil rig,
North Slope of Alaska, 1969

Barrow. Likewise, my office led the successful opposition to the effort
to build a huge new Miami international airport which would have
significantly damaged the Everglades National Park. On such matters,
I developed a good working relationship with John Ehrlichman, assistant to the president for domestic policy. He was extremely helpful.

We succeeded in supporting strong coal mine health and safety legislation on the Hill despite White House opposition led by Arthur
Burns. We combined with the Army Corps of Engineers to condition
the permits for the Marco Island development off the west coast of
Florida to protect a substantial amount of wetlands, bald eagle nesting
sites, etc. In my office, John Quarles took the lead on this as well as
other dredge and fill permit issues and worked closely with Bob Jordan, general counsel of the Army. (John was later to become deputy
administrator of EPA.)

The friendships I made then at the Cabinet level were part of the
fun of my job, and they stood me in good stead over the years. The
Under Secretaries, in particular, were a fairly close-knit group. I suppose being number two provided us with a common bond! We lunched

together two or three times that year and the occasions were mostly social. The group was informally chaired by my old friend Elliot Richardson, as Under Secretary of State, the senior department. There was Dave Packard at Defense (co-founder with Bill Hewlett of Hewlett-Packard), Charls Walker at Treasury, Dick van Dusen at HUD, Rocco Siciliano at Commerce, Jim Hodgson at Agriculture, George Shultz at Labor, and others.

Another rewarding experience was to get to know and work with some of the top professional career people in the department, such as Bill Pecora, director of the U.S. Geological Survey, and George Hartzog, director of the National Park Service. These were individuals of great ability and total dedication to the public interest. I was always unhappy when partisan politics intruded on the tenure of such people. It has become politically fashionable in recent years to attack Washington and "bureaucrats," but this has been cheap politics that, in my opinion, has been self-defeating and has actually kept good people from entering public service.

The only meeting that I recall with President Nixon that year was when I presented Interior's appeals on the budget decisions. The meeting was in the Oval Office and, much to his unhappiness, Hickel was sick with the flu in Alaska and unable to be there. I represented the department at a joint U.S.-Japan Cabinet meeting in Tokyo, giving Aileen and me our first of many visits to Japan. On that occasion, we met Emperor Hirohito at a reception at the Imperial Palace.

The National Environmental Policy Act legislation, which The Conservation Foundation had helped develop, reached the public hearing stage in 1969. I was designated to present the official administration position and testified against the legislation before the Senate Interior Committee on the ground that it was unnecessary since the administration had established an interagency Environmental Quality Council. Every member of the committee was well aware that I was testifying directly contrary to my personal convictions. Fortunately, I (and others) was subsequently able to persuade the administration to change its position and was able to testify in the House in favor of the legislation. These were some highlights of a busy and satisfying year.

Surprising Secretary
Hickel Quiets Critics
By Showing Great Zeal
For Conservation Effort

Skeptics Are Still Dubious
On Interior Chief, but He
Acts on Oil Leaks, Parks

Leaning on a Powerful Aide

The *Wall Street Journal* headline that,
together with the article that followed,
precipitated the rupture with Hickel

Of key importance to this record was my own immediate staff—
Boyd Gibbons, Buff Bohlen, Jack Horton, John Quarles, and Marian
O'Connell, my longtime secretary.

Unfortunately, my relatively high visibility led to trouble with
Hickel, and our relationship went from bad to worse. While it was
easy to blame Hickel's considerable ego, the fault was not all one-
sided. He was not the only one with an ego! I had not learned that a
"number two" in an agency should keep a low profile, and I was doubtless a bit insensitive to the situation.

However, the event that brought about the final rupture in our relationship was the publication of a long article on Hickel in the *Wall
Street Journal*.[1] It was the lead article in that day's issue and occupied
the right-hand front-page column and most of a page inside. After the
main headline about Hickel, a subhead declared: "Leaning on a Powerful Aide." The article appeared to have been written by two or more
reporters. The first part of the article concerned the management of
the department and quoted one of the assistant secretaries as saying, in
effect, that when you need a decision, you go to Train. The second half
mocked Hickel for his malapropisms and general lack of polish. Quite

1. *Wall Street Journal*, June 18, 1969.

understandably, Hickel blew his top. I had no sooner sat down at my desk that morning than Hickel was on the phone. My only recollection of the conversation was his statement that "this [expletive] has to stop!" I had not seen the article and neither I nor anybody else in my office was aware that it had been written. No matter. That was the end of any effective working relationship.

President Nixon announcing to the White House press his appointment of the author as chairman of the new Council on Environmental Quality and Gordon MacDonald and Robert Cahn as members, 1970

In any event, with the passage of the National Environmental Policy Act at the end of 1969, which included creation of a new Council on Environmental Quality (CEQ) in the Executive Office of the President, I persuaded the White House to name me the council's first chairman, a position of equal rank to that of Under Secretary. (Hickel himself finally came to odds with the White House, where he had never been popular, and was fired at the beginning of 1971.)

Council on Environmental Quality

I WENT TO CEQ just as the environmental issue burst in full force
on the public stage. Nixon chose to sign the National Environmental
Policy Act into law on January 1, 1970, as his first official act of the
decade of the seventies, a symbolic act but one which presaged the
explosion of environmental initiatives that followed. Nixon personally
introduced the new council to the press with the assurance that CEQ
would act as the environmental conscience of the nation. That description, of course, implied that CEQ would be occupying a sort of "bully
pulpit"—hardly practical given the fact that CEQ was part of the
White House. In addition to myself as chairman, the council consisted
of Dr. Gordon MacDonald, a geophysicist, and Robert Cahn, a Pul-
itzer Prize-winning newspaperman. (Later, Bob Cahn's wife, Pat, was
my public affairs assistant at EPA.) MacDonald made a major contribution on international environmental matters and Cahn took the
lead in putting together our annual report to the Congress.

We secured an executive order from the White House giving CEQ
the responsibility for monitoring and overseeing agency compliance
with the Environmental Impact Statement (EIS) process mandated
by NEPA. This was a crucial authority as a number of agencies, such
as the Federal Highway Administration, were doing their best to
avoid compliance. We issued guidelines for compliance and were successful over time in securing the agencies' conformance with the law.
Citizen suits, authorized by NEPA and brought by public-interest law
firms, were also influential in reaching this result. Thus, the Natural
Resources Defense Council (NRDC) sued the Agency for International Development (AID) and succeeded in getting the courts to
reject AID's argument that NEPA did not apply to its projects abroad.

In practice, CEQ led the administration's policy response to the
environmental issue, a process that required quiet, behind-the-scenes
staff work. In all cases, it was essential to involve in the process all
those executive agencies which had an interest in the subject matter of
a particular initiative. The Environmental Protection Agency (EPA)

The author holds his first press conference as chairman of CEQ while standing behind his desk. Hanging behind him is a portrait of an orangutan (by Hug) whom he described to the press as "an early chairman of CEQ." This Associated Press photo was carried widely throughout the U.S.

was created in late 1970 and became the focal point for the implementation and enforcement of environmental laws. I had personally urged in testimony before the President's Council on Reorganization of the Executive Branch—the so-called Ash Council named for its chairman, Roy Ash—that the government's environmental responsibilities be concentrated in a single, independent agency (such as EPA became) rather than submerged in a new Department of Natural Resources favored by the White House at the time. I felt strongly that environmental issues needed a sharp, cutting edge in government, one that had high visibility to the public, and this view finally prevailed.

Following the creation of EPA with William Ruckelshaus at its head, CEQ continued to be responsible for coordinating the development of new policy initiatives, both domestically and internationally, and often was responsible for the initiatives themselves, as in the case of the Toxic Substances Control Act (TOSCA). In addition to TOSCA, there was new legislation to regulate pesticides, fungicides, and herbicides; to provide controls on surface mining and ocean dumping; to

protect marine mammals; to protect water and air quality; to manage
solid waste; to ensure safe drinking water; to provide noise controls; to
institute a tax on sulfur oxide emissions; to inaugurate a national land
use policy; and much else, including many initiatives of an executive
nature, such as a ban on the use of DDT on federal lands.

While a few of the CEQ initiatives, such as the proposal for national
land use policy legislation, were not acted upon by the Congress, we
certainly succeeded in keeping the Nixon administration out front
on environmental issues. My two associates on the council—Gordon MacDonald and Bob Cahn—were valuable colleagues. Our staff,
which reached 54 at its peak, was absolutely superb, led by Alvin (Al)
Alm as chief of staff. Al proved to be a master in dealing with the
intricacies of the issues and, even more important, with the competing
bureaucracies involved. Perhaps CEQ's greatest accomplishment was
its success in achieving interagency agreements, and Al Alm is due the
lion's share of the credit for that success. Of course, White House support was also a critical factor in that regard, and we had that support in
full measure.

Boyd Gibbons, who had been my deputy at Interior, was secretary
of the council and took a particular lead on land use, assisted by Bill
Reilly, whose specialty this was. Timothy Atkeson was general counsel, and Bill Lake and Chuck Lettow left clerkships at the Supreme
Court to join him as assistants. Lee Talbot (later director-general of
the International Union for the Conservation of Nature) was senior
scientist. Heyward Isham (later ambassador) was detailed from the
State Department to advise on foreign affairs, as later were Otty Hayne
and Jack Perry. Clarence (Terry) Davies joined us from the Princeton
faculty and became the principal author of the Toxic Substances Control Act. Stefan Plehn, Bill Dircks, Steve Jellinek, Roger Strelow, Eric
Zaussner, Harry Blaney, and Bill Matuszeski were other members of
this extraordinary group. That we attracted such talent was due in
large part to the excitement that the environmental cause engendered
at the time.

International Involvements

MY INTRODUCTION to the conservation/environment world had been through African wildlife and, later, world wildlife. Thus, it was not surprising that I continued to be deeply interested while at CF and later in international conservation opportunities and in the international dimensions of environmental problems generally. While I was at CF, we funded surveys of marine sanctuary opportunities along the East African coast and the conservation of vicuña in the highlands of Peru, and I promoted the World Heritage Trust concept described later.

At CEQ, we developed and pursued numerous international environmental initiatives. Clearly, we could not have done so without White House support. It was helpful, in this regard, that the White House insisted on looking to us rather than the State Department to lead on such matters. With the line of responsibility thus clearly established, Chris Herter, Jr., the senior environmental officer at State, and his staff were always helpful to us and never failed to support us from a foreign policy standpoint, as well as doing a fine job on their own initiative. At CEQ proper, my fellow council member Gordon MacDonald was an enthusiastic player in the international environmental field, with Lee Talbot playing a major role with respect to international wildlife and related matters. Overall, however, I have to state the conviction that my own strong personal interest and involvement in international environmental matters were key factors in building the record we did. Thus, when I moved from CEQ to EPA, I took the international "portfolio" with me with the full support of the White House.

International Conferences and Agreements

WHILE, OF COURSE, others did most of the work, I headed the U.S. delegation to the U.N. Conference on the Human Environment at Stockholm in 1972, headed the U.S. delegation to the conference in London that adopted the Convention on Ocean Dumping in 1972, represented the president at the International Whaling Commission

meeting in London in 1972 (presenting the U.S. proposal for a mora-
torium on hunting whales), represented the U.S. in negotiating with
Canada the Great Lakes Water Quality Agreement of 1972, co-chaired
two U.S. delegations to conferences in London that adopted international conventions to control the discharge of wastes at sea, was the
U.S. representative for six years to the NATO Committee on the Challenges of a Modern Society in Brussels, headed the U.S. side of the
U.S.-Soviet Environmental Agreement of 1972, was involved in several other bilateral environmental agreements, and led the U.S. delegation to the Washington conference in 1974 that wrote the Convention
on International Trade in Endangered Species (CITES).

Most of those international activities were the result of U.S. initiatives and several were generated by CEQ. The U.S. became the clear
world leader in terms of both domestic environmental policy and international environmental cooperation.[2]

Aileen, Bowdy, and Errol had accompanied me to the Stockholm
conference in June 1972 and spent two weeks there sightseeing, demonstrating on behalf of whales, sailing with friends, and visiting the conference. Together with Bill and Jill Ruckelshaus, we had all spent a
weekend bicycling on the island of Gotland.

World Heritage Trust

WHEN I FIRST went to CF in the fall of 1965, I was invited to participate in a White House Conference on International Cooperation,
and I became a member of one of its working units, the Committee on
Natural Resources, chaired by Dr. Joseph Fisher, then president of
Resources for the Future (RFF), a private nonprofit organization dedicated to economic analysis of natural resource issues. (I was later to
become a trustee of RFF.)

I was probably the only conservationist on the committee and

2. For a summary of the environmental accomplishments of the administration over
the years 1969-1974, see Train, Russell E. "The Environmental Record of the Nixon
Administration." *Presidential Studies Quarterly* 26, no. 1 (Winter 1996), pp. 185-196.
Published by the Center for the Study of the Presidency (New York).

Fisher approached me with an idea for "a trust for the world heritage." His thought had its genesis in the fact that our first national park at Yellowstone had been established almost a hundred years before in the belief that the area possessed natural values of such importance that they transcended the interest of any state and, indeed, belonged to the heritage of the entire nation. In the same fashion, reasoned Fisher, there were natural areas around the globe of such value that they should be part of the heritage of all peoples everywhere. It was a great idea, and I quickly espoused it. The concept was endorsed by the committee and became one of the recommendations transmitted to the Johnson White House by the conference.

Not long afterward, I went to a World Wildlife Fund conference in Amsterdam, chaired by H.R.H. Prince Bernhard of the Netherlands, and gave a speech outlining the world heritage idea and expanding it to include great cultural areas such as the Acropolis, Angkor Wat, the Pyramids, etc. There the matter lay for several years although there was some activity in the International Union for the Conservation of Nature (IUCN) and in the International Council on Monuments and Sites (ICOMOS). The Johnson administration never took up our proposal.

Finally, in 1971, opportunity came. CEQ had responsibility for developing the president's annual message to the Congress on the environment. Accordingly, we included the World Heritage Trust in the 1971 message and on February 8, 1971, President Nixon espoused the concept, declaring:

> It would be fitting by 1972 [the centennial of Yellowstone] for the nations of the world to agree to the principle that there are certain areas of such unique worldwide value that they should be treated as part of the heritage of all mankind and accorded special recognition as part of a World Heritage Trust. Such an arrangement would impose no limitations on the sovereignty of those nations which choose to participate, but would extend special international recognition to the areas which qualify and would make available technical and other assistance where appropriate to assist in their protection and management . . .

At the Stockholm Conference on the Human Environment in June 1972 and on the motion of the United States, the delegates unanimously endorsed the World Heritage concept, and the following year an international conference convened by UNESCO adopted the World Heritage Convention. Several hundred sites around the world are now part of the World Heritage and it has proven a useful tool in upgrading or maintaining the quality of management of the areas in question and, in some cases, has proven critical in preventing the degradation or even destruction of an area. It is not an earthshaking program but one of which, I believe, we can be proud. It takes a very positive American contribution to world culture—namely, the national park concept, and builds on it to create a new shared value of common interest to all peoples of the world, a world in which such common interests seem all too rare. There are a number of World Heritage sites in the United States, such as Yellowstone National Park, Everglades National Park, and Independence Hall. Americans are generally unaware of the World Heritage Trust designation but in many nations World Heritage status is a matter of pride. Unfortunately, the WHT Committee in Paris has few funds and is unable to assist poorer countries around the world in their effort to establish and maintain WHT sites.

Sadly, the U.S. has been extremely weak in its support of the World Heritage and that has been true under all presidents. In several years the budget submitted to the Congress has "zeroed" the WHT. On those occasions, I contacted the key people on the appropriation committees of the Congress and was usually successful in getting a modest appropriation restored.

I am sometimes described as the leader in initiating the World Heritage.[3] It is Joe Fisher who really fathered the concept. Unfortunately, Joe died quite suddenly after serving in Congress from northern Virginia while still a relatively young man. As chairman of CEQ, I was fortuitously placed to make the concept a reality.

3. See, for example, *Masterworks of Man and Nature: Preserving Our World Heritage,* published by UNESCO's World Heritage Committee and the IUCN (1992); preface, p. 7. This massive tome provides a complete history of the World Heritage Trust (WHT), including an essay by myself at pp. 377-379 as well as a listing and a description of all WHT sites worldwide as of 1992.

The Dan Schorr Affair

I SUPPOSE THAT all White Houses "play games" at times with the press and the public, and perhaps the Nixon White House played more than most. I had personal experience with only one such situation and that was while I was at CEQ.

Dan Schorr was a well-known and widely respected national affairs reporter for CBS. He tended to be politically liberal in his views and was no admirer of Richard Nixon. Reportedly, the White House instigated an FBI investigation of Schorr, a report which got wide coverage in the press and put the White House very much on the defensive. I assume that I was aware of the situation through the press coverage but it had nothing to do with me.

In any event, at some point, when I was in John Whitaker's office in the southwest corner of the Old Executive Office Building, John told me that, at a staff meeting that morning, Bob Haldeman had said that the administration should be doing more to publicize its environmental record and that CEQ should hire a top television news personality to take charge of such an effort and to develop a documentary series on the environment. The idea sounded great to me although in retrospect the idea of CEQ putting together its own television series was pretty nutty. As I recall it now, I went from Whittaker to Chuck Colsen and Fred Malik to discuss the idea further, to get specific suggestions on possible candidates for the job—Schorr was never mentioned—and to figure out how to deal with the matter within CEQ's budget and personnel ceilings.

Back at CEQ, I immediately started talking to several individuals I knew who had national television stature. The conversations went well although I found no immediate takers. A bit of time went by and I had a call from a reporter for the *New York Times,* as I recall, who said that the White House was explaining the FBI investigation of Dan Schorr as being related to CEQ's effort to recruit a major television news personality and asked whether I could confirm that. With that statement, a great light dawned in my naive brain. To put it simply, I had been "had," and I had swallowed the bait—hook, line, and sinker. I confirmed that CEQ had been trying to recruit a major television news personality and went on to describe my efforts in that regard. There was no mention of Schorr. The reporter did not pursue the matter any further, and the next day his article reported that I had confirmed the basics of the White House story. That was the end of the matter so far as I was concerned. I certainly did not do any more "recruiting" and I do not recall ever mentioning the matter again to White House staff or they to me. The Dan Schorr story pretty much died in the press. Good old naive Train was left feeling like a jerk. In 1998, at least a quarter century later, Dan Schorr told me that when he had talked to Nixon after the latter had left office, Nixon had said to him with a grin: "We tried to hire you once!" I concluded that Nixon had been privy to the entire affair.

A Cruise on the Sea Star

A WELCOME BREAK in the tensions of those years came in February 1973 when Aileen and I joined Laurance and Mary Rockefeller on board their large, three-masted motor sailer Sea Star for a week's cruise in the Caribbean. There were just the four of us, and it was a very intimate time. Laurance's younger brother, Winthrop, was dying and the boat received frequent radio messages of his condition. I recall Mary leading us in prayer at the dining table. We also had lots of fun and laughs as we cruised from St. Thomas, through the British Virgins, to St. Martin.

CHAPTER 17

Environmental Protection Agency

THE FIRST administrator of EPA was William Ruckelshaus who, together with his wife, Jill, became and remain close personal friends of Aileen and me. After Bill left EPA in April 1973 to head the FBI in the continuing turmoil that followed Watergate, I decided that I wanted to succeed him at EPA. CEQ had had an exciting "run" as the environmental policy initiator in the government but now the action had moved to EPA. It was hard to identify new policy initiatives, and focus had shifted to implementation and enforcement. Both Haldeman and Ehrlichman had left the scene by then in the wake of Watergate, and my discussion at the White House about my EPA ambition was with Major General Alexander Haig, who had become chief of staff. I evidently satisfied Al that I would not be a wild-eyed radical at EPA, and I was nominated that June by Nixon to take Ruckelshaus' place, which I finally did in September 1973.

My confirmation was held up for three months by "holds" put on my nomination by two senators—Cliff Hansen of Wyoming and William Scott of Virginia, both Republicans. My friend Hansen was presumably acting at the behest of the coal industry which doubtless looked upon me with a pretty jaundiced eye, based upon my support of coal mine health and safety legislation when I was Under Secretary of Interior and also CEQ's sponsorship of surface mining legislation requiring the reclamation of mined sites.

The reasons for Scott's opposition were more obscure. At my confirmation hearing before the Senate Public Works Committee, Scott, a member of the Republican minority, picked up my *Who's Who* biography and noted that I had described myself as a "conservationist." He asked me why I had listed myself that way when I had been a federal judge. "Are you ashamed to have been a judge?" he asked. He went

Being sworn in as
EPA administrator
by Attorney General
Elliot Richardson

around and around on this question and plainly could not be satisfied
no matter what I said. (At some point unrelated to these proceedings,
the Senate press gallery had voted Scott the dumbest member of the
Senate. He had responded by calling a press conference to deny the
charge.) When the Senate finally voted on my nomination, I was
approved with only one dissenting vote as I recall.

In a private meeting with Nixon in the Oval Office, I asked the
president to swear me in at EPA. He replied: "That's probably the very
worst thing I could do for you!" and, of course, he was right. By the
time I was sworn in, Ruckelshaus was deputy attorney general, and the
attorney general was Elliot Richardson. Elliot administered the oath
to me at EPA with Bill standing by. They were both about to be fired
by Nixon in the so-called "Saturday Night Massacre." Aileen was there
for the ceremony with Errol, as well as Cuth and Mid, Audry and
Sandra. There was also Bob Fri, who had been Ruckelhaus' deputy and

who had been acting administrator for the past six months.[1] Aileen and I went to the farm that evening and on the way I suffered an attack of kidney stones—perhaps an omen of the travails ahead.

Ruckelshaus had done an outstanding job at EPA, and his was a tough act to follow. However, I thoroughly enjoyed my years there. The job was a highly visible one, which I admit to liking. The agency had overall responsibility for carrying out the nation's anti-pollution laws dealing with air and water pollution, toxic wastes, solid wastes, radiation, pesticides, noise pollution, etc. It was an enormous challenge. The country was only just beginning to feel its way in the area. The science for understanding the problems and the technologies for dealing with them were in their infancy. Economic impacts were poorly understood. At the same time, the public demanded aggressive action to address environmental problems, particularly those with perceived adverse health effects.

Two of the most difficult issues that I inherited involved the banning of most uses of certain pesticides such as aldrin, dieldrin, heptachlor, and chlordane, and the regulation of auto emissions. Ruckelshaus had led the way in the pesticides area by banning DDT, and I followed with a number of other similar actions. Inevitably, these decisions brought me under attack by the agriculture committees of the House and Senate and also by EPA's appropriation subcommittee in the House chaired by Jamie Whitten of Mississippi. While Whitten inevitably criticized the decisions in public, I discovered that giving him a few hours' advance notice did much to reduce his rancor. It was Whitten who said publicly that "Train has more power than a bad man should have, or a good man would want!"

One contentious issue in the pesticide field which I inherited was whether to permit the emergency use of DDT to control the tussock moth, which was in one of its cyclical population explosions and was devastating the forests of the Northwest, primarily in Washington,

---

1. Fri became Deputy Secretary of Energy, then headed the nonprofit Resources for the Future (of which I was a director after leaving government), and, as I write this, is director of the Museum of Natural History of the Smithsonian Institution—a superb public servant.

Oregon, and Idaho. I was petitioned by the governors of all three states, by all six of their senators, and their entire congressional delegations to permit the emergency use of DDT. It was a tough issue. On the one hand, I could do nothing and pray that the moth was at the end of its growth cycle and would disappear naturally. If that did not happen, there could be devastating economic impacts throughout the region. On the other hand, if I permitted the use of DDT, there could be adverse ecological impacts. It was a classic EPA issue with inadequate scientific data on which to base the decision. Moreover, it was not a case where I could just "wait and see." The upshot was that with great reluctance I permitted the use of DDT, imposing such restrictions as we could in order to limit any ecological damage. I chose to make the announcement at a press conference in Seattle, at the heart of the region and of the controversy. It was an emotional occasion and I can remember to this day the weeping of some members of the audience as they heard the decision. As it turned out, the threat of the tussock moth ended—but was it the DDT or was it the natural end of its cycle? Who knows?

The major auto emissions issue was whether to set standards that, in effect, mandated the use of catalytic converters. These were opposed by the auto industry primarily on the basis of cost. Surprisingly, however, there was a strong difference of opinion on the matter within EPA. The Office of Mobile Sources, the implementing office, urged the use of catalytic converters. However, the agency's health experts warned against their use, predicting that they would produce a sulfuric acid aerosol that would penetrate deeply into human lungs with seriously adverse health effects. I finally decided in favor of requiring the catalytic converters and, fortunately, the health concerns were never borne out.

Of course, catalytic converters would be rendered ineffective if used with leaded gasoline. That fact, together with the adverse health effects of lead itself, led to the elimination of lead in gasoline. EPA issued a regulation mandating a fuel-tank design for vehicles equipped with catalytic converters which made it impossible to insert the nozzle from a leaded-fuel gas pump. This led to a telephone call which I received one winter night at home. The conversation went something like this: "Is this Mr. Train?" "Yes, it is." "The Russell Train who heads the Environmental Protection Agency?" "Yes, it is." "Well, Mr. Train, I have something to tell you." "You know, it is almost 3:00 a.m. here in Washington. Could you call back later?" "No, Mr. Train, this is something I want you to know about right now." "Okay, go ahead." "Mr. Train, it's a very cold, snowy night out here in Minnesota. A few hours ago, my wife and I were driving home and our car ran out of gas out in the middle of nowhere. I walked about two miles through the snow-drifts to a filling station where I was able to get a tank of gas. I carried it the two miles back through the snow, took off the cap of my gas tank—and you know what, Mr. Train?" His voice was deceptively soft. "The nozzle wouldn't fit the gas tank," and here his voice rose to a crescendo as he yelled, "all because of your g—d— stupid EPA regulations." I mumbled something to the effect that I didn't blame him for being mad. "I just thought you ought to know about it, Mr. Train," he said in a calm voice and hung up. While many public officials have unlisted home phone numbers, I never did, and so far as I can recall, this particular call was the only one of this nature I ever received.

Just about the time I went to EPA, the Arab oil embargo signaled the beginning of the energy crisis—and also the end of the environmental "honeymoon." The whole emphasis within the Nixon administration changed. It was exactly as if the White House had done its environmental "thing" and was now going to do its energy "thing." And, of course, there were real energy shortages, and the public was unhappy about them. In Chapter 22, I recount several energy/environment conflicts in both the Nixon and the Ford administrations and I will not repeat them here. I managed to keep good personal and working relationships with the various energy "czars"—John Love, Bill Simon, Frank Zarb, and John Sawhill. But there were major confrontations and, while EPA granted some short-term variances to meet some localized problems, we succeeded in holding the line against any broad rollback of environmental standards. In some ways, I feel that our success in that regard may have constituted our most important achievement during my time at EPA.

When I went to EPA, I brought with me, with White House agreement, the several international hats I had worn at CEQ. I have already referred to these, and those involvements continued throughout my tenure at EPA. This led, of course, to a great deal of travel, notably some six trips to the Soviet Union, on most of which Aileen was able to accompany me. My Soviet counterpart during most of those years was Yuri Izrael, head of the Hydrometeorological Agency (Hydromet). We became good friends and Yuri spent a weekend with us once at our farm on Maryland's Eastern Shore—and without a KGB watchdog!

With all the conflicting interests involved, it was amazing how much progress we were able to make. In addition to an outstanding staff, I was almost always fortunate in having a very friendly press and was usually able to muster bipartisan support in the Congress. In the House, Congressman Paul Rogers of Florida, chairman of the Commerce Committee subcommittee on health and the environment, was always helpful. I maintained a positive working relationship with Senator Ed Muskie of Maine, the leading Democratic spokesman on environmental issues, and with his chief of staff, Leon Billings. I have little doubt but that an important motivation for President Nixon's advocacy of environmental programs was his desire to take the issue away from Muskie.

On the Republican side, Senator Howard Baker, the ranking Republican on the Senate Public Works Committee, was a true friend and supporter. While relatively junior on the committee, Senator Jim Buckley of New York, a longtime personal friend, was supportive on environmental issues, an important asset considering his very conservative political credentials. I do not really recall any important issue in that committee ever becoming the subject of partisan contention.

By the end of the Nixon administration, the White House was almost entirely preoccupied with its Watergate problems and left me pretty much alone. The Ford White House was generally friendly although, of course, conservative. With all the above, the EPA job was exciting, fun, and enormously satisfying. I enjoyed working with the men and women in the agency. They were a dedicated, competent group.

Deputy EPA administrator
John Quarles

I was fortunate in having an extremely able deputy administrator, John Quarles (a brother of John Harper's wife, Barbara). In addition, among many other associates to whom I was indebted, Al Alm was outstanding. He had been the chief of staff at CEQ, and at EPA he filled the critical position of assistant administrator for Planning and Budget (deputy administrator in the Reagan administration). He played a vital role in helping formulate policy and then steering it through the bureaucratic complexities of government. Both at CEQ and at EPA, Al was my right hand. At EPA, I was also blessed by very able administrative assistants, including Bill Dircks (later executive director of the International Atomic Energy Commission in Vienna), Roger Strelow, and Stefan Plehn (later an EPA assistant administrator). And, of course, there was my secretary of many years, Marian O'Connell.

Assistant EPA administrator
Al Alm

Trustee of Princeton

DURING MY years in government, I avoided any outside commitments and resigned from the various boards of which I had been a
member. However, while I was at EPA, I was elected an alumni trustee
of Princeton and accepted with enthusiasm despite my general counsel's admonition that it would be a conflict of interest because of government contracts that Princeton doubtless had. I served as trustee
from 1975 to 1979 and never was aware of any conflict situation. Given
the demands of my job as EPA administrator, it was about all I could
do to get to the meetings proper, which I generally did by chartered
aircraft. (Maryland Airlines out of Easton on the Eastern Shore had
become my regular way of commuting on weekends and I used their
planes to get back and forth to Princeton.) However, I did serve on
some of the departmental committees, particularly after I left government in early 1977. One of these was the comparative literature visiting
committee; a member of that committee whom I met and enjoyed was

Lillian Hellman. One of my fellow board members was Susan Savage Speers, my first cousin once removed, who was the first woman to serve on the board. A charter trustee, Sue was an active and effective member of the board. Manning Brown, chairman of New York Life, was a senior member of the board. He was also a member of the Union Carbide board and I credit him for my being asked to join that board several years later.

Threatened by the Manson Gang

ONE OF THE odd experiences I had at the time was to have my life threatened by "Squeaky" Frome, a member of the notorious Charles Manson gang, who was in federal prison in California for participating in one of the cult killings in which the gang was implicated. She wrote me a letter from prison threatening that I would be knifed to death by one of the Manson gang still at large. Given the bloody insanity of the Manson killings, I took the threat seriously. I complained to Attorney General Ed Levy over Frome's use of government stationery and the franking privilege, and he told me that these were rights which the courts had upheld and, moreover, that the government was not entitled to read the letters she wrote, all of which struck me as pretty ridiculous. EPA had a security detail and for some time I had an armed agent stay at our house on Woodland Drive during the night and also accompany me in my car. Finally, I ended the security watch. I never did hear anything further from Frome and she is still in prison.

Experience with Investigative Reporting

WHEN I WENT to EPA, Aileen and I were required to put all of our investments—mostly hers at that time—into blind trusts. The trustee of our trusts was John Davidge, in whose conservative judgment we had great confidence. For the duration of the trusts—presumably until I left government—neither Aileen nor I were to have any knowledge of the securities we held or of any transactions that might occur in our accounts. Income, if any, was simply to be deposited in our respective bank accounts.

All went smoothly in this regard until one day when we were taking a brief winter break at the Mill Reef Club at Antigua. I had a call there from a Washington reporter whose name I no longer recall but who I believe worked for UPI. He told me that *Washingtonian* magazine was trying to get the press to pick up on a story about our profiting from oil stocks. I explained our blind trust arrangement, and he said that he did not intend to publish anything on the matter.

What had happened was this: Unbeknownst to us, *Washingtonian* magazine had apparently for some time been collecting the trash we placed at the curb outside our Woodland Drive house. The trash was then delivered by *Washingtonian* to a free-lance photographer living on Capitol Hill. He would sort through the trash, photograph anything of possible interest, and deliver the results to the magazine. *Washingtonian* went public with an article charging me with profiting from the energy crisis. The article displayed a large blown-up photo of a crumpled notice of a security transaction in which 100 shares of Exxon had been purchased for Aileen B. Train. Aileen, in fact, recalled that while opening her mail one day, she had seen that notice, knew we were not supposed to get it, and had crumpled it in her hand and dropped it into the wastebasket. She had thought nothing further of the matter and never mentioned it to me. The notice had been mailed in mistake by the bank that handled the transaction. So far as I am aware, it was the only such mistake ever made.

I had a call at EPA from Les Whitten, an assistant to the columnist Jack Anderson, and I explained the blind trust arrangement to him and told him of Aileen's recollection. He said it was a non-story so far as he was concerned. In fact, none of the press ever picked up the *Washingtonian* story, and I was always grateful for their responsible treatment of the matter.

We learned the truth about the magazine picking up and photographing our trash as I have recounted above as the result of an extraordinary coincidence. It turned out that the photographer to whom the trash had been delivered was a friend of a secretary in John Davidge's office. Without making any connection between the investment notice he had photographed and John Davidge, as trustee, he told her the whole story. Our friend Rowland Evans subsequently visited the photographer at his home on Capitol Hill and got a full account from him at first hand.

That's really the end of the story. I learned later that others had had their trash rifled in the same fashion—Judge John Sirica and columnist Betty Beale, among them. The owner and publisher of *Washingtonian* magazine at the time was Laughlin Phillips, son of the founders of the Phillips Gallery in Washington and a substantial member of the community. I had known him, although slightly, since he was a child. He told me once that he had known nothing of the magazine's activity in my regard, and I have no reason to doubt him. However, I have always avoided contact with him since the affair.

When I left EPA at the outset of the Carter administration in January 1977, it was with genuine regret. It was the biggest and toughest job I would ever have. I have only touched on a few highlights here. Environmental issues were relatively new, and fresh and unexpected dimensions of those problems, such as the impact of chlorofluorocarbons on the ozone layer, were constantly being revealed. The economic interests concerned—energy companies, steel companies, auto companies, chemical companies, agricultural interests, etc.—typically opposed regulatory action.

The environmental community led the charge for such action, and public-interest law firms were constantly initiating legal proceedings to force it. Some of these were doubtlessly "sweetheart suits" connived in by crusading young EPA employees. The politicians pushed and pulled in all directions. Other agencies usually were antagonistic toward EPA, as it almost always posed a threat to their entrenched positions. Finally, the White House, supported by the Office of Management and Budget, usually took a conservative, pro-business and pro-energy stance. That was the "environment" in which decisions had to be made affecting the economic, health, and public welfare interests of the American people.

Reunion at our Kalorama Square home of some of my key associates during my years at Interior, CEQ, and EPA, c. 1990. There were some important absences. Seated: Terry Davies, Marian O'Connell, the author, Chuck Lettow, and Janet Bohlen. Standing: Boyd Gibbons, Lee Talbot, Roger Strelow, Al Alm, Buff Bohlen, Bill Reilly, Tim Atkeson, Frank Bracken, Stefan Plehn, and Steve Jellinek

Departure from EPA

WHEN I FINALLY did leave EPA, it was probably just in time. I was pretty stressed out and my back was in such bad shape that I could barely get up and down steps. Examinations at George Washington and Johns Hopkins Hospitals pinned the problem on old damage to a vertebra which I myself traced back to the time at St. George's School when at the age of 12 and as the result of a dare I had jumped about 20 feet from a roof to the ground. Regular back exercises every morning since have kept the problem at a manageable level. Shortly after I left EPA, Aileen and I joined our friends Peter and Carol Black on their 46-foot ketch, *Caroline,* for a cruise in the Bahamas—from the Exumas to the Out Islands and on down to Pine Cay in the Turks and Caicos Islands—a highly beneficial "unwinder."

My successor at EPA when the Carter administration took office was Douglas Costle. I knew Doug well, as we had worked together when he had been on the staff of the Ash Council. I left with the confidence that he would do a good job and he did.

CHAPTER 18

Return to Private Life

AFTER I LEFT EPA at the beginning of 1977, I spent the next year settling back to earth after the heady years in government. Leaving government and the power I had enjoyed for eight years, especially losing my secretary and my car and driver, was a shock to the system!

We sold 3101 Woodland Drive in March 1977. The first home of our married life where all our children grew up, it had been a happy place. Leaving it was a wrench. However, we bought a far more manageable house at Kalorama Square, a new development of 25 condominium townhouses at the corner of S Street and Phelps Place where the Holton Arms School gymnasium had once been located.

While out of government, I kept involved with public affairs. Early in 1978, I became part of a task force entitled the Light Metal Fast Breeder Reactor (LMFBR) Review Steering Committee charged by the White House (specifically, by President Carter's assistant for energy affairs, James Schlesinger) with reviewing federal policy toward a fast breeder reactor program. Four of us filed a separate view strongly opposing the development of the fast breeder reactor and I filed my own additional views in opposition. The program never went forward.

I went on the boards of the Natural Resources Defense Council (NRDC), a leading public-interest law firm, and the Union Carbide Corporation, both headquartered in New York and each representing a rather diametrically opposed environmental perspective. As it turned out, I left the NRDC board after a couple of years and remained on the Carbide board for 15 years, finally retiring in 1992. I was and am an admirer of NRDC, including its longtime executive director, John Adams, but I brought little to their board that they did not already have. I was "more of the same."

Bob Kennedy, chairman and CEO of Union Carbide, presenting me with a painting by John Guille Millais on my retirement from the Carbide board at a dinner in my honor at the St. Regis Hotel, New York City, 1992

The Carbide board was a great experience. It gave me an exposure to business operations that I had never had, and it gave me a close relationship with a number of prominent businessmen and women, all of which added a new dimension to my life. Moreover, the directors' fees, which were in the neighborhood of $50,000 per year, were a welcome addition to my meager income. My most active involvement on the board was as chairman of its health, safety, and environmental affairs committee set up after the tragic accident on Carbide's agricultural chemical plant at Bhopal, India, in 1984.

My Financial Circumstances

AT THE CONCLUSION of my EPA service, I had been shocked to find that I was not entitled to any federal retirement benefits despite over 30 years in federal service (including military service). The problem was due to the fact that, when I had gone on the Tax Court, I had elected to be covered by the Tax Court retirement plan which was a generous one and, in so doing, waived any benefits under the Civil Service retirement system. When I left the court after eight years, my rights under the judicial retirement plan had not yet vested so that I ended up with nothing under either system. Everyone concerned agreed that this result was an outrage but that nothing could be done about it under the law as it stood. The upshot was that the Congress enacted an amendment to the Internal Revenue Code which was general in its language but which, in effect, applied only to me. My former law clerk Herb Chabot had a hand in shepherding the amendment through Congress while he was on the staff of the Joint Committee on Internal Revenue Taxation. I owe him a large debt of gratitude. I draw a Civil Service pension today, but the issue was not resolved until mid-1978. In the meantime, my circumstances were fairly penurious. To help make ends meet, I went on the lecture circuit, earning somewhere between $2500 and $5000 an appearance.

My financial circumstances resulted in large part from my disinterest in entering the practice of law. I knew that my principal currency in such a pursuit would be as a lobbyist, more than likely for clients who opposed particular environmental legislation or regulations. Of course, I was enabled to take such a principled stand because of Aileen's private income, which kept us afloat. Indeed, had it not been for her income, it would have been difficult for me to pursue the combination of nonprofit and government roles which I did.

One very welcome windfall in March 1977 was the Tyler Prize for Environmental Achievement. The prize carried with it a check for $150,000 which was not subject to income tax under the law as it then stood (since changed). I received the award at a big dinner at the Beverly-Wilshire Hotel in Beverly Hills, California. My good friend Dr. Ruth Patrick, distinguished limnologist and president of the Philadelphia Academy of Natural Sciences, was my sponsor for the award. I will always be grateful to her. I was expected by a good many, I suspect, to contribute the prize money to some worthy environmental cause. I decided, however, that my personal upkeep was my most worthy and urgent cause at that moment in time.

Speaking of awards, I received a good many in those days, certainly due in part to the public enthusiasm for environmental programs. In the early 1970s, I received twelve honorary degrees, the most satisfying of which from a personal standpoint were from Princeton and Columbia. In that time of student unrest and antagonism toward U.S. involve-

The author receiving honorary degree of doctor of public service at fall convocation, Washington College, Chestertown, Maryland, 1996. College president John Toll is at the right (Kent News photo by Gibson Anthony)

ment in the Vietnam War, I always suspected that I was the only government official that a university dared invite to its commencement. I "sang for my supper" on a number of these occasions and delivered a lot of unmemorable commencement addresses. Years later, in the fall of 1996, I received an honorary degree from Washington College at Chestertown on the Eastern Shore at its fall convocation. I was able to note at the time that George Washington had received the college's first honorary degree and that I had received the most recent. In my address, I stated: "We will never achieve excellence in government by trashing it at every opportunity."

World Wildlife Fund

IN EARLY 1978, I was approached by my old friend Dillon Ripley, Secretary of the Smithsonian Institution as well as chairman of the board of the World Wildlife Fund, John Hanes, another good friend, and Joseph F. Cullman, 3rd, both also members of the board, to ask

With Joe Cullman at
Runnymede on the
Restigouche, 1999

whether I would be interested in becoming the paid president and chief
executive of WWF-U.S. (Later, Joe Cullman and I became warm
friends. We share a love of the African wilds, and Aileen and I have
fished for salmon at Runnymede, his camp on the Restigouche, and at
Two Brook, his camp on the Upsalquitch, both in New Brunswick, on
several occasions. As I write this, Joe is in his mid-eighties and is a
director emeritus of WWF. He seldom misses a meeting and his enthusiasm for WWF is an inspiration to the entire organization. He has
been and is a great force for conservation of the Atlantic salmon and of
African wildlife as well as of nature in general. He is a fine and generous man.) This sounded like just the right combination of worthwhile
endeavor and fun that I was looking for, together with reasonable compensation. After fairly brief negotiations, I accepted and renewed an
association that went back to 1961.

During the 17 years of its existence, WWF had remained a relatively minor player among U.S. environmental organizations despite
that, aside from the African Wildlife Leadership Foundation and
the New York Zoological Society, it was the principal organization
involved in international conservation and the only one with a truly
global outreach. Whatever the cause, in 1978, WWF's income was
only about $2 million a year, its membership about 30,000, and it had

Tom Lovejoy
(Photo by Patricia Barrow)

about 12 employees. WWF-International (WWF-Int.) and other national WWF organizations were highly critical of the U.S. performance.

From the beginning, it went well. We had an excellent board and a fine, although small, staff. Tom Lovejoy was our senior scientist who led our program initiatives and did a superior job in that regard. Perhaps the time was simply ripe for international conservation. Whatever the reasons, income, membership, and program grew rapidly. In the beginning, WWF-U.S. had been largely a fund-raising, grant-making organization. I was convinced that unless we pursued a more proactive approach with our own program which we ran with our own professional staff, our credibility and our fund-raising potential were limited. We increased our program staff and the move immediately began to pay dividends.

Moreover, while WWF-U.S. had been limited by an agreement with WWF-Int. to managing projects directly outside the U.S. only in the Caribbean and Latin America, we broke out of that mold and began operating in Nepal and Southeast Asia including the Philippines, and in Africa. At some point during that period, I became the

North American vice president of the International Union for the Conservation of Nature (IUCN), which shared its headquarters with WWF in Switzerland. I was a member of its bureau or executive committee.[1]

Today, WWF-U.S. has a membership of about 1.3 million and an annual operating budget of about $100 million. It is active all over the globe and provides between 30 and 50 percent of the funding for the total international conservation program of the overall WWF family of organizations. With the success of WWF-U.S., frictions began to build with WWF-Int. headquarters in Switzerland. Ironically, while WWF-U.S. had been criticized for years for being weak, it now was criticized for being too aggressive in its outreach.

Hudson River Peace Treaty

IN 1979, I WAS asked to mediate a set of environmental issues involving Consolidated Edison of New York (as well as other utilities), the New York State Power Commission, the federal EPA, and a group of environmental organizations, including the Natural Resources Defense Council, Scenic Hudson, and the Hudson River Fishermen's Association. After months of negotiations, starting in August 1979, we hammered out an agreement canceling the Storm King pumped storage project on the Hudson River, setting up systems to minimize fish kill at the water intake facilities of the power plants along the river, and establishing and funding a Hudson River Foundation to research and monitor the environmental health of the river. The agreement was signed at a public meeting in New York on December 10, 1980.

The *New York Times* in a lead editorial called the agreement the "Hudson River Peace Treaty." I got a lot of credit for the agreement but I think my most valuable contribution was to keep the parties meet-

---

1. Martin Holdgate, Director General of IUCN between 1988 and 1994, has written a fine history of that organization entitled *The Green Web. A Union for World Conservation.* Earthscan Publications Ltd., London (1999). The book makes a number of references to me, including my role in starting the World Heritage Trust.

ing on the issues and to keep the negotiations going. Chuck Luce, my predecessor as Under Secretary of the Interior and at the time of which I write the chairman and chief executive officer of Con Ed, was determined to get the issues behind us and was a major reason the mediation was successful. Ross Sandler, attorney for NRDC, and Albert Butzell, attorney for Scenic Hudson, were the principal protagonists for environmental interests. It had been Luce who had called Laurance Rockefeller and asked him to persuade me to take on the job of mediator. George Lamb in Laurance's office had then called me and I had accepted the challenge. (I had first become involved in mediation matters back in 1977 when I became the first chairman of RESOLVE, a nonprofit organization designed to promote mediation and other alternative dispute settlement mechanisms in disputes between environmentalists and other interests, usually business, in the resolution of natural resource controversies. RESOLVE was merged into The Conservation Foundation in 1980 and then with the latter into WWF. It is once again an independent organization and doing well.)

An involvement that closely related to my mediation experience was the chairmanship of Clean Sites, Inc., which I undertook while at WWF and continued for a number of years. Clean Sites was the product of discussions between members of the environmental and business communities who sought a constructive dialogue and a non-adversarial approach to addressing the many problems associated with the cleanup of toxic waste dumps under the so-called Superfund legislation. The discussions had been held with the active encouragement of Bill Reilly, then EPA administrator. I became the first chairman of the Clean Sites board, an extraordinarily broad-gauge group of former EPA administrators, former state environmental agency heads, environmental organization heads, leaders from industry (particularly the chemical industry), scientists, representatives of local government, etc. We had superior executive leadership: Charles (Chuck) Powers at the outset, followed by Tom Grumbly and then Toby Clark.

The premises on which Clean Sites was founded—namely, the need to promote dialogue rather than controversy, the need to provide alternatives to adversarial approaches to problem solving—were all

Bill Reilly

concepts in which I believed wholeheartedly and have tried to practice in public life. It was a natural fit. When I finally retired from the chairmanship, Bill Reilly, who had recently left EPA, succeeded me.

The Conservation Foundation Merges with WWF

IN 1985, Bill Reilly, then president of The Conservation Foundation,[2] and I had a fateful discussion. We were lunching together at Vincenzo's Restaurant on 20th Street just above Que. Bill was telling me of being approached by the National Audubon Society in New York to become its new president and, at the same time, making clear that he

2. William K. Reilly had been on the staff of the Council on Environmental Quality during my chairmanship and was the principal architect of the National Land Use Policy Act which President Nixon submitted to the Congress but which was never enacted. Bill left CEQ in July 1972 to head the Rockefeller Brothers Fund Task Force on Land Use and Urban Growth, chaired by Laurance S. Rockefeller. In 1973, he became president of CF, succeeding Sid Howe, who had in turn followed me. Reilly's tenure at CF had been highly successful.

did not want to move to New York and also that he was unhappy about the lack of international dimension to the Audubon job. As he talked, I had a flash of inspiration which I immediately expressed more or less as follows. "Bill, I am about to be 65 and should start winding down. You are 45 and ready for a new and bigger challenge. Why don't we merge CF into WWF; you become president and CEO of the combined organization; and I become a full-time, active chairman of the board but compensated, as I cannot afford to give up the income." And that is essentially what we did with the full approval of our respective boards, the affiliation taking place in October 1985.

Bill Reilly became president of WWF/CF in 1985 and I became chairman, blessed with an office and a secretary, Catherine Williams, who had replaced Marian O'Connell when she retired in March 1981. (Marian died after a long illness April 28, 1999.) Without executive responsibilities, my life became much less hectic. My understanding with Reilly was that I would be helpful on WWF matters whenever I could but that I would not interfere in any way with his exercise of executive authority. It was an agreement I stuck to, and Bill and I never had any difficulties on that score so far as I was aware. He did an outstanding job and continued to build the program, membership, and financial base of the organization. WWF was by far the major conservation organization on a global scale and WWF-U.S. was the principal player in the WWF family.

WWF-International Board

I BECAME A member of the WWF-Int. board, one of two vice presidents, and a member of EXCO, the executive committee. All of this required about four meetings a year, two of the board and two of EXCO. In view of the fact that Prince Philip, the Duke of Edinburgh, was president (chairman in U.S. terms) of the WWF-Int. board, one or two of the meetings each year were apt to be at Buckingham Palace and I attended two or three EXCO meetings at Windsor Castle. All of that, of course, was great fun. There were other WWF-Int. board

Prince Philip,
the Duke of Edinburgh
(Photo courtesy of Central
Office of Information, London)

meetings that I recall in Washington, Hong Kong, Vienna, and Buenos
Aires. There was an interesting meeting at Assisi where WWF brought
representatives of the world's great religions together to address the
issue of conservation.

Travel was a constant reality. As a vice president of IUCN, I had to
travel at least twice a year to Switzerland and then to the IUCN General Assemblies held every two years. These took me to Madrid and to
Christchurch in New Zealand. Aileen accompanied me to New Zealand, and we stopped for a few days at Bora Bora and more briefly at
Tahiti en route. I had also become a member of the Trilateral Commission headed by David Rockefeller. I attended meetings of the commission in London, Washington, Rome, and Bonn, but I was not a
very active participant. However, it was an interesting enterprise, and I
met under relaxed circumstances extremely prominent political and
business leaders from North America, Europe, and Japan.

Meeting Pope John
Paul II at the Vatican
during a meeting
of the Trilateral
Commission,
Rome, 1983

Working for Bush

DURING THE Republican National Convention in New Orleans in
August 1988, I testified on environmental issues before the platform
committee. Then, during the Bush-Dukakis campaign that fall, I co-
chaired with Bill Ruckelshaus an Environmentalists for Bush Committee. I accompanied Bush on Air Force One on a campaign swing to
Michigan, and I wrote a couple of environmental campaign speeches
for him. In his acceptance speech at the nominating convention, he
had highlighted education and the environment as two areas where
he was going to put a lot more emphasis than had Reagan. Following Bush's election, he asked Bill Reilly to become EPA administrator.
He did not know Reilly but acted on Ruckelshaus' recommendation,
which I fully supported. Reilly accepted and went on to do a stupen-
dous job at EPA. Not only did he do a great job domestically, but he
also made the U.S. once again a principal player in the international

A light moment in a meeting with Vice President Bush to discuss environmental issues for his forthcoming presidential campaign, 1992. Former New Jersey governor Tom Kean is on the far left, and next to him is Boyden Gray, counsel to the vice president and (later) to the president. Pollster Bob Teeter has his back to the camera. Facing, at left, are Frank Blake, EPA general counsel, and Bill Ruckelshaus, former EPA administrator.

Kathryn Fuller

environmental field. Kathryn Fuller, an environmental lawyer and a marine biologist who had been a member of the U.S. staff for some years, became WWF president in the place of Reilly. She, too, has done a superb job, and she remains leader of WWF-U.S. today.

Friction with WWF-International

IN THE MEANTIME, relationships between WWF-U.S. and WWF-Int. had continued to worsen. I could never accept the constant putting down of WWF-U.S. by the WWF-Int. Director General Charles de Haes, always supported by Prince Philip. The latter and I had a number of confrontations over such matters and each side finally employed counsel, WWF-Int. doing so first. Lloyd Cutler of the Washington firm of Wilmer Cutler & Pickering represented us. Lloyd may well be the most highly respected member of the bar in Washington, and he represented us with great skill and tact. I shall always be grateful to him for his successful help. In any event, de Haes finally resigned in 1993. I decided not to seek reelection to the WWF-Int. board in 1994, as I was retiring as chairman of WWF-U.S. later that year, and finally Prince Philip retired in 1996. It is gratifying to note that the relationship between the two organizations today is very positive. WWF-U.S. has fine representation on the WWF-Int. board in the persons of my good friends Roger Sant, my successor as chairman of WWF-U.S., and Rodney Wagner, who has recently retired as vice chairman of J. P. Morgan.

Medal of Freedom

IN THE SPRING of 1992, I was greatly honored by the presentation to me of the Presidential Medal of Freedom, the highest civilian honor bestowed by our government. There were a number of other recipients and the ceremony was held in the East Room of the White House. President Bush presented me with the medal and the First Lady, Barbara Bush, hung it around my neck. After I had shaken hands with the president and was about to leave the platform, Barbara said in a voice that carried to the furthest corners of the room, "Aren't you going to kiss your old friend?" And so, of course, I did. All of us had lunch in the State Dining Room. I sat on Barbara's left and on her right was Tip O'Neill, the retired Democratic Speaker of the House. Our daughter

Presentation of the Medal of Freedom by President Bush, assisted by Barbara Bush, in the East Room of the White House, 1992

Nancy sat next to Secretary of State Jim Baker and the rest of the family were scattered around the room.

All of our children and their spouses were there as well as our grandson Alex, who represented his generation. My sister-in-law Noël was there, as were Mid and Audry. It was a fine moment for all of us. We posed for a formal picture of the family in the front hall of the White House and then for a family snapshot on the steps of the East Wing as we left.

The citation for the medal read:

As Chairman of the World Wildlife Fund, Russell E. Train has devoted himself to protecting our precious natural heritage. He has served the Nation as Administrator of the Environmental Protection Agency, as the first Chairman of the President's Council on Environmental Quality, and as Under Secretary of the Interior. Over the years, he has helped shape society's growing environmental awareness into sound policy. America honors an ardent conservationist, whose efforts help preserve Nature's treasures in this country and around the world.

National Commission on the Environment

IN 1991, WWF sponsored a National Commission on the Environment to undertake a broad review of the nation's environmental programs and to make recommendations as to the direction they should
take in the future. I chaired the commission and put together its membership of 19. It was a remarkable group representing a broad spectrum
of the interests involved—including industry, science, economics,
international finance, religion, environmental organizations (both
national and "grass-roots"), public health, and government. No one
currently employed by government was included. Four of the five
former EPA administrators (excluding only Anne Gorsuch) were
members.

A principal focus of our recommendations was on shifting environmental and public policy in general toward a sustainable course. We
emphasized the desirability of using market mechanisms to this end;
two of our more controversial proposals were for a carbon tax on fossil
fuels and a substantial increase of $1 per gallon in the federal gasoline
tax. Terry Davies was creative director, assisted by Amy Salzman.

Our commission's report, entitled *Choosing a Sustainable Future*,
was issued in late 1992 shortly after the presidential election.[3] I had
timed its release after the election to avoid possible collapse of biparti-
sanship within the commission if it or any part of it had become an
issue in the election campaign. I probably need not have worried, as the
report did not get widespread public attention which was, of course, a
disappointment. At the same time, I am persuaded that the report was
and will continue to be an extremely useful document.

Retirement from WWF

MY RETIREMENT from WWF in September 1994 after nine years
as chairman of our board was mandated by our by-laws, and at 74 I was

3. *Choosing a Sustainable Future*, the Report of the National Commission on the Environment. Island Press, Washington, D.C. (1993), 180 pp.

ready to step down. I was elected chairman emeritus, which authorizes me to attend all board meetings and to participate in the discussions but not to vote. One of my more irreverent fellow board members said, "Russ, you know what 'emeritus' means, don't you? The 'e' means you're out and the 'meritus' means that you deserve it!" WWF gave me a fantastic retirement party at Union Station in September 1994 after I had presided at my last board meeting. Walter Cronkite, who had been CBS evening news anchor for many years and who was often called "the most trusted man in America," was master of ceremonies. He and his wife, Betsy, are old friends, and he presided with humor, alternately roasting me and saying nice things about Aileen and myself.

"Trains" was the motif of the whole evening—the invitations, the program, and the decor. A video and two large books contained wonderful messages from old associates around the world. The entire evening, attended by about 300, was both entertaining and moving. A highlight was the announcement of a $10 million (now $20 million) Education for Nature (EFN) Fund launched in my name to provide scholarships, fellowships, and institutional grants for environmental education around the world and particularly in those developing countries where most of the WWF program is concentrated. Over $6 million had already been raised. No more gratifying way to honor me could have been chosen, given that the wildlife management training of Africans had been how I had started my environmental career. Grants of $300,000 were made by the Russell E. Train Education for Nature Fund in 1996 and $500,000 in 1997, 1998, and 1999, all the result of an international application process and selection by an independent committee of international education experts.[4]

Now, in 1999, the EFN is part of WWF's Living Planet Campaign and approximately $14.5 million has been either given or committed to the EFN endowment.

---

4. In late 1996, I established a charitable remainder trust funded by stock gifts valued at $2 million which, following the death of both my wife, Aileen, and myself, will go to WWF-U.S. as additional endowment for the Education for Nature Fund.

CHAPTER 19

Grace Creek Farm

IN 1967, while I was at The Conservation Foundation, Aileen and I bought Grace Creek Farm, a 170-acre waterfront property near Bozman in Talbot County on the Eastern Shore of Maryland. (We had sold the Nonquitt house shortly before that.) We had cruised the Eastern Shore on many occasions over the preceding ten years on our ketch, *Traveller,* and we had come to love the tranquil landscape with its flat fields and woods, its creeks and coves where we had spent many a happy night at anchor. On one of those occasions when we were cruising alone, Aileen suddenly said: "Why don't we find a farm over here?" And so we did.

We engaged a real estate agent in Easton, Maryland, named Nesta Weir, an elderly lady who was a member of the Goldsborough family—one of the Eastern Shore's old colonial families. She drove us around in her ancient car to visit properties. Most of them were too grand or did not have enough land. We had no intention of acquiring a mansion on the Eastern Shore with all its attendant problems of upkeep and staffing. And we wanted land to walk on, perhaps to hunt over. Finally, after several weekends of fruitless search, Nesta Weir said she had one more place to show us—in the "lower county," with considerable acreage, and a fairly modest but old house badly in need of repair. Of course, we fell in love with the place and bought it.

We bought the property from Francis Berry, a mover headquartered in Denton, Delaware, who had bought it four years previously on speculation from the estate of Jesse Eldot, a somewhat mysterious New York entrepreneur. Eldot in turn had acquired it from a Willie Smith in satisfaction of a $5000 poker debt. Smith was a national billiard and/or pool champion who I am told had a heavy drinking problem and had an Asian wife known as "the Princess." Eldot had been an

Nancy, c. 1968

Emily as a debutante, 1968

Bowdy, c. 1975

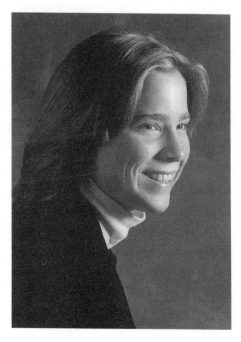

Errol, c. 1980

orphan left in the proverbial basket on the doorstep of an orphanage in New York City. The note the mother left was signed "L." and from this came the child's last name, "Eldot." I understood that Eldot had been in the printing business and had also at one time owned the building in which was located the Roseland Ballroom in New York, which I had patronized on occasion while at college. The rumor among his Bozman neighbors was that he was "Mafia-connected," but without any foundation of which I became aware.

Prior to all that rather exotic history, the place had been a working farm and back in colonial and nineteenth-century days had been an isolated subsistence farm. The land is quite low and fairly marginal for agriculture. The size of the property is described in the deed as "170 acres more or less" and I used to say that at high tide it was mostly less. The central house was probably built about 1720. We paid what was considered a high price for the property at the time; for several years our Washington friend and Eastern Shore neighbor Ella Burling used to entertain her houseguests by driving them over to see the property for which the Trains had paid so much.

The house is what is sometimes called "a shotgun house"—a shot fired into it from one end would pass through all the rooms. We added a large glassed-in room on the water side which became our principal dining and living area, although in cold weather we are apt to enjoy the original living room with its two fireplaces. We built a swimming pool and a tennis court and these have been frequently used by family and friends. Unfortunately, I have become too arthritic to enjoy tennis anymore. Several years ago, we tore down our bedroom wing and replaced it with a two-story addition. Together with the guest house, we can sleep up to fourteen in a pinch. However, one of the things that appealed to us most about the place was that the house was not "grand." While attractive and very liveable, it is also low-key and eminently manageable. At least two knowledgeable people have told Aileen that it is the most attractive house they know on the Eastern Shore.

The house looks southeast over what is called "broad water" on the Shore. Grace Creek marks the northerly boundary and Leadenham Creek the southwesterly. The two creeks come together at Broad

The house at Grace Creek Farm (the kitchen wing is not visible)

A winter view from the house

Creek, which we look down. It is a beautiful spot and a peaceful one. Each season has its particular joys—the ducks and geese, the nesting ospreys, the shorebirds and other spring and autumn migrants. We often enjoy our own oysters, eaten on the half shell with champagne or just plain white wine in the garage where Tom Adler, our gardener for 30 years, opened them until his death in 1997 at 83. Richard Willey, our manager, now does the honors.

Aileen is an accomplished gardener and spends countless hours making the area around the house bright with bloom for at least six months of the year. The spring bulbs are her particular joy, and the daffodils in great variety are a thrilling sight in the early spring. Some years ago, she tried her hand at dried flower arrangements and soon became an expert. Now our houses in Washington and on the Eastern Shore have marvelous arrangements of dried flowers and plants, most of which Aileen has collected from our own garden and fields. These give special pleasure during the six months of the year when the garden is not producing fresh blooms. At one time, Aileen did dried flower arrangements for friends and for the benefit of charities but now confines her effort mostly to our own needs. She uses a room in one of the farm outbuildings we call the Duck House—probably because I store duck decoys there—for drying flowers and doing her arrangements. The blooms in these are often so bright that it is difficult to believe that they were picked months earlier. The art has given Aileen, her guests, and family much pleasure over the years.

The vegetable garden and fruit trees also get a great deal of attention from Aileen. She selects the varieties and seeds from the vast number of catalogues she receives in the mail and either does the planting herself or supervises it. As a result, we have fresh vegetables for much of the year. Nothing from the stores tastes as good. Among the fruits, raspberries are a favorite and demand a great deal of attention, as they have proven difficult to grow at Grace Creek. Aileen is constantly planting new stock and cutting out old canes. She does much of the picking herself and comes back to the house with scratches on arms and legs and even an occasional wasp sting. Among the products of all this industry are marvelous raspberry jam, damson plum jam, chutney, sour cherries, applesauce, tomato juice, etc. In season, our kitchen is a hive of activity as fruits and vegetables are prepared, cooked, seasoned, and put into jars. As anyone who has ever done this knows, it requires an enormous amount of work.

Aileen's jams are much appreciated at Christmastime by our friends. When we drive back to town at the end of a weekend, the car is almost always loaded with fresh vegetables, eggs, cut flowers, etc., which we share with our children and their families.

With young Russell and Bowdy at the farm, c. 1994

I have to confess that, apart from enjoying all this bounty, I play very little role in its production. Weeding and digging just do not seem to be part of my natural tastes. I do prune on occasion and rather enjoy it. However, during my government years in particular, I used to carry a heavy bag of paperwork to the country with me, and much of my time was spent at my desk. I am afraid the habits of those years have stuck with me, except now I keep busy working on a book such as this.

When we first bought Grace Creek Farm (called Pine Shore Farm then), I used to do a bit of duck and goose shooting there as well as some quail hunting. The latter, in particular, was never very good and our Labradors are not bird dogs. A number of years ago, we bought 190 acres of an old property known as Lostock, which was not contiguous with Grace Creek but very close by. It had a couple of old goose pits which we refurbished and Bowdy and I and our friends had quite fair sport there. With that opportunity available to us, we ended any waterfowl hunting at Grace Creek and, for a number of years now, it has been a principal sanctuary or rest area for waterfowl in the area. Every day in the fall and winter, we throw out a couple of buckets of corn into the cove right in front of our house, and, as a result, we have a constant scene of waterfowl coming and going. A flock of about 25 Canada geese seem to consider our cove their home base, and it is our definite impression that they head straight for it when they arrive from the north in the fall. At times, we have up to several thousand geese in our fields.

Lostock had first been settled by the Caulk family in the seventeenth century. An old brick house on the property was in a state of total disrepair. The property had been about to be divided into one-acre parcels, and we bought it to keep it from being developed. We made one or two efforts to restore the old house but never made a serious commitment in that direction. We put environmental easements on the property so that it could never be divided into more than three parcels and finally sold it in 1992 as one piece. We have never resumed shooting at Grace Creek Farm.

Our crops have always been corn and soybeans and recently we have added winter wheat, which seems to have done well despite the geese. We often see deer feeding along the edges of the fields, but they seem to do little real damage. In recent years our place has become home to a large number of deer, including a snow-white doe. Our main worry is that the deer are infested with the tiny ticks that carry Lyme's disease, an extremely disagreeable malady. In 1996, we started the practice of inviting a local waterman / house painter, Joe Ostrowski, to organize a deer hunt and take off a number of deer. In return, Joe provides us with as much venison as we want. Despite the culling, the deer herd remains large. (In 1998, we took off 18 deer and immediately after the season counted 22 at one time in the field behind Richard and Diane Willey's house.)

We have always enjoyed eating food that comes from our own land. On Thanksgiving, when a large number of family gather around the table at Grace Creek, the oysters, vegetables, relishes, chutneys, and sour cherry pie all come from our own land (or water). For many years, there were a couple of wild geese as well but our children finally rebelled and announced that they wanted turkey. Integral to that feast was Viola Chase, who cooked for us at Grace Creek Farm on weekends and other special days for almost 30 years until health problems forced her to retire in 1996. Her place has been taken by Faith Palmer.

We keep our own chickens, and nothing can compare with the

Tom Adler and Alex Smith, c. 1974

fresh eggs they produce. There was a time when we kept ducks as well, and Errol, then a small child, spent so much time with them that she became known as the "duck girl."

We have always had a horse or two as well as a pony at the farm. Aileen is a keen rider; Errol went through a major "horse period" as a young girl; and even I had my own horse at one time. However, an allergic reaction to horses and ever-more arthritic joints have taken the pleasure out of riding for me. The grandchildren have all enjoyed the pony, and we have a cart to which he can be hitched for a trip to the general store in Bozman. We had one pony that insisted on a Coca-Cola when he arrived there.

It must be plain that Aileen and I have not run Grace Creek Farm all by ourselves over the years since 1967. Indeed, we have had a wonderful support system over that time. Tom Adler, gardener and general handyman, was with us from the beginning until his death in 1997. It was Tom, who was illiterate and explained that "schooling just never took," who kept the garden, mowed the lawn, fed the chickens, watered the horses, cut the firewood, laid the fires, took care of the swimming pool, and shucked the oysters, among other chores. Tom was a devoted friend and helper. We miss him.

We have a tenant house at the farm, situated about a hundred yards from the main house. It is of somewhat curious design since it was once a restaurant/pool hall in neighboring Claiborne. It has been occupied by three families since we have owned Grace Creek. The first tenants were Howard and Clara Johnson, who were on the place when we bought it. Howard worked at the *Star-Democrat* in Easton as a pressman and did a few odd jobs for us. Later, he organized the Talbot Printing Company which Aileen and I financed. It was not a successful venture and finally folded. The Johnsons had moved away from the farm and built their own home by that time.

Our next tenants were Dave and Jane Thompson. Dave was a young lawyer in Easton and Jane taught school there. They had nothing to do with managing the farm. They finally bought their own house in the neighborhood, and Dave handles legal matters for us on the Eastern Shore.

Since their departure, the tenant house has been occupied by Richard and Diane Willey, both of whom have roots deep in the Eastern Shore. Richard works full time for us and acts as our manager as well as doing just about everything that needs doing. He is good with mechanical problems and there always are a lot of them. He and Diane are both interested in animals and train guide dogs for the blind. They do a fine job of taking care of our Labrador when we are traveling, and, of course, the horses and chickens on a daily basis.

We have always operated the actual agricultural activity of the farm through sharecropping, at first on a 50-50 basis but more recently 60-40. (We get the 40.) Our first farmer was Horace Hambleton, a rather laid-back local farmer/waterman. We had planted some clover in the horse pasture near the house and one day Horace and I were leaning on the rail fence looking at the horses and talking casually. "Horace," I said, "why don't the horses eat the clover?" "Mr. Train," said Horace, removing the hay stalk from his teeth, "that's just the way horses is nowadays!"

Horace was not much of a farmer, and we replaced him with Earl

Richard and Diane Willey
with "Yaller," 1999

Harrison, a retired state trooper, who lived across Cooper Point Road
from us at the head of Caulk Cove. His five acres lay between Grace
Creek Farm and the Lostock property we acquired. Earl was a hard
worker and he farmed our land until his death about ten years ago. His
wife, Cora, remains a good friend and neighbor. Earl was an old "red-
neck" whose attempts at humor were generally too politically incorrect
to be repeated today. But we got along well, and we missed him when
he died.

Later farmers have been more businesslike and better farmers but
my communication with them has generally been by telephone. One
of our farmers was young Mac Stinchcomb. He lived down at Tilgh-
man, where his family had farmed for generations. He married Julie
Johnson, the daughter of our erstwhile tenants. Mac did a fine job and
we made a little money from the land for the first time but he finally
had to give us up when he became the full-time resident manager of
John and Suzanne Whitmore's Langdon Farm. Our current farmer is
Christopher (Chris) Metz, who has recently taken on the job. The fact

With Walter Cronkite
at Grace Creek

Cy Vance and Elliot
Richardson at the farm

is that it is difficult today to find an experienced farmer with whom to work in this area. The land has been so cut up for development that the old farm economy has all but disappeared.

As I mentioned earlier, our effort to keep our ketch, *Traveller*, off our farm did not work out. However, for several years now, we have had a 15-foot catboat, unpretentiously named *Flying Cloud,* which we bought from the Marshall boatyard in Padanaram, Massachusetts. We keep her at our dock and Aileen and I enjoy taking her out for an hour or two on the neighboring creeks. Grandchildren occasionally accompany us. For those who do not know the Shore, the word "creek" can cover almost any waterway, such as Broad Creek, even if a mile wide.

Grace Creek Farm has been a haven of peace and renewal in a fairly hectic life. I remember that when I was Under Secretary of Interior there was a time when I would charter a helicopter at National Airport and fly direct to the farm. (The charter was, of course, at my expense. It was not cheap, and the helicopter company finally went broke. I said it had been a race as to which one of us would go broke first.) As I saw Chesapeake Bay beneath me on those occasions, I always felt as if a great spring within me were unwinding. The tensions of the week—and there were plenty—would seem to slough off as I got to the farm. Bowdy and Errol spent a great deal of time there when they were growing up, but Nancy and Emily less so, as they were away at school. It is a delightful place for us to spend a relaxed time with our children and our grandchildren, and the farm has added a wonderful dimension to all our lives. The grandchildren all seem to love their visits to the farm and the activities it affords: pony rides, hayrides, jumping on the trampoline, climbing the jungle gym, swimming, fishing and crabbing off the dock, playing in the caboose, enjoying a tree house in the woods, collecting eggs in the chicken house, helping Gran pick fruit and vegetables and helping her make jams, etc.

When we first bought land in Talbot County, there was at least a possibility in the back of our minds that we might one day make this our principal residence. That thought has pretty much evaporated over the years. We have made many wonderful friends on the Eastern Shore and always enjoy ourselves there. But the fact is that we do not want to give up our Washington life. At least half our children and grandchildren are there, and Aileen in particular sees them quite often during the week. She sees her old friends with considerable regularity, plays tennis twice a week, sees her personal trainer twice a week and enjoys entertaining in our home. We both enjoy the cultural opportunities of

With Virette and Bill
Finlay from Dublin

Peter Ramsbotham,
Cynthia Helms,
Zaida Ramsbotham,
and Dick Helms at
Grace Creek

Ella Burling

With Peter and Virginia Blond in southern France, where Aileen and I, along with Harry and Leslie Hambleden, visited them at their house in the countryside in 1999

Washington—the galleries and their art exhibitions, the theater and concerts. I have my book collection in Washington which I enjoy working with and would find difficult to move to the country. I also have all my sources for writing there, as well as my office at the World Wildlife Fund which keeps me in touch with environmental activities. Aside from all that, however, Washington is an exciting place in which to live, with close friends in and out of government, reporters and columnists, diplomats, and interesting new people that one is constantly meeting.

We made many close friends on the Shore when we first bought our farm—Peter and Carol Black, Shep and Nora Krech, Rog and Anne Morton, and John and Louise Walker, to name a few. Later came newer but no less close friends such as Dick and Mary Manegold, Jim and Peggy Calvert, and John and Suzanne Whitmore. And, of course, there is a growing contingent of Washington friends we see more often on the Shore than in the city—Ella Burling, Frank and Tricia Saul, Tom and Jane Nigra, Alec and Peggy Tomlinson, Nevin and Liz Kuhl, Buff and Janet Bohlen, Gil and Margot Hahn, Dick and Sheila Griffin, David and Randy Hunt, and Jack and Donna Pflieger, among others.

Very special among the new friends that the Eastern Shore has brought into our lives are Peter and Virginia Blond, who are from En-

At Grace Creek with
Judge, 1995

gland and who several years ago bought a house on Leadenham Creek
looking across at our land. They make two visits of about two weeks'
duration each during the year, and we see them at least once a year in
England. They are always great fun to be with.

At the close of 1998, we put conservation easements on Grace Creek
Farm which will prevent any development of the property beyond that
which was then there. Structures can be replaced or moved but essentially nothing new, particularly residences, can be built. The 600-acre
Sheehan property across Leadenham Creek has been deeded to the
National Audubon Society so that our two properties together will
constitute in perpetuity a large natural area in a region where development pressures are tremendous. Since the property can no longer
be divided and developed, there is a significant diminution in market
value. However, our children are all supportive of our action. Aileen
and I have received many gifts from the Grace Creek land: natural
beauty, peace, spiritual refreshment, and joy in countless ways. We feel
glad to be able to give back to the land some small measure of what we
have received.

CHAPTER 20

Hobe Sound

ABOUT THREE years after acquiring Grace Creek Farm, we bought our house on Jupiter Island at Hobe Sound, Florida. Aileen's father had had a house there, and I had visited Aileen there first in early 1953 before we were married. When her father died in 1967, Aileen and her two sisters inherited his property. For at least two years, our three families tried to make a go of using the property jointly. That was not easy as, of course, we all wanted to use the house at the same time, namely, during our children's school vacations. One Christmas, when we were all there—about 16 strong—Aileen spent a half-hour squeezing a large pitcher of grapefruit juice, almost enough for the entire family. She put it into the refrigerator to chill. Returning to the kitchen some time later, she was just in time to see her nephew Joe Spaulding, Helen and Si's strapping oldest son, finish the entire pitcher in about three gulps. Aileen found me and said, "We need our own house!"

That same day we contacted Alita Reed, who was in the real estate business, and almost immediately located a house at 114 Gomez Road that had just come on the market. The price was high for the time but the house seemed perfect—relatively small and manageable, well built and in near-perfect condition, facing the inland waterway rather than the ocean, and located conveniently close to the Jupiter Island Club, tennis, golf, and the beach. And so we became owners of our own home at Hobe Sound, in our view the most attractive resort in Florida. The Spauldings and Keys finally tore down the old Bowdoin house, divided the property, and built their own separate homes.

Of course, I was far from retirement at the time and, over the years, we have rented the house out for most of the "season," using it ourselves for nearly a month over Christmas and New Year's and about two weeks at the beginning of April. The house has always been in

Houseguests at Hobe Sound:
Roger and Vicki Sant,
Albert and Madzy Beveridge,
Bill and Jill Ruckelshaus

Antony Acland

"B.A." and Lloyd Bentsen
with Aileen

Jenny Acland

Stan Resor and Louise Walker
just before their marriage

Nan and Paul Ignatius,
Sandy Trowbridge, Jill
Ruckelshaus, and Ellie
Trowbridge

Kay and Rowly Evans—
obviously between visits to Hobe Sound

George and Sally Pillsbury—
plainly on their way to Hobe Sound

Kate Davis Quesada

Jeff Wheelwright, Lucy Moorhead, and
Mary Wheelwright with Aileen

Nelson and Ruth Mead

demand by renters, and the rents have substantially helped carry the house financially. Even today, we have little thought of using Hobe Sound as a full-time winter home, although we have begun to use it during March, because we have grandchildren who can enjoy it then during their school vacations.

Some years ago we added a two-bedroom guest house, and we are able to accommodate a reasonable number of our children and grand-children or friends. It has been our custom in April to have house parties over two successive weekends with three other couples each time. These are pleasant reunions with old friends—long breakfasts and lunches on the terrace with lots of laughter, tennis, swimming, and usually a dinner party. Our guests have included Lloyd and "B.A." Bentsen, Bill and Jill Ruckelshaus, Roger and Vicki Sant, John and Caroline Macomber, Bill and Susan Kent, John and Suzanne Whitmore, Gary and Joan Jewett, Sandy and Ellie Trowbridge, Paul and Nan Ignatius, Rowly and Kay Evans, Bob and Louisa Duemling, Woody and Liberty Redmond, Ebersole and Sheila Gaines, Dick and Cynthia Helms, and Bill and Lynda Webster, among others. At one time, all or most of our children would join us over Christmas, but, as they have gotten older, married, and had children of their own, they have tended to celebrate Christmas in their own homes and then perhaps visit us at Hobe Sound after Christmas. Emily and Jim Rowan usually go to their house on Nevis, frequently drawing other members of the family with them as well. When Bowdy and J.C. are with us, we can hunt quail together, as I belong to the High Point syndicate which operates a shoot on ranch land west of Hobe Sound.

High Point was organized and is managed by Nat Reed, whose parents, Joseph Verner Reed and Permelia Reed, were responsible for creating the Jupiter Island Club and the wonderful community around it. Recently, the club members have bought out the Reed interest. Hobe Sound is a wonderful place, and the Reeds are owed a large debt of gratitude for its creation and development.

Nat Reed has been a strong force for conservation in Florida, and in 1975 he was appointed by President Nixon as Assistant Secretary of the Interior for Fish, Wildlife, Parks, and Outdoor Recreation. He did a superb job in that capacity and was a major contributor to the fine environmental record of the Nixon-Ford administrations. (He had been a member of the task force which I had chaired in 1968 to advise President-elect Nixon on environmental affairs.)

We have many good friends in Hobe Sound. Aileen plays tennis quite regularly and is in great demand to help make up a doubles game. We swim before breakfast in the saltwater pool at the Beach Club, swim there again about noon, hopefully in the ocean, and frequently lunch there at the snack bar. Since we are fairly irregular visitors, we tend not to be involved in the Garden Club, Bridge Club, Yacht Club, or Whiz Kids kinds of activities. However, we dine out a lot, entertain at our home with some frequency, and otherwise keep pretty active in the Hobe Sound social scene, which is considerable. Add about five walks a day for our Lab and the demands of a book such as this plus all of Aileen's household chores, and you get a very full schedule. Fortunately, dinners are almost invariably early affairs. Old-timers insist that the Hobe Sound motto is "HBT"—"Horizontal by Ten."

The back terrace of our house, shaded by a spreading ficus tree, looks out over the inland waterway. The lawn slopes down to the tropical planting that shields us from the passersby on the "Ramble" along the waterway. Thick vegetation protects us as well from the houses on either side. Grapefruit, orange, lemon, and lime trees add to the pleasure of the place. Hopefully, an avocado tree will eventually start bearing.

CHAPTER 21

Long Point

IT SHOULD BE apparent to anyone reading this book as well as *The Bowdoin Family* and *The Train Family* that duck hunting has been an enthusiasm of both Bowdoins and Trains. My own father and his father, as well as my brother Mid, loved nothing better than to be in a duck blind on a cold winter's dawn. My father-in-law, George T. Bowdoin, shared this enthusiasm, and duck hunting was one of our common interests. I have already mentioned duck hunting at Long Point, Canada, in connection with both my own life and that of my father-in-law, who was a member from 1945 to 1967, when I acquired his shares. I have continued as a member since that time, and my son, Bowdoin Train, became a member in 1994. My son-in-law, Errol's husband, J.C. Giordano, has been a regular guest. Since Long Point has played such a part in the lives now of three generations of the family, it seems appropriate to set out something of the history of the Point and, more specifically, of the Long Point Company.

Long Point is situated on the north shore of Lake Erie, about a third of the way from the lake's eastern end and opposite to Erie, Pennsylvania. It is about 20 miles in length and runs roughly west to east in the lake, whose general orientation is from southwest to northeast. Long Point is a readily identifiable feature on almost any map of the Great Lakes.

Geologically, Long Point is essentially a long sand spit, with forested sand ridges transecting the last third of it, and with a vast marsh making up its inner reaches toward the mainland. In the old days of the early to mid-nineteenth century, the Point was an isolated wilderness, largely unvisited except by hunters, trappers, fishermen, fugitives from the law and various other unsavory characters. Legend has it that a bordello operated on the Point at one time and that gambling barges

were anchored off the Point, drawing most of their clientele from the
U.S. side of the lake. Having had some experience of the violence of
the storms which can suddenly strike Lake Erie, I marvel at the risk-
taking involved on the part of the customers of these establishments.
Market hunters shipped thousands of waterfowl from the Point and
timber operators ravaged its forests.

In any event, a group of sportsmen, primarily Canadian, acquired
title to most of Long Point, and, in 1866, they organized the Long Point
Company. Erstwhile poachers were hired as punters and keepers. The
company proceeded to bring law and order—or at least an approxima-
tion of it—to the area. Miraculously, over the past 130 years, Long Point
has been maintained, nurtured, and protected as one of the prime
waterfowl habitats on the North American continent. At times, the
area has been devastated by a combination of low water and extreme
drought conditions, turning the marsh into a semblance of the Dust
Bowl. At other times, extreme high water combined with heavy storms
has threatened the Point with massive erosion and has, in fact, washed
away some of the company facilities. The company has dug ditches to
improve the circulation of water in the marsh as well as to provide better access to parts of the marsh and has constructed a massive berm
along the south shore to keep the lake from overwhelming the marsh.

Typically, the company shoots a much shorter season than permitted by Canadian law and also substantially shorter hours during the
day. It has renovated and rebuilt its facilities and today the company
property is in splendid shape and the marsh is flourishing. Indeed, the
Long Point Company has over the years been a shining example of
conservation by private initiative. In 1977, through various gifts involving the Nature Conservancy and the Canadian Wildlife Service, about
8000 acres at the eastern end of Long Point were transferred to the
Canadian government to be maintained as a fully protected wildlife
refuge. Today, the company property consists of 7840 acres of prime
marshland.

Along the northern edge of the marsh facing on the inner bay, a
deep "creek" runs into the marsh, and along the west side of that creek,
the company docks and buildings as well as the members' "cottages"

are situated—all on piles and connected by a boardwalk. The buildings are painted red with white trim. The oldest building houses the members' dining room, kitchen, staff dining room, and quarters for the head keeper and his family.

The dining room with its one long table is where much company memorabilia are enshrined. The room is entirely paneled in chestnut. Over the large fireplace hangs a steel-engraved portrait of Prince Arthur, a son of Queen Victoria, who shot here as a young man in 1869. The record of his day's bag together with that of the other guns on that occasion is framed on the wall. He was the "low gun." (A long-circulated rumor that Prince Arthur was Jack the Ripper appears to be without foundation. He had a distinguished military career and later became duke of Connaught. His brother, Prince Rupert, who never came to Long Point, would make a more likely suspect.) Another shooting record on the wall is that of King George V, who was a guest at the Point in 1883, when he was Prince of Wales and a midshipman. He shot 141 ducks over two days and was the second-highest gun.

Over the sideboard is an attractive oil painting of the Long Point buildings by Field Marshall Lord Alexander of Tunis, who visited there a number of times when he was governor general of Canada and who was a favorite of the members. There is a photograph of him in his punt. The earl of Athlone, another governor general, who was married to the Princess Royal, is also pictured in his punt and is resplendent in shooting tweeds and a necktie. A framed letter from him on the wall is addressed to "Dear Bowdoin," my father-in-law, George T. Bowdoin, who was apparently his host, thanking him for a "delightful time." A huge four-gauge shotgun hangs high on the wall.

There are also pictures of three generations of Ferrises—Walker, Hanson, and Norman—head keepers from 1889 to 1973, as well as a portrait of John (Buck) Wamsley, who was head keeper from 1973 to 1991. His son, David, has been head keeper since that date. These men, with their families, have devoted their lives to the Point, and its survival and fine condition today are due in great measure to their dedication. It is important to emphasize the family contribution because, going back to at least Hanson Ferris, the wives of the head keepers have been an integral part of the whole operation. David Wamsley and his wife, Penny, are fully in that tradition and do a marvelous job. There are also pictures of three generations of the Reeves family—Phineas, Charles, and Jack—who were punters and decoy makers of extraordinary skill.

I have examples of the work of all three Reeves craftsmen at my cottage, situated at the extreme end of the boardwalk. From its windows, one can look far to the east and see the dark line of the trees on Ryerson's Island, which forms the eastern boundary of the marsh. Reverend Edgerton Ryerson, who owned Ryerson's Island in the mid-nineteenth century and who had shot at Long Point as a boy, wrote the Canadian government that "it was impossible for a respectable man to go there and ruin for any young man to shoot there; that immorality, drunkenness and a low tone was prevalent throughout the place."[1]

It seems in full keeping with that tradition that my cottage is known as "the Sin Center." The name goes back to about 1929 when Junius Spencer Morgan, the son of J. P. Morgan II, became a member. When he visited the Point as a guest, he was horrified to find that there was little socializing among the members and that they all kept to their own cottages for a drink before dinner. Upon becoming a member, he instituted the practice of having all members and guests present come to his cottage for cocktails each evening before repairing to the dining room for dinner. His cottage was promptly dubbed "the Sin Center," and the name has stuck, although today the practice is to have cocktails rotate among the different cottages.

History and tradition are an important part of the Long Point experience. Each member's shares in the company trace back to its origin in 1866 and their passage from owner to owner over the years since is all carefully recorded. My own shares were derived in 1967 from George T. Bowdoin, my father-in-law, who had acquired them in 1945 from Wilton Lloyd-Smith who acquired them in 1931 from Harry Payne Whitney who acquired them in 1914, etc., etc. Whitney and

1. This quotation comes from a small volume published by the Long Point Company in 1966 on its 100th anniversary.

Aerial view of "The Cottages" at Long Point, a photo taken a number of years ago, but the layout remains essentially unchanged. The "Sin Center" is the nearest structure.

Henry W. Sage, who became a member at about the same time, together built the Sin Center.

When I became a member in 1967, I had already been a guest at Long Point on a number of occasions dating back to 1954. I shared the Sin Center with Jack Morgan (John Pierpont Morgan III), who acquired his shares the same year and whom I had known for a number of years. Jack had acquired his shares from his father, Junius S. Morgan,[2] who had acquired them from Henry W. Sage, etc., etc. When Jack decided to resign from the company in 1994, his shares were offered to and bought by my son, Charles Bowdoin Train (Bowdy), who now occupies the other half of the Sin Center. While my schedule in retirement gives me far greater freedom than he has to visit Long Point in the fall, we have managed to be there a fair amount of time together, opportunities which I cherish and which are all too rare in our hectic world.

Although I became a member of Long Point in 1967, it was only

2. Technically, Jack acquired his shares from the Estate of George T. Bowdoin who had acquired them when Junius died and essentially held them for Jack.

two years later that I entered the government as Under Secretary of the Interior, and for the eight years of the Nixon-Ford administrations, during which I held positions of considerable visibility, including responsibility for fish and wildlife, I decided to forego the pleasures of Long Point. Since the fall of 1977, I have not missed a season and, starting in 1982, with only one exception due to an unexpected freeze-up, Bowdy accompanied me as a guest until he became a member in his own right.

Our cottage is at the end of the boardwalk and has a large living room with windows looking out on the marsh in three directions, two bedrooms, and a bathroom running the width of the building with a toilet at each end—in the sociable tradition of the Sin Center. The cottage has its own connecting boathouse with a ramp down to a loading dock. My old wooden punt lies on one side of the boathouse. The punt is no longer used but is redolent of memories of earlier days. On shelves on either side of the boathouse lie our decoys—mallards, blacks, pintails, baldpates (wigeon), bluebills (lesser scaup), redheads, and canvasbacks. Some of these were made for me by Jack Reeves and others by his father, Charlie Reeves, before my time. Each of my decoys is branded on the bottom. Some carry the mark of Harry Payne Whitney, plus the initials of WL-S, GTB, and RET. Thus, the older decoys go back at least to 1927 and possibly to 1913 or thereabouts. It gives me pleasure to have these old-timers still at work.

The interior of the cottage is all dark-stained chestnut—now a vanished wood. A large fireplace provides the only heat, with a world-record Barren Ground caribou head, collected by Wilton Lloyd-Smith at Rainy Pass, Alaska, presiding above it. High on shelves at the far end of the living room, three mounted snowy owls unblinkingly observe the proceedings. Bookshelves, desk, workbench, bar and cabinet, woodbox, retired decoys, a ship's clock, and an enormous sofa facing the fire with large overstuffed easy chairs to each side complete the picture. A recent addition is a small refrigerator. In 1998, I also added the skin of a leopard that I had shot in 1956 in the Northern Frontier District of Kenya. The skin had at one time resided on our living room floor at 3101 Woodland Drive in Washington but had been a bit chewed over by our Labrador.

However, change is not the name of the game at Long Point. Junius Morgan's sailmaker's kit still stands on the workbench, and I have only recently discarded a can of his smoking tobacco. Bowdy often wears his grandfather's shooting coat, the tattered condition of which would embarrass a Bosnian refugee. Prior to my purchase of the fridge, the most radical change had been the introduction of electric blankets by my guest the late Jack Dorrance, who had sent to the mainland for them after his first night in the cottage. Back in the 1930s when the marsh dried up and there was no shooting, Junius Morgan and Wilton Lloyd-Smith brought their wives up. The story is that Mrs. Morgan ("Aunt Louise" to Aileen) changed all the furniture around in the living room. Junius made no protest. However, as soon as the ladies left, he and Wilton simply moved everything back to where it had been. And so it remains today.

The daily routine is equally immutable. The day begins about 6:30 when your punter arrives to make a fire and leave a thermos of hot coffee (decaf in my case). In due course, I wander into the living room wrapped in an old flannel bathrobe. It is cold, and I stand in front of the fire, warming long underwear and wool shirt before donning them. I watch the sun rise over Ryerson's Island and try to gauge the weather from the looks of the sky. I scan the latter for ducks on the wing. Occasionally, a couple of mallard dabble in the creek below the window. At 7:00, I turn on my portable Sony radio and listen to the "Morning Edition" broadcast by the NPR station in Erie, Pennsylvania, directly across the lake from Long Point. I sit in front of the fire with my coffee.

Breakfast is at 8:00 and, perhaps accompanied by Bowdy or a guest, I walk up the boardwalk in time to stop for a few minutes at the "Office," a small, one-room building where the head keeper oversees the entire operation and where the punters forgather after their own breakfast. It is a moment for good-natured banter among members and punters and also for picking up some informed opinion as to the prospects for the day. Breakfast itself is an impressive meal. The senior member present sits at the head of the table, serves the plates, and rings the bell to mark the passage of the courses—fresh orange juice, oatmeal with cream and brown sugar, followed by eggs in various guises or by pancakes and maple syrup, accompanied in all cases by both Canadian and strip bacon, toast, marmalade, and/or comb honey and coffee. It is not a meal to take lightly, and it provides a solid base for the morning's work.

At the very outset of the meal, as soon as everyone is seated, the head keeper comes in and carries a small cloth bag around to each person, starting with the table head. You stick your hand in and take out a numbered die which determines the order of choice for shooting positions. (The maximum number of guns permitted in the marsh under company rules is seven at any one time to avoid undue pressure on the marsh.) However, by time-honored tradition, it is not the member who gets to make the choice but his punter. After breakfast, we all stop by the office and check the large printed chart which shows all the thirty or more shooting positions—Bulmer's, Pearson's East, Behind Second Island, Between the Ridges, Back of Bayside, Trapper's, Leary's, etc. The wind direction is a major determinant of your punter's choice.

I go back to the cottage to complete preparations for the day. My punter puts the punt into the water with a pile of selected decoys and helps carry my gear out. By 9:00 (hopefully) I am in the punt, settled in the swivel seat, complete with hip boots and shooting gear. The other "guns" are also in their punts circling around on the creek. At 9:00 sharp, the head keeper rings a large bell outside the Office and off we all go. (This is long after shooting begins in the public gunning areas in the park at the base of Long Point, where shots ring out at first light.)

When I first visited the Point, punts were propelled by poling, which had the advantage of causing little disturbance in the marsh and the disadvantages of being relatively slow and requiring a lot of work. Actually, it was quite remarkable how fast an experienced punter could pole a boat through the marsh. In any event, small "seagull" outboards

The author and Ross Kenline about to head into the marsh. The "Sin Center" is in the background.

were introduced a number of years ago and worked well with the old wooden punts. However, the outboards had a vertical drive which put them at a disadvantage in the very shallow water we frequently encounter. We then procured so-called "go-devils," which have a lengthy drive shaft that sticks out behind the boat, just below the horizontal, and require no more water than the boat itself. They are noisy and cannot be used with the old punts such as the one I have lying retired in our boathouse. We recently experimented with electric motors but have abandoned them as too weak for the often rough conditions and have returned to traditional outboards, although quieter ones, which work fine in relatively high water.

Traveling through the marsh in the early morning is exhilarating, particularly if you are the first away at the starting bell. Big mallards and blacks jump from the reeds nearby as the sound of your motor puts them up. Further off, large flocks of ducks get up and you strain to see to where they move. You are full of eager anticipation. The marsh is beautiful—still green in early season, brown and sere but golden in the sunlight toward the end of the season. The open water is filled with celery and other choice duck food. You finally reach your allotted location—hopefully a large bunch of ducks got up there and will return over the course of the morning. You select the exact spot depending on the wind, put out your decoys, and shove your punt into the reeds, arrange as much cover as you can, and settle down to wait. Depending upon the location, you are generally set up by at least 9:45. The rest is unpredictable. If the ducks are not flying or not decoying, you may move after at least a half-hour at your assigned spot.

Even in the absence of ducks, the marsh is endlessly beautiful. It is like being on the prairie or at sea. The sky is enormous overhead and constantly changing, as are the colors of the marsh and the shadows that move across the reeds and the water. There are great blue herons, gulls and terns, an occasional bittern, marsh hawks wheeling low over the marsh, a distant bald eagle high in the sky, shorebirds on the mud-flats early in the season, curious marsh wrens that approach through the reeds within inches of your punt, and monarch butterflies flutter-ing by on their way to their wintering grounds in Mexico.

A luncheon pail and thermos bag are tucked away in the bow of the punt and, depending on the shooting, one eats in the marsh or returns to the cottages. If the ducks have been few and far between, try put-ting a cup of soup on one knee and a sandwich on the other. A flight of ducks is bound to arrive—and usually depart unscathed—at such a time.

Of course, the punters do most of the work, and one's success in the marsh is largely a product of their skill. In earlier days, the punters could be described as "marsh rats." They were trappers and often poachers by profession and knew the marsh like the backs of their hands. They were colorful characters. As their breed has died out, the punters recruited today are apt to take on the job because of their love of the outdoors and of hunting and as a break from their regular occu-pations. Thus, my punter on most visits today is Ross Kenline, a sub-stantial tobacco farmer in the area who loves to hunt and who finds the time to punt once his tobacco crop has been harvested. Other punters include a retired school principal, a world-class taxidermist, and a boat builder.

Our company rules require us to be back at the cottages no later than 5:00 p.m., which usually necessitates picking up the decoys about 4:00. Thus, we shoot a good deal shorter day than Canadian law permits. Once back at the cottage, it is time for a bath, a change of clothes and a bit of relaxation before the fire. By 6:45, members get together for cocktails at whatever cottage was agreed upon in the morning, there to share accounts (all true, of course) of our exploits or lack thereof.

We are expected to be in the dining room at 7:30. We troop in and take our places and the senior member bangs the bell. The evening's menu is written on a slate at his place, and he reads this aloud to the group. Soup, liberally laced with sherry, is first. Then comes the fish course—sometimes planked whitefish but more often fried perch or other fish caught fresh that day in the marsh. Then the pièce de résistance—a whole roast duck for each person. Each is cooked to order—rare, medium, or well done. The woodstove in the kitchen is stoked up to 750 degrees so that a rare duck is cooked six minutes, a medium nine, and a well-done duck twelve minutes. Several vegetables accompany the ducks, all invariably delicious. White and red wine flow during the meal, served by the junior member present. Finally, the repast closes with dessert and coffee.

Discussion at dinner tends to be lively, and the decibel level is apt to rise toward the end of the meal. With twelve American members and eight Canadians, there is a good deal of political discussion, and almost everyone seems more conservative than the Trains.

On one of my visits to the Point in 1995, I was delighted to be there at the same time as Bob Winthrop and his nephews, Fred, Grant, Rob, and Jonathan, the latter two now members. Bob had been a member since 1945 and was 92. He had slowed down a bit, but he was alert, clear-headed, and still getting his share of the ducks. We had some talk of the Bowdoin-Winthrop connection and, without checking a genealogical table, I would guess that Bob and George Bowdoin were fourth cousins. Bob became managing director of the company in 1940 and filled the role until 1975 when Danny Davison took on that responsibility. The managing director really runs the show on behalf of the members and keeps in regular contact with the head keeper. Both Bob and Danny have done a superb job. Danny's father, Trubee, was Assistant Secretary of the Army for Air in the Hoover administration and a friend of my father's. Sadly, Bob Winthrop died in 1999, and we lost a true friend and a great sportsman.

With dinner over, there is time to call home, stop for a glass of port or just some more talk at another cottage, but early to bed is the routine. So ends another memorable day at Long Point.

While Long Point has always been a male enterprise, Aileen came up with me in the fall of 1994 a few days before the season opened. She had, of course, known of the place for years—first from her father and then from me. We had three nights and two full days together there, traveling the marsh with Ross Kenline, walking the south beach, hiking along Cortright Ridge, picnicking out of our lunch pails with Harry Barrett at the keeper's cabin at Jeremy's, and eating breakfast and dinner in the main dining room. She enjoyed the visit and I think has an understanding of why I love the Point. At least, when she is a "duck widow" in the fall, Aileen will have a good picture of where I am.

At the end of the 1993 season at the Point, Bowdy arranged, entirely unbeknownst to me, to have the well-known waterfowl artist Chet Reneson visit the Point and paint a picture of me there. It was a complete surprise when Bowdy presented it to me some months later. The large watercolor shows Ross Kenline and me putting out our decoys as a flock of canvasback come flighting in. The colors are very evocative of late autumn in the marsh. The painting is a possession I treasure. It hangs at Grace Creek Farm along with Ogden Pleissner's painting of Aileen's father, George, also shooting at the Point.

I have been a member of Long Point for over 30 years now. The Point provides an experience that is unique today in North America. I feel blessed in having had the opportunity to enjoy that experience and also to play a small part in helping preserve the Point for the future. That I have been able to share this with my son, Bowdy, and my son-in-law J.C. on so many occasions has added immeasurably to my enjoyment.

CHAPTER 22

Recollections of Presidents

WHILE MOST of my contacts with presidents are without historical significance and some are quite trivial, any president is a central figure of his time, and I have tried to record here any memories of them which I have not recorded elsewhere. Thus, I have already told the story of staying with my brothers at the White House and breakfasting with President and Mrs. Hoover in 1932. Roosevelt and Truman I never met, but Aileen recalls meeting the latter, which seems likely since her stepfather, Ed Foley, was Under Secretary of the Treasury in the Truman administration.

President Eisenhower

I ALSO NEVER met Eisenhower although he appointed me to the Tax Court and I knew a number of senior members of his administration. Aileen and I were invited to the Eisenhower White House following a dinner honoring the justices of the Supreme Court and including other senior judges of the federal courts. Judges of the Tax Court, the Court of Claims, other specialized federal courts, and, I assume, the district courts were invited to come after the dinner. We all arrived on schedule—about 9:00 p.m.—at the south entrance and spent the next hour milling about in the downstairs rooms, waiting for the dinner to end. Finally, an aide appeared and said: "You may go up now." We walked up and were guided into the south end of the East Room where we found seats. The Eisenhowers and their dinner guests were already seated with their backs to us. At the far end of the room from us on a low stage were 24 women seated at golden harps who played "Rudolph the Red-Nosed Reindeer." It was a high point of

Washington cultural life. The Eisenhowers did not receive us at any point. I suppose such arrangements were par for the course and I recall my grandmother Train writing extremely critically of a similar experience at the (Franklin) Roosevelt White House.

President Kennedy

I HAVE ALREADY mentioned President Kennedy in various contexts. My acquaintance with him was almost nonexistent, although many of our friends were intimates of the Kennedys. There was the time we both paced up and down the waiting room at Idlewild (later JFK) Airport waiting for Aileen and Jackie Bouvier on their return from the coronation of Queen Elizabeth in 1952. While he was still a senator, we met at a large party at Walter and Marie Ridders' and at a small dinner at Rowly and Kay Evans'. At the latter, talking in a small group, Kennedy made a very disparaging remark about the legal profession as a whole. It was not said facetiously and I took exception to the remark.

Aileen and I went to at least one state dinner at the Kennedy White House. I happened to sit at a table with Robert Kennedy, then attorney general. Since it was a small table, I went around to introduce myself to him. My recollection is that he looked at me a moment and then turned to the person next to him without saying anything to me. Manners were not the Kennedys' long suit. Several years after Robert's tragic assassination in Los Angeles, his widow, Ethel, whom I always liked, asked me to arrange an African safari for their eldest son, Joe. I did so, using my network of contacts in East Africa, and the trip was a great success. Ethel was very appreciative and young Joe sent me a thank-you letter.

President Johnson

MY ASSOCIATIONS with Lyndon Johnson were almost entirely with his wife, Lady Bird, a delightful person. That association came about primarily as the result of Laurance Rockefeller co-chairing with her the White House Conference on Natural Beauty. Surprisingly, the first time I met Johnson, he was in his pajamas. This unusual circumstance occurred when there was to be an opening of the film "Born Free" based on Joy Adamson's book of the same name about the lioness Elsa whom we had met along with Joy while on safari near Iseolo in the Northern Frontier District of Kenya.

I had arranged the opening as a benefit for AWLF. Alice Roosevelt Longworth, then well into her eighties, was honorary chairman. She and I drove to the White House in her limousine after she picked me up at the CF/AWLF office building at 1250 Connecticut Avenue. We drove to the southwest gate of the White House per instructions, and the guard tried to get some sort of identification from Mrs. Longworth. He asked for a driver's license, and she replied that she did not drive. He then asked for a credit card, and she said she did not have such a thing. Finally, in exasperation, she said: "Young man, I grew up in this house!" When we finally gained admittance, Mrs. Johnson met us in the Blue Room where a number of publicity shots were made of the three of us inspecting an album of still pictures from the film. Mrs. Johnson then took us upstairs to the family quarters for tea. We sat in the same center hallway where Aileen and I would have an extraordinary meeting with George and Barbara Bush some thirty years later.

As we sat talking over our tea, suddenly down the hall came the president, garbed in his pajamas and wearing slippers. He had been taking his regular afternoon nap on doctor's orders following a heart attack. He greeted Mrs. Longworth warmly, and I was introduced to him by Mrs. Johnson. It seemed odd that he had not bothered to at least put on a bathrobe before greeting someone like Mrs. Longworth. Perhaps it was an admirable naturalness and perhaps it was just plain Johnsonian crudity. He more or less ignored me, which was understandable, and chatted for a few minutes with Mrs. L. Then the president stood up and padded back down the hall to his room, presumably to dress and return to his office.

I have an unclear memory of being in the Blue Room (the central state room of the White House) with Laurance Rockefeller when LBJ

With Lady Bird Johnson
at the LBJ Ranch, 1978

was pointing out the windows looking toward the south at the planes
taking off from National Airport and explaining the steps being taken
to reduce their noise. I met him again more officially when the National
Water Commission presented our report to him in the Cabinet Room.
The meeting was not very substantive and mostly a "photo op."

After Johnson's death, Aileen and I spent a couple of nights at the
LBJ Ranch near Austin, Texas, as the guests of Mrs. Johnson. Barbara
Ward (Lady Jackson)[1] was also there and was to be the principal speaker
at a symposium at the LBJ Library. I was also to be a speaker. The four
of us drove around the ranch and visited the old Johnson homestead. I
remember being impressed by Mrs. Johnson's statement that she slept

1. Barbara Ward was an English economist who focused on resource issues. She co-
authored with Rene Dubos the book *Only One Earth* (W. W. Norton and Company,
New York), which provided much of the intellectual underpinning of the 1972 U.N.
Conference on the Human Environment at Stockholm. She had acted as a principal
advisor at the conference to its chairman, Maurice Strong. She became head of the
International Institute for Environment and Development (IIED) of which I was a
Fellow for a brief period in 1977-1978. Aileen and I spent a delightful couple of days
with her during that time at her home in Sussex.

in each of her guest rooms at least once a year in order to assure herself that they were all in order. I have seen Mrs. Johnson many times since those days, particularly at meetings of Laurance Rockefeller's American Conservation Association and Jackson Hole Preserve, Inc.—sometimes at Jackson Hole, Wyoming, or Woodstock, Vermont. She is a great person.

President Nixon

WHILE I HAD little or no contact with Nixon during the year I spent at Interior, when I became chairman of CEQ at the beginning of 1970, I began to see more of the president, starting with his introduction of my two colleagues on the council and myself to the press, something he rarely did. At the outset, I was invited to Cabinet meetings and would sit along the wall facing across the Cabinet table toward the president, sitting alongside such persons as Henry Kissinger (national security advisor), George Bush (CIA director), and Paul McCracken (chairman of the Council of Economic Advisors). Vice President Spiro Agnew's back was toward us, as he always sat facing the president.

A somewhat chilling episode so far as I was concerned occurred at a Cabinet meeting when the President introduced a new energy "czar"— Bill Simon (later Secretary of the Treasury). The latter sat at the president's immediate right. Nixon emphasized the necessity for his energy boss to have broad authority at a time of severe energy shortages and for the other agency heads to accept that authority. To illustrate his point, Nixon picked up a copy of Albert Speer's *Inside the Third Reich* and read aloud Hitler's directive to Speer as head of the German procurement effort during the war. It seemed an unfortunate choice of an example. Nixon always had a fascination with power, particularly as it was exercised by heads of state. It would not have surprised me if he had had a sneaking admiration for Hitler in that respect. I suspect that his fascination with the exercise of power helped explain, at least in part, how an otherwise intelligent person got himself into the fiasco of Watergate.

I had not attended more than a few Nixon Cabinet meetings when John Whitaker, assistant to John Ehrlichman, called me on very short notice and asked me to make a presentation to the Cabinet explaining the environmental impact statement (EIS) process that had been mandated by the National Environmental Policy Act. I did so with the help of a chart prepared by Whitaker's office. Deciding that it would be helpful to use a real-life example, I looked straight at Mel Laird, Secretary of Defense, and said something to this effect: "Mr. Secretary, the Army is about to conduct a series of tests at Amchitka in Alaska of the Spartan missile carrying a five-megaton nuclear warhead. That program clearly requires an environmental impact analysis." I was wrong in one respect—the tests would be undertaken by the Atomic Energy Commission, whose chairman, Glenn Seaborg, was not at the meeting. I was also wrong in picking a highly controversial example. As it turned out, the president later asserted the right to exempt activities from the EIS process for national security reasons and the courts upheld him. Be that as it may, I can still see Mel Laird's jaw drop as I cited my example.

Shortly after that event, I stopped receiving notices of Cabinet meetings. When that first happened, I called chief of staff Bob Haldeman to see whether a mistake had been made. He said there was no mistake and that I was not being invited anymore on a regular basis.

Despite that setback, I saw Nixon from time to time during the year. Most of these meetings were fairly pro forma. CEQ was required by law to prepare an annual report on the state of the environment, and its presentation to the president was the occasion of an annual meeting of the council with him. These were usually occasions of a certain amount of light banter. Once he said he had just seen the show "Hair" in New York. I said, "That has a lot of nudity in it, doesn't it?" He looked up at me and said, "What's wrong with a little nudity?"

I occasionally saw Nixon in the Oval Office before going off to an international meeting. That was a useful device, as it enabled me to say at the meeting that I had just met with the president and, by implication, that I had his support for whatever position I was taking. Because of the strength and scope of his domestic environmental program,

1972 meeting with Nixon in the Oval Office immediately after my return from the Soviet Union (*Washington Post* photo)

Nixon was widely recognized abroad as an environmental leader—about the only head of government that could be so described. On one occasion, after some international session, I met with Nixon and told him, rather apologetically, how I had "used" him at the meeting to influence a decision. He immediately replied, "That's exactly what you should have done!"

I had few really substantive meetings with Nixon. About twice a year I would have what the White House staff described as a "stroke session" with him. (I was the one being "stroked.") I recall one such meeting with no one else present, which was highly unusual. He sat in a chair to the right of the fireplace and I sat on the end of a sofa to the left. I took the opportunity to try to interest him in land use planning, in part because the U.S. tends to be deficient in that area, but also because I thought he might welcome the departure from discussing the regulation of industrial pollutants.

I described the differences between the English countryside landscape and the strip development and urban sprawl that tends to afflict so much of our own landscape. I did not get much of a reaction to that but he did pick up the overall subject. He said, "You know, when I am playing golf at Key Biscayne with Bebe [Rebozo], there are mangroves growing along the water's edge which obscure the view. We wanted to cut just a few vistas through the mangroves but we were not allowed to. Yet those mangroves aren't good for anything except gooney birds!"

As he said this, his longtime valet, Manuel, entered the room with a fresh cup of coffee for the president. "Isn't that right, Manuel?" said Nixon, looking up at him. "No, Mr. President," said Manuel, "that's not right. You know that when I have my day off down there I go fishing. I know that the fish I catch need those mangroves to grow up in. If you cut down those mangroves, there won't be any more fish." Manuel picked up the empty cup and turned and walked out of the room while Nixon stared at him. From then on, whenever I saw Manuel around the West Wing of the White House, I would ask him whether he had been giving any more ecology lessons to the president.

Nixon never did become a personal proponent of land use planning although he twice submitted to the Congress a proposed National Land Use Policy Act which was drafted by CEQ. I have no doubt that some Republican real estate developers took strong exception to the language in the president's 1971 environmental message to the Congress which supported the need for such legislation. I understood that Nixon said at some point in reference to that language: "Who is the son of a bitch who wrote this stuff for me?"

Aileen sat next to Nixon at one White House dinner, and he launched into a discussion of how to run a big city. He cited New York Mayor John Lindsay—a Republican and our good friend—as an example of how *not* to run a city. He said John was just too open and accommodating and that the transit unions and others just did what they wanted and got away with it. On the other hand, Democratic Mayor Daley of Chicago was his ideal of a big-city mayor. Daley was the boss and everyone knew it. He did not fool around with endless discussions but made decisions and saw to it that these were carried out. Here was another case of Nixon's predilection for a strong-man approach to governing. Literally months later, Aileen met the president again in the receiving line at a White House reception. The moment they shook hands, Nixon said, "That was a very interesting discussion you and I had that night at dinner about Lindsay and Daley!" He proceeded to repeat some of the same points, leaving Aileen flabbergasted at the man's memory.

I recall meeting with Daley once in his office in Chicago to promote several matters of EPA interest. I sat next to him at his desk and just beyond us were four or five of his principal minions, sitting in a row. As I would raise an issue with Daley, he would make up his mind about it and then turn toward one of his subordinates and say, "Joe, take care of that!" And so it went.

Actually, one of the more colorful times I spent with Nixon was just as I became CEQ chairman at the beginning of 1970. I had been in the job about one day, if that, and I flew on Air Force One to Chicago with the president, Haldeman, Erhlichman, and others for a meeting at the Field Museum with five Great Lakes state governors to discuss the environment. The White House had been drafting, while I was still at Interior, a Clean Air Act, which I knew absolutely nothing about. I had not been involved in its development and had not been briefed on it. Nor had anyone told me the agenda at the Field Museum.

So there we were: the president and his staff on one side of the table and the five governors, Laurance Rockefeller as chairman of the Citizens' Advisory Committee on Environmental Quality, and myself facing the president across the large oval table. After a few introductory remarks, the president introduced me as the new head of environmental matters at the White House and then asked me to summarize the new Clean Air Act amendments for the governors. The only problem: I knew nothing about the subject. Thank God for John Ehrlichman. He knew I knew nothing of the matter and stepped in to fill the breach. I survived that but it was not a good moment. When I walked out with the president, I tried to interest him in the Carl Akeley sculptures in niches in the walls but he would have none of it. I explained that Akeley had been with Theodore Roosevelt in East Africa but he still was not interested.

The next morning I helicoptered with Nixon to the town of Hammond, Illinois, where a tertiary sewage treatment plant had been built. We walked into the plant and gathered around the top of a large white tank full of clear water which was the treated effluent from the plant. An employee on the far side of the tank held a long pole with a glass set in the end. He dipped the glass down into the pool and then swung the full glass over to Nixon. He was urged to have a drink but shook his head politely and said, "I am sorry but I never take a drink before lunch."

Traveling back to Chicago on the helicopter, Nixon and I sat knee-to-knee facing each other. Haldeman sat on a bench to one side and Ehrlichman toward the back of the craft. Nixon was quiet, tired, and seemingly dispirited. As he stared glumly down into the back yards of Chicago's slums, he suddenly shook his head and said: "Lyndon Johnson will be remembered for [saving] the redwoods. I will be remembered for sewage treatment plants." I thought to myself later: you should be so lucky!

After Nixon won the 1972 election and I had been CEQ chairman about three years, every presidential appointee was asked to submit his or her resignation. I was in London on official business when Aileen called me to tell me the news report of the resignation directive. I wrote out my resignation at the U.S. Embassy and mailed it to the White House. It was a strange, unpleasant time when no one knew where they stood, whether they were going to be kept on board or not. Obviously, all of us served at the president's pleasure anyway but the process being used was a sort of unattractive exercise in raw power.

At some point in early December, not having heard where I stood and because Aileen and I were going away the next day for about a week, I called John Ehrlichman and said I would like a decision on my status before I went away. He called back the following day to say that I was to stay. It was good to know, but what an odd way to run a railroad!

Somewhat later (Aileen says the date was December 17), we attended a dinner at the White House for members of the administration. I suppose it was meant as a Christmas celebration of sorts. It was anything but joyous. Aileen believes that I was one of the few in the room that knew he was staying on. A woman next to me—whose name I do not now recall—was the wife of a top official in the Justice Department who had only recently accepted the appointment. They had sold their home in the San Francisco area and had moved their six children to Washington. He had no idea what the future held. (His resignation was accepted.) Aileen sat at a table between John Ehrlichman and Secretary of State Bill Rogers. The latter did not know whether he would be continued or not and, in fact, he was replaced by Henry Kissinger. Aileen recalls the hatred between Ehrlichman and Rogers as "palpable."

When I went to EPA in September of 1973, the Arab oil embargo had made the energy/environment equation a sensitive and contentious issue. Energy became the president's top priority and EPA became pretty beleaguered on the issue. The Departments of Energy, Commerce, and Transportation usually opposed the EPA position. At one meeting in the Cabinet Room with the president, it was argued that sulfur oxide emissions standards should be relaxed to permit power plants to shift from oil to coal. I opposed the move as unnecessary and would not agree. Following the meeting, Nixon, without my knowledge, went before the press with his energy "czar" and announced that emission standards would be relaxed and that I had agreed. When I was called later by members of the press, I denied any agreement. We did make some case-by-case, temporary adjustments but never changed the standards.

There was one entertaining (in retrospect) occurrence at that meeting. I had been suffering from sciatica and was subject to sudden, acute pains in my leg. In the middle of the meeting, while Nixon was talking, I was hit by such a pain and involuntarily screamed. General Al Haig, sitting across the table from me, looked at me as if I had lost my mind. The president was pretty startled but finally went on with the discussion.

I am probably biased on the subject but I am quite certain that the environment represented the single most important area of accomplishment of the Nixon administration in the domestic arena. Indeed, its environmental initiatives in the international sphere were also of major importance. Yet Nixon either did not understand this or preferred to ignore it. His book on domestic policy written after he left office never mentions the environment.[2] He never mentions EPA—his creation—in over 1000 pages. He mentions Bill Ruckelshaus and the banning of DDT in one three-line footnote. However, I also have to say that Henry Kissinger, his foreign policy expert, likewise never mentions the environment in his major tomes on foreign policy during the Nixon administration.[3] In almost 3000 pages, the subject is never mentioned, unless I have missed a passing reference. Likewise, Nixon does not refer to the environment in his own later book on foreign policy. It strikes me as nothing less than extraordinary that these two men, at the epicenter of U.S. domestic politics and U.S. involvement in international affairs, each brilliant in his way, appear to have been either totally oblivious or totally uncaring of an issue that swept our own country as well as countries abroad in the 1970s. It is even more extraordinary in that the issue was one in which the United States both at home and abroad took a highly active leadership role.

Lest my own close association with the Nixon administration's environmental record makes my very positive evaluation of that record somewhat suspect, it can be pointed out that Theodore H. White, a close observer of the presidency who became thoroughly disenchanted with Nixon, described environmental policy as one of the two major accomplishments of his administration—the other being the successful invasion of Cambodia.[4] White goes on to declare that, by the summer of 1970,

> a masterful three-part plan for environmental reorganization had been designed—it had a research branch, NOAA, the National Oceanic and Atmospheric Administration, which pa-

2. Nixon, Richard M. *The Memoirs of Richard Nixon.* Grosset & Dunlap, New York (1978).
3. Kissinger, Henry. *White House Years.* Little, Brown and Company, Boston (1979). *Years of Upheaval.* Little, Brown and Company, Boston (1982).
4. White, Theodore H. *Breach of Faith: The Fall of Richard Nixon.* Atheneum Publishers, Readers Digest Press, New York (1975), p. 131.

trolled oceans, seas, sun, air, coastal zones scientifically; a three-man council on Environmental Quality to guide the President personally; and a new tough policing branch, the Environmental Protection Agency. The scheme was already in operation and would shortly make America the world's leader in environmental management.[5]

Later, in writing of Nixon's 1972 election, White said: "He had launched the most advanced environmental program in American history, and both air and water were being rid of filth."[6]

Toward the close of his presidency, Nixon became increasingly crippled by the Watergate mess. This state of affairs had already arisen when I was first nominated for EPA in June 1973. Haldeman and Ehrlichman had already resigned—dumped by Nixon—and Al Haig was chief of staff. With the weakened condition of the White House, I was probably able to get away with setting an independent course to an extent that never would have been possible otherwise. When the *Wall Street Journal* did a front-page story on how Watergate had affected the operation of the executive agencies, I said something to the effect—somewhat facetiously but also with considerable truth—that "it's the best thing that ever happened to EPA!"

President Ford

WITH THE succession of Gerald Ford to the presidency after Nixon's resignation, the energy issue remained critical but the whole atmosphere changed. The White House became more open, relaxed, and less confrontational. Ford's several chiefs of staff—Mel Laird, Donald Rumsfeld, and Dick Cheney—were all people I could work with and with whom I maintained a positive relationship. Bill Seidman on the domestic side became a good friend.

Once Ford was in office, I made an appointment to go and see him.

5. Ibid., p. 139.
6. Ibid., p. 334.

We met without staff and had a good discussion. I recall that there had just been an anniversary celebration at Yellowstone of its creation as the first U.S. national park (and the world's first, for that matter). Ford had planned to speak but at the last moment asked Secretary of the Interior Rogers Morton to present his speech for him.

Rog did so and apparently the speech spoke of the importance of achieving balance between the supposedly competing needs of the environment and the economy. A *New York Times* editorial blasted the speech, particularly the emphasis on "balance" which was interpreted as probably being anti-environment.

Ford was both puzzled and annoyed by the editorial and said: "Russ, don't you believe in balance?" I said: "Yes, Mr. President, I do believe in balance but I am afraid that, when a Republican speaks of 'balance,' it is apt to be understood as a code word for 'tilt toward business.' I suggest that you leave the balancing to me and, when you make a statement on some environmental occasion, you just be four-square for the environment." He listened but I don't recall that he made any comment.

By the time I became head of EPA, Nixon had done away with direct budget appeals to him by agency heads. Ford restored the process. As I recall it, we would meet in the Cabinet Room, just the president, his director of the Office of Management and Budget, Roy Ash until 1975 and then Jim Lynn, and myself. I would usually appeal about three items in the hope I might win one of them.

In 1975, I had a better crack at the proposed budget while it was still in a formative stage. President and Mrs. Ford were at Vail, Colorado, over Christmas and New Year's. I was invited out and put up at a nearby house for a couple of nights. Jim Lynn was there (as Secretary of HUD), as well as Roy Ash and probably about ten others including White House staff. There is no point in taking up in a family memoir the substantive issues discussed.

However, I remember one relaxed conversation involving just the president, Ash, and myself. We were in a study by ourselves and I was sitting on the floor in front of an open fire. Somehow we were on the subject of nature and the outdoors. I got talking about the winter pop-

With President Ford on
Air Force One, Russell
Peterson at left

ulation of Canada geese on the Eastern Shore and how this had fluc-
tuated over time. It quickly became apparent that Ford and Ash were
not outdoor people at all. Ford had played football, golfed and skied
but neither he nor Ash had ever hiked, fished, hunted, camped, sailed,
bird-watched, gardened, or done any other of the myriad activities
that take one into the out-of-doors. The same had been true of Nixon.
I am quite sure that people's lack of such an exposure makes it more
difficult to interest them in environmental matters. Of course, outdoor
experience does not guarantee that an individual will be environmentally sensitive but it definitely helps.

I traveled with Ford on Air Force One on at least one occasion
when we went to Cincinnati for the dedication of a new EPA water-
quality laboratory. I have a photo in my office of several of us convers-
ing with Ford in his cabin on the plane; we are all in shirtsleeves but I
am the only one wearing suspenders. Ford instituted so-called "town
meetings" around the country when he and several Cabinet officers and
agency heads would speak and answer questions. I took part in a number of them. It was a good idea although time-consuming.

As I have said, my relations with the Ford White House were generally good. I was in Kansas City, Missouri, staying at the old Muehlbach Hotel while on a visit to the EPA regional headquarters there. I had been placed for the night in the hotel's presidential suite where Harry Truman used to stay. There was a piano in the suite, which Truman used to play, and in the corner of the living room was the desk on which he had signed the Marshall Plan into law. That evening, sitting at the desk, I took a call from Melvin Laird, then Ford's chief of staff. He explained that the regulations that EPA was about to promulgate which dealt with reducing the lead content of gasoline were receiving a lot of opposition from the petroleum industry. I said we had taken all of their comments into account. He asked me whether I felt the regulations were reasonable. When I told him that I did, he replied, "Russ, that's all I need to know."

On another occasion, potentially unpleasant, EPA's regional administrator in Dallas had resigned and I had made a choice of a highly qualified professional to succeed him. I received a call from Donald Rumsfeld, Laird's successor as chief of staff. He said that Senator John Tower of Texas (Republican) had notified the White House that he wanted me to appoint someone else, a member of EPA's Dallas staff whom I knew but whose name I do not now recall.

I said to Rumsfeld that the individual in question was totally unqualified, which he was, and, what was more, was a Democrat. Rumsfeld said that Tower was very important to the president and was to be his floor manager at the next Republican national convention (1976). I said I certainly would not want to hurt the president in any way but that supporting the man Tower wanted would be an embarrassment to me, EPA, and the president. When Rumsfeld pushed a bit more, I said that if the president really wanted me to appoint the guy, I would do so and resign. The president could not have both of us. Rumsfeld (or "Rummy," as he was often called) said, "Russ, forget it but you make your peace with Tower."

So I went to see Tower in his Senate "hideaway" office. A member of his staff sat in the background making notes. Tower told me he wanted me to appoint his guy and made clear that he (Tower) was in a position to make life difficult for the president at the convention. I in return made clear that I was not going to appoint his man because he was totally unqualified. The meeting ended in a standoff, with Tower angry and unpleasant. A few days later, I called him and said I was ready to appoint a third individual—neither his choice nor mine—and he accepted that. Thus, we both saved face. However, my fall-back choice was also eminently qualified so I was quite happy with the result. It was one of the few incidents of that kind I had in all my years in government.

The Clean Air Act had given rise to a rule—not expressed in the act but the result of court decision—called "no-significant deterioration." This rule meant in practice that in an area where the ambient air quality was already higher (or cleaner) than the standards required by law, the state could not permit new industrial development that would lead to significant deterioration of air quality even if the latter was still within legal limits.

The purpose of the rule was to protect so-called "pristine" areas, particularly in the West. While the overall objective was desirable, the rule was highly contentious in practice. In any event, probably in 1975 or thereabouts, the White House Office of Legislative Affairs without any consultation with me collaborated with some Western senators on the introduction of legislation effectively killing the no-significant deterioration rule. Not only did they not consult with me, they failed to consult with the Republican minority side of the Senate Public Works Committee (now the Committee on Environment and Public Works), which had jurisdiction over the matter. I called Howard Baker, the ranking minority member of the committee, and he was outraged. He said, "Russ, leave this to me!"

A few days later, all five minority members of the committee (Senators Baker, Domenici, McClure, Buckley, and one other I cannot recall) came to the White House and met with the president. I was in the meeting, as was the head of the White House congressional staff. The senators sat on the president's side of the table and I across from them. Actually, led by Baker, they did most of the talking and told the president in no uncertain terms that the kind of legislative maneuvering by the White House that had gone on behind my back and behind the committee's back was intolerable and unacceptable. There was no indication whether the president had been privy to the whole affair or not and no one asked. However, he stated that it would not happen again and that the White House would not support the bill in question.

I said very little as I recall except to answer a question or two. The senators were careful to protect my relationship with the White House and made clear that it was they, not me, who were complaining. Nor did they reveal that I had blown the whistle on the White House. The whole affair illustrates the good relations I was able to establish and maintain on the Hill and how important those relations were in building and protecting our environmental program.

Aileen and I were not invited to the White House during the Ford administration until the very end. During my visit to Vail on budget business in 1975 described above, I had found myself one evening seated next to Betty Ford at dinner. Jim Lynn, then HUD Secretary, was at the same table and said to her how much he appreciated the frequency with which Cabinet members and their wives were invited to state dinners. I could not help but add my two cents—"but don't forget the heads of independent agencies such as EPA who never get invited at all!" We finally were invited to a farewell dinner at the White House given for members of his administration just before Ford left office. As we left the dining room that evening and said good night to the president, he was most friendly and expressed regret that he had seen so little of us. The remark was genuinely meant and he certainly paid little or no attention to official guest lists, for which I do not blame him. The trouble was that no one else did either.

In January 1998, while attending an AES Corporation board meeting in Palm Springs, California, with Aileen, I paid a call on former President Ford at his home in Rancho Mirage, a fairly posh community next to Palm Springs. He and Betty Ford have lived there since leaving government in 1977, spending five months a year at a home in Vail.

We met in his office, part of a quite large, one-story office complex just inside the gate to the compound in which he lives. He said he would be 85 that year but looked little changed from when he left

Washington. He sat behind his desk, and we talked for about half an hour. He asked me what I had been doing and I told him of my involvement with WWF ever since I had left government. Characteristically, he expressed no interest in WWF or in environmental matters generally. We talked about the sex scandal rocking the Clinton White House at that time. He said that he, Carter, and Bush should keep their mouths shut publicly on the subject. I told him I had just heard former Senator Alan Simpson say on television that Clinton suffered from an addiction, just like an addiction to alcohol or drugs. Ford agreed completely and added that "he is sick." Ford also expressed the view that it is a compulsion that is impossible to cure.

We also talked about the state of the Republican Party. He had given an extensive interview to the *New York Times* the week before in which he had said that the GOP would never recapture the White House unless it stopped espousing extreme views on matters such as abortion. I certainly agreed. We talked about possible Republican presidential candidates. He said he hoped the party would not go for some "warmed-over has-been" like Dan Quayle. I asked him what he thought of young George W. Bush, then governor of Texas. He said very positive things about George. I saw the latter two nights later at the Alfalfa Club dinner in Washington and mentioned Jerry Ford's friendly remarks. The senior Bushes were also there and we had a chance to talk briefly as well. Young George was the Alfalfa presidential candidate that evening and was very entertaining. Toward the close of his remarks, his mother, Barbara, went to the mike across the room from him and began to attack him for being ungrateful. Then father George appeared on the steps and joined in the fun. It was a family act that they had carefully rehearsed earlier that day, I later discovered.

With Ford, I took the occasion to ask him about his choice of Bob Dole as his running mate at the 1976 GOP convention at Kansas City. I had understood that Bill Ruckelshaus had been his choice but that Bryce Harlow, representing the conservative Reagan forces, had told Ford the night before the vote that the nomination of Ruckelshaus would precipitate a floor fight at the convention and that, as a result, Ford had accepted Dole.

When I told Ford all this, he said that was not entirely right. He said that the Democrats were expected to carry the South and that it was essential that he carry the farm states between the Mississippi and the Rockies. He said there were three candidates—Ruckelshaus, Dole, and one other he did not name—and that the choice fell to Dole, as he was believed to provide the best chance of carrying those farm states.

"And we did," he said, "with the exception of Minnesota which went with Mondale [Carter's running mate] and Texas which we lost by just a few votes." I replied that the election had been extremely close and that I had always felt that Ford would have won with Ruckelshaus, who would have been a very attractive candidate. I said it seemed likely to me that he would have won the farm states in any event. "Perhaps," said Ford. He went on to say that he had no criticism of Dole's performance, that he had done a fine job.

When I described this dialogue to Bill Ruckelshaus, he generally confirmed my original understanding of the matter. He said that Senator John Tower had been with Harlow in the discussion of the vice presidency with Ford. Bill also told me that Bob Teeter, a Republican pollster and longtime friend of his, had been present at all the discussions and had been the one who called Bill at his motel to tell him that he was to be the vice presidential nominee. It was also Teeter who called him again three hours later to say that it was going to be Dole..

A question I did not ask Ford involved my own non-participation in the 1976 GOP convention. In 1972, preceding Nixon's second term, Aileen and I had attended the convention in Miami, staying at the Doral Beach Hotel with all the principal party figures. We attended all the events, and I discussed Nixon's environmental record before at least one group of delegates. I recall that we rode to the convention hall itself with George Bush in his limousine. Afterwards, Nixon wrote thanking me for my participation.

In any event, as the 1976 convention approached and I had heard nothing of any involvement by me in the proceedings, I called Martin Anderson, the White House staffer making all the arrangements. I told him I had heard nothing and wanted to know what plans I should make for attendance. "Russ," he said, "you are not being invited." I never pursued the matter any further. I could only assume that in their concern over conservative opposition at the convention, the Ford people did not want to be identified with an environmentalist.

The story illustrates the continuing ambivalence of the Republican Party toward environmental issues. The actual environmental record of the Nixon administration was on the whole outstanding. The White House was sensitive to the groundswell of public support for environmental protection during the early Nixon years. While he had no real interest in the issue from a substantive standpoint, Nixon was willing that we preempt the issue and prevent the Democrats and particularly Senator Ed Muskie, a potential presidential candidate, from making it *their* issue.

That effort sometimes led to somewhat ludicrous situations, such as when Muskie was not included among the members of Congress invited to the White House for Nixon's ceremonial signing of major clean air legislation in 1971. Muskie had long been identified with such legislation and had in this case been the principal Democratic voice in the Senate helping to guide the legislation. When I was asked by the White House press at a briefing after the signing ceremony whether the exclusion of Muskie was not unusual, I had to agree that it was.

In the Ford White House, there was even less interest in the environment. However, the White House staff were not idealogues and were a moderate, middle-of-the-road group like their leader. In most cases, they avoided confrontation and accepted my decision on environmental issues. I have already described one instance when the White House congressional staff tried an end run around me. A somewhat similar case arose when Roy Ash, director of OMB, developed a proposal to take the auto vehicle fuel economy testing responsibility away from EPA and give it to the Department of Commerce, which presumably could be relied on to be more sympathetic to the auto industry. I learned of this development through the staff grapevine and was appropriately outraged, especially since Ash had made no effort to discuss the matter with me. Although not a route I would normally take, I saw to it that the story was leaked to a sympathetic reporter. The story was widely covered, and I never heard another word from OMB. The proposal simply died.

OMB had become a major force, and often an obstacle, in the

review and promulgation of regulations which EPA was required by law to issue. On one occasion—and I cannot recall the issue—we had proposed regulations and received public comment and had then revised the "regs" in the light of the public comments (and also those of other agencies). Before publishing them as final, they went to OMB for review as required by presidential order.

In this particular case, literally months went by without action by OMB. No amount of pleading on our part could dislodge the regs. Finally, in desperation and in defense of the credibility of EPA before Congress and the public, I addressed a memorandum to President Ford setting out the history of the matter and stating that I had no alternative but to say that, unless I received a direct order from the president to the contrary within 48 hours, it was my intention to issue the regs as final.

I heard nothing from the White House during that period and we did go ahead and publish the regs in final form. Jim Lynn, who was OMB director at the time, told me that it had been outrageous of me to "hold a pistol to the president's head" in that fashion. I never saw it that way. If anyone had been acting outrageously, it was OMB. I never heard from anyone else on the matter.

I played no role at all in Ford's reelection campaign. That had also been true in the Nixon campaign, and it suited me fine. As the head of an agency with major regulatory responsibilities, I always found it preferable that I not become actively and visibly engaged in partisan politics. However, my non-participation was not a matter of my refusing to help. I was simply never asked. Later, during the Bush administration, EPA head Bill Reilly made campaign speeches and appearances for both congressional candidates and Bush. During Nixon's reelection campaign in 1972, Aileen joined a committee of wives of Cabinet members, headed by "Obie" Shultz, to campaign for the president. She recalls going to Kansas City, Missouri, on that mission with two other wives and also appearing on television.

President Carter

I HAD VERY little contact with Jimmy Carter and, of course, I had left the government with his inauguration in January 1977. I had met him for the first time a year or two before that when I was in Mobile, Alabama, for a meeting of the Southern Governors' Conference. The governors were meeting around a horseshoe table and several members of the Ford administration appeared before them individually, including myself. I spent an hour or so sitting at a table in the open end of the horseshoe, mostly responding to attacks on EPA by conservative governors of both parties. Seldom did anyone have a kind word in this sort of session.

Carter, then governor of Georgia, was not present when I spoke but as I left the room I met him arriving. We stopped and shook hands and then he suggested we sit down and talk just outside the meeting room. We spent at least a half-hour talking about environmental issues and he displayed a strong interest. When I suggested that perhaps he ought to join the other governors, he brushed off the suggestion and said our conversation was more important. How could I not fail to like Jimmy Carter after that?!

I recall another occasion in Washington when I was invited to attend a meeting at the White House of representatives of the coal and railroad industries, mostly the former, who filled the East Room. I did not have a speaking role nor was I asked to respond. I simply sat and listened and made occasional notes while one speaker after another vilified EPA and the entire environmental movement. Finally, Arch Moore, Republican governor of West Virginia, got up and called attention to the fact that I had sat there listening to all the attacks on EPA and said that he thought the audience should be grateful to me for my patience and courtesy in listening to their complaints. I got a round of polite applause. (Arch later went to jail for misconduct in office.)

Later, after Carter had become president and I had left EPA, I became a member of the National Commission on Coal Policy, spon-

sored by the National Academy of Sciences and chaired by Carroll
Wilson of M.I.T. I was not much of an expert on coal but sought to
ensure that the work of the commission paid adequate attention to
environmental factors. It was evident that coal was the world's cheap-
est and most abundant energy source and I became satisfied that the
technology existed to permit in most cases the utilization of coal in
environmentally responsible ways. (This premise fit well into my later
association with the Mellon Institute Energy Productivity Council, a
nonprofit which evolved into the AES Corporation.)

I testified before at least one congressional committee on the commission's findings. It is somewhat startling today when global *warming* is an increasingly important international concern to find in my
testimony a cautionary statement about the possibility of global *cool-
ing*. When Carroll Wilson presented the commission's report to President Carter at a brief meeting in the Oval Office, he asked me to
accompany him. Wilson handed a copy of the report to the president
and gave a brief summary of its findings. I was somewhat dumb-
founded when Carter turned to me and said, more or less, "Russ, is this
report all right?" I replied that it was. He then said, "Then it's okay by
me!" That was the only time I was to see Carter during his administration. His choice of Doug Costle to head EPA was an excellent one and
Doug did a fine job. However, despite Carter's sympathy for environmental programs, his administration was not remarkable for its environmental achievements.

After he left office, Carter established the Jimmy Carter Center at
Emory University in Atlanta to promote dialogue on policy issues,
including the environment. One day, while I was at my desk at WWF,
my secretary, Catherine Williams, said to me, "President Carter is on
the phone." I found myself standing up to take the call. He told me of
the Jimmy Carter Center and said he would like me to serve on its
advisory board. I had been suggested to him by Gus Speth, who had
been chairman of CEQ during the Carter administration and who
was then actively engaged in promoting the establishment of what
became the World Resources Institute, an independent, private sector,
environmental "think tank."

I had tried to initiate something of the sort during the Nixon administration when I was at CEQ. The idea then had been a free-standing institute jointly funded by the government and private foundations. McGeorge Bundy, then president of the Ford Foundation, supported the idea and was helping put together a consortium of foundations to fund the private share. George Shultz, then OMB director and later Secretary of State in the Reagan administration, was interested, as he saw such an institute bringing a much-needed economic dimension to the analysis of environmental problems. However, the whole project finally collapsed when the White House vetoed our tentative selection of a director of the institute, Alain Enthoven, and effectively withdrew its support of the project.

With that background, I was glad to help Speth develop and promote his concept of an environmental institute and was a member of an informal committee, which included Robert McNamara, to think it through and help secure its funding. The latter eventually came from the MacArthur Foundation. I served for several years as a director of the World Resources Institute (WRI) but never became closely engaged in its work. Under Speth's direction, it became a well-respected institution and produced a number of excellent studies. (When Gus left WRI, he became head of the United Nations Development Programme [UNDP] and subsequently dean of the Yale School of Forestry and Conservation. Jonathan Lash succeeded him as head of WRI.)

When Carter asked me to join his center's board of advisors, the Reagan administration's environmental record was coming under attack. With key environmental appointments perceived to be antagonistic toward environmental programs—primarily James Watt as Secretary of the Interior and Anne Gorsuch as administrator of EPA—the environment was rapidly becoming a hot political issue. I told Carter that, as president of WWF, I felt it important that I not get involved in a partisan political situation. He assured me that the Jimmy Carter Center would be nonpartisan and then said: "Russ, will it help if I tell you that Jerry Ford and Howard Baker have already agreed to be members of the advisory board?" I said, "Yes, it helps very much and I am delighted to accept!"

I went to two meetings at the center. The first was in March 1984 and was called a "leadership retreat." I knew most of the group: Gerard Smith (disarmament negotiator and longtime friend from Washington and the Eastern Shore), Frank Press (president, National Academy of Sciences), Lloyd Cutler (distinguished Washington attorney), Patricia Harris (former Secretary of HEW, whom I did not know), Irving Shapiro (retired CEO of Du Pont), and Jim Schlesinger (former director of CIA, Secretary of Defense, Secretary of Energy). Senator Howard Baker was joining us the following day.

We met on arrival at the Woodruff Library at Emory for drinks and dinner. A sign down the hall read, "Office of Professor Jimmy Carter." Carter said he was "honored" to have me there. After dinner, he talked about his aspirations for the center, where major world issues could be studied in a bipartisan fashion. "I have had extraordinary experience as president," he said, "and I have access to just about any leader in the world." There were several questions and then we adjourned for the evening.

In the morning, we were picked up at our hotel and driven to the home of Emory President Laney where we were to have breakfast and meet. As luck had it, while the others shared a van, I ended up in a car with the former president and Mrs. Carter. The three of us sat in the back, with the driver and a Secret Service agent in front. Carter immediately asked me about the World Wildlife Fund. I described some of our projects, including protecting the wintering grounds of the monarch butterfly in Mexico. We talked about Mexico more generally, and he asked me about population problems. We talked about the fact that Mexico City then had 18 million living there.

At breakfast, I sat between Carter and Schlesinger. Bert Lance had also joined us. Somewhat tongue in cheek, Schlesinger, a dedicated birder, asked me what I was doing to save the Blackburnian warbler in its winter habitat in Colombia! So I gave a short discourse on the WWF migratory bird program, including a recent trip to Yucatán that involved a migratory bird project we were funding. The conversation moved on to Watergate. Jim had been at the CIA at the time and said that at the beginning he could not conceive that Nixon had had any pre-knowledge of the affair. His assumption had been that it was an

Ehrlichman/Haldeman operation. He said that he had always felt that having so many Christian Scientists in the White House had contributed to the problem. "Christian Scientists don't believe evil exists if you don't accept it." Thus, there was no wrong done in Watergate unless you thought it was wrong. He said that Haldeman never did understand what was wrong in what they did. Carter made no comment on all this.

The conversation was wide-ranging, including the story of how a young Mormon yeoman at the White House allegedly removed and photographed documents from Henry Kissinger's briefcase and wastebasket and delivered the copies to Admiral Tom Moorer, chairman of the Joint Chiefs of Staff. This led Lloyd Cutler to tell the following story. He recalled that at one time Mormons were often refused public office. Senator Smoot (of Smoot-Hawley Tariff Act fame) had had trouble being seated in the Senate when he was elected from Utah. He was attacked for his belief in polygamy. Senator Reed of Pennsylvania ("Puddling Jim") rose to his defense more or less as follows: "Senator Smoot may believe in polygamy but the fact is he has only one wife and has never had more than one wife. We should be willing to accept into the Senate a man who believes in polygamy but who doesn't 'polyg' just as we accept members who believe in monogamy but who don't 'monog'!" Smoot was admitted.

Prior to the meeting at Emory I had had what I felt was an interesting idea concerning U.S.-Soviet relations. These were far from good and Reagan had made his "evil empire" speech citing eight alleged violations by the Soviets of arms agreements. (Carter said he did not accept most of the violations cited by Reagan.) The U.S.-U.S.S.R. environmental agreement was still on the books but pretty moribund. Détente was all but dead. My idea was to go to the Soviet Union as a private citizen, perhaps wearing a WWF hat, renew old acquaintances, and try to reactivate a dialogue on environmental matters. Such a dialogue would be nonthreatening to both sides, yet of mutual concern, and just might blow new life into détente.

During a break in the meeting at Emory, I tried the idea out on both Schlesinger and Frank Press, who thought it was worth pursuing.

Back in Washington, I called Jack Matlock on the staff of the National Security Council. I had met him in Moscow where he had been chief political officer in our embassy. He listened to me and said he would talk to others about it and get back to me. He never did. Later he became our ambassador in Moscow. The whole idea was probably pretty naive, and I guess it had no place in the cold-war thinking of the Reagan administration. I certainly had no interest in pursuing a political objective in the Soviet Union that was not supported by our own government.

At the meeting I brought up the matter of conflict resolution which Carter had discussed the evening before as one of the areas of interest of the center. I said I thought there was a real opportunity for identifying new or emerging issues and for bringing together different groups with opposing interests in those issues in order to explore possible common ground. I spoke of the need to find "convergences" and cited Latin America as a fruitful area for such an effort. I said that the pressure of population growth on the natural resource base was having a direct impact on political stability in many areas (for example, in Haiti). I told Carter that I thought Latin America not only was of great importance to the U.S. but that it presented many opportunities for positive action on our part, while I seriously doubted that we would ever solve the Mideast problems. I do not think Carter was too happy with this last opinion, as he rather featured his Mideast experience and potential role as peacemaker there.

Carter told me that the center was having a meeting in about six months to bring together environmentalists and businessmen and invited me to come. I did attend the meeting in September 1984 but have very little recollection of it. Several presentations were made followed by discussion. One very vocal commentator was Ted Turner. That was the last time I went to the Jimmy Carter Center. I was invited on two subsequent occasions involving non-environmental issues but schedule conflicts prevented my attending.

As I have already indicated, I liked Carter as a person. He was always warm and friendly on the few occasions that we met. He was articulate in private conversation. Most of all, he was interested in the environment and took the trouble to draw me out on the subject. He was not a great president, a judgment evidently shared by many others, as borne out by the results of his 1980 campaign against Reagan. Since leaving office, he has led an exemplary life. He and Rosalynn live simply. He has gone on no business boards and has not made a career out of speaking for fees. He has undertaken a variety of rather thankless international missions, such as monitoring elections. In the U.S., he has devoted a substantial amount of his time to volunteer charity work for organizations such as Habitat for Humanity. He is a very decent human being and sets a fine model for his countrymen.

President Reagan

I HAD EVEN less contact with President Reagan than I had with Jimmy Carter. Of course, I had been out of government for four years when he became president. I met him for the first time in his office in Sacramento while he was governor of California. It was familiar ground, as I had met there with Jerry Brown when he was the Democratic governor. On that occasion, Brown had come out of his office to greet me in a large anteroom where I was waiting by myself. He sat down there and we proceeded to talk for a couple of hours. An assistant came in to remind Brown that he was late for a cabinet meeting of his agency heads, and he simply waved her off. I missed a plane and an appointment in San Francisco. I recall nothing of the conversation and, frankly, doubt that it raised any matters of great moment. I recall feeling somewhat trapped and unable simply to get up and end the session. Brown, I think, was anxious to establish his environmental credentials.

The meeting with Reagan was quite different. We really did not talk much substance, if any. It was primarily a courtesy call so far as I was concerned. What I remember most clearly is that as soon as Reagan and I were seated, a photographer came in and Reagan asked that he and I change places, as he preferred his left profile to his right.

Two nights before his inauguration, Reagan was the guest of honor at a dinner at the Renwick Gallery at the corner of Pennsylvania Avenue and 17th Street, N.W., given by Time-Life. When I met the president-elect at the reception before dinner, he showed no sign of recognition. Aileen sat on his right and on her right was Henry Gruenwald, chairman of Time-Life. It was an extraordinary seat. Gruenwald said to Aileen that Nancy Reagan was very interested in drug treatment programs and suggested that she talk to Reagan about Second Genesis. She did so and found little interest. Reagan leaned past her and started talking to Gruenwald about his old movies, which Aileen recalls was the principal subject discussed during dinner. At one point, Gruenwald asked Reagan whether he felt nervous about taking on the presidency and Reagan promptly replied, "No, not at all!"

I had few contacts with the White House over the next eight years. With Jim Watt as Secretary of the Interior and Anne Gorsuch at EPA, the Reagan administration's environmental credentials were just about zero. After the first Reagan budget was submitted, I wrote an op-ed article for the *Washington Post* detailing how proposed budget cuts would cripple EPA. The *Post* entitled the piece "The End of EPA." It got quite a lot of attention—including from Gorsuch, who called me up. It was our first contact. She said that my analysis was unfair and that perhaps she should have gotten together with me earlier. I said I would be glad to see her if she wished and that is what we did in due course. We had a half-hour meeting alone in my old office, and she described and defended what she was doing at EPA. None of her explanation altered my perception that the ability of EPA to carry out its statutory mission was being significantly prejudiced.

The next time I saw her was in Nairobi where she was co-chairing the U.S. delegation to the international meeting marking the tenth anniversary of the 1972 U.N. Conference on the Human Environment held at Stockholm where I had led the U.S. delegation. I was a member of her delegation but understood she had said concerning me (or words to this effect): "I don't want to sit next to that old man!" I would then have been 62!

Fortunately, the White House came to realize that the administration's anti-environment image was hurting the president politically, and Gorsuch was replaced by Bill Ruckelshaus, who returned to EPA for a second tour. He restored the agency's credibility and morale and then left in January 1985, just before Reagan's second inaugural. Lee Thomas replaced him and did a fine job.

In July 1984, the White House scheduled a luncheon meeting between President Reagan and the heads of a few selected environmental organizations.[7] I do not believe there was any particular agenda other than to have Reagan be able to say that he had met with a group of environmentalists. For reasons known best to the administration, the White House had announced that morning the appointment of Anne Gorsuch, late of EPA, as chairman of an air quality advisory commission at the Department of Commerce. It was pretty much a non-job but the environmental community took it as a kick in the teeth and went up in smoke. Jay Hair of the National Wildlife Federation announced that he would not attend the luncheon that day. He eventually did—about a half-hour late—after attacking the Gorsuch appointment at an impromptu press conference on the lawn of the White House.

At the lunch, Reagan was his usual affable self and told several stories. I was worried that the occasion would pass by without the environmentalists having an opportunity to address their concerns. Therefore, at an appropriate point, from my seat next to him, I broke in on the president. I thanked him for inviting us to meet with him and then said: "Mr. President, I am sure you have a very busy schedule this afternoon, and I know that several of your guests have matters that they would like to bring to your attention." He seemed somewhat startled and looked at me as much as to say, "What do you know about my schedule that I don't?" In any event, everyone had a chance to say their bit and the meeting ended. It was pretty much a non-event. It was the only time in the eight years of his presidency that I had any contact with Reagan.

7. Bill Reilly of The Conservation Foundation; Jay Hair of the National Wildlife Federation; Paul Pritchard of the National Parks and Conservation Association; Jack Lorenz of the Izaak Walton League; and myself (WWF). Bill Ruckelshaus of EPA; Jim Baker, the president's chief of staff; and Ed Meese, the attorney general, were also there.

When WWF launched a "Pennies for Pandas" campaign among schoolchildren, partly as a fund-raiser but primarily as a conservation education vehicle, I went to the White House and drove to the National Zoo with Nancy Reagan to visit the pandas there and meet with a group of schoolchildren. She was a good sport about it and did a good job with the youngsters, but I found making conversation in the car was an uphill struggle.

President Bush

I FIRST KNEW George Bush when he came to Washington as a member of Congress in 1967. Aileen and Barbara became good friends and met frequently on the tennis court. When Bush became president, Aileen often played on the White House court until some health problems interfered with Barbara's playing. In 1970, when Bush ran for the Senate against Lloyd Bentsen—and lost—I had gone to Houston to make a campaign appearance on Bush's behalf, about the only time I recall doing so for any candidate. (Ironically, the Bentsens became close friends and "B.A." and Aileen had a tennis game together every Tuesday for 22 years, only stopping when Lloyd left government and the Bentsens returned to Houston.)

When Bush was U.S. ambassador to the United Nations in 1971-1973, Aileen and I stayed with them at their official residence in the Waldorf Towers and attended a diplomatic reception there. Since I was EPA administrator at the time, I assume there was some meeting at the U.N. that I was attending. Later, Aileen and I, together with Bowdy and Errol, visited the Bushes in Beijing in 1975. When Bush ran for the Republican nomination for the presidency in 1980, I was an early and enthusiastic supporter. When he visited Hobe Sound in April of that year, he asked me to talk to him about the environment, which I did. However, when I was approached to be his finance chairman in the District of Columbia, I demurred, in large part because I had no experience with that kind of effort. I was an alternate delegate for Bush at the convention but, of course, Reagan was the winner and Bush was nominated as his running mate.

I played no part in the Reagan-Bush campaign. One week before the 1981 inaugural, we gave a dinner at our Kalorama Square house for the Bushes. It was a fun evening with lots of old friends and music provided by Howard Devron for a bit of dancing. Somehow we squeezed 32 of us into the dining room and still had room—barely—to dance in the center.

The Bushes were always helpful to me in the ensuing years of the vice presidency. They entertained our WWF-U.S. board at their house, and they gave a big bash when WWF-International came to Washington for its annual meeting with all the national organizations. It was then that we got to know Harry Hambleden (more formally Viscount Hambleden) who was accompanying Prince Philip. He and his wife, Leslie, have since become good friends. After the Bush reception and "picnic" at the vice presidential mansion, I drove with Harry back to his hotel. He said he was going to the country to spend the weekend with unnamed friends. That weekend, while we were at the farm, the international meeting having concluded, the telephone rang and our near neighbor and close friend Peter Blond said, "We have someone staying with us for the weekend who says he knows you." It was Harry.

As vice president, Bush was given the task of reviewing and, hopefully, simplifying or eliminating some of the vast array of government regulations. Not unexpectedly, the process targeted EPA regulations for particular scrutiny. I had always looked with a pretty jaundiced eye at the various efforts to superimpose a presidential-level review on the promulgation of agency regulations.

The Nixon administration, for example, had instituted a "Quality of Life Review." All too often, that sort of review seemed designed to give affected private interests another crack at proposed regulations outside the normal regulatory procedures which were carefully designed to provide public hearing, comment, and an open process. An executive office review was a chance for special interests to gain through political clout what they had failed to get in the normal process.

I have described earlier my problems as EPA administrator with OMB review when the effort was made not to achieve modification of the proposed regulations but, in effect, to quash them by simple inaction. At the same time, having said all that, there is no question there are cases of regulatory abuse or excess which should be corrected. I felt strongly that the agency itself needed to make the corrections and that Congress, which had given the regulatory authority in the first instance, should monitor performance. The president, of course, retains the ultimate authority of dismissing the agency head if he disapproves of his or her performance.

In any event, I was invited one day to the vice president's office, in the Old Executive Office Building (EOB) across from the West Wing of the White House, to join a small group of environmental organization heads to be briefed by the vice president on the progress of his regulatory review effort. We sat at a small table with Bush at one end, myself at his left, and about four other organization heads, including Bill Reilly of The Conservation Foundation. Boyden Gray, the vice president's counsel, and a couple of OMB staffers sat off to one side. Bush made a short statement explaining what his office was trying to do and laying out some of the actions already taken. When he was through, he turned to me and said something like: "Russ, what do you think of that?" I said, "Mr. Vice President, if that process was applied to me as an agency head, I would resign!"

In early 1988, as Reagan entered his last year in office, Bush geared up his own presidential campaign. I was then chairman of WWF and felt comfortable agreeing to co-chair an Environmentalists for Bush Committee with Bill Ruckelshaus. He and I met with Bush in his EOB office, along with other close supporters such as pollster Bob Teeter, to discuss strategy. I had drafted a proposed speech for Bush designed to put him out front on the environmental issue. The draft committed him to the submission of Clean Air Act legislation by the White House, to the objective of no net loss of wetlands, and to a strengthening of the Superfund law to achieve the cleanup of toxic waste dumps. During the campaign, I flew with Bush to Michigan and heard him deliver an edited but quite acceptable version of the speech I had drafted. On the plane on the way out, he had asked me to explain the "ozone layer" problem, which I did fairly inexpertly.

As co-chairman of the Environmentalists for Bush Committee, I made one "surrogate" appearance that I recall in Ohio but otherwise had no role in the campaign beyond what I have described. Of course, when Bush selected Bill Reilly as his EPA administrator, I felt very positive about the direction in which Bush was moving insofar as the environment was concerned. At the same time, however, he named Manuel Lujan of New Mexico as Secretary of Interior, an extremely conservative choice, and made the same sort of appointments at Agriculture, particularly with respect to the Forest Service.

Lujan had been the most junior Republican on the House Interior Committee when I had testified there frequently as Under Secretary of Interior and CEQ chairman. He was always friendly to me when he was Secretary but he was a man of fairly limited scope. Bush went to Reilly's swearing-in, and Bill asked me to be there and act as sort of a master of ceremonies. I did so and did my best to warm up the crowd as we waited for the president. Meeting in the run-down old EPA building on Maine Avenue, I got a roar of approval when I asked: "Don't you think it is time that EPA got a new building?" Bush heard this as he walked in and appeared a bit startled.

The Under Secretary of Interior was Frank Bracken from Indianapolis. He had been legislative counsel at Interior when I was Under Secretary and essentially reported to me since the Secretary had made me responsible for legislation. Frank and his wife, Judy, although much younger, became good friends, as they did of the Bushes who lived near them on Palisades Lane. Frank was a moderate and believed in protecting the environment. At Interior during the Bush administration, he was for all practical purposes frozen out of decision-making by Lujan and his arch-conservative inner circle. The White House just left him hanging out to dry.

I tried to send messages to Bush on several occasions, but I do not think they ever got through. I recall that when I heard that he was considering an appointment of a particular individual as the Assistant Secretary of Agriculture who would have responsibility for the Forest Service, I wrote him that the nomination, if made, would prove highly controversial and would be strongly opposed by the environmental community. On that occasion, I did get a reaction, not from the president but from whoever ran personnel matters for him. It was pretty much a form letter thanking me for my interest. The nomination was made, proved highly controversial as predicted, and ultimately was withdrawn.

I found this sort of thing mystifying and frustrating. In public appearances and in private contact, Bush seemed a moderate, middle-of-the-road Republican. However, much of the White House apparatus seemed to be in the hands of the conservative wing of the party. I finally reached the conclusion that that is where George Bush's heart really lay.

Bill Reilly, as head of EPA, found Bush accessible and generally supportive although John Sununu, White House chief of staff, was notoriously negative toward the environment. The Bushes and Reillys became good friends. However, I thought that Reilly was shockingly poorly treated by the White House when he headed the U.S. delegation to the U.N. Conference on Environment and Development at Rio in 1992. When Bill succeeded in negotiating a highly sensitive agreement with the Brazilians on a biological diversity convention and communicated that agreement privately to the White House, the White House leaked a report to the press repudiating Reilly's proposed action. The leak was widely believed to have been engineered by David McIntyre, a very conservative and consistently anti-environment member of Vice President Quayle's staff. While Bush publicly repudiated the leak and said he would punish the leaker, he never did. In any event, the damage had been done.[8]

Bush often seemed disengaged to the point of apathy. When the *Exxon Valdez* went aground and spilled millions of barrels of oil in environmentally sensitive Prince William Sound, Alaska, I called Marlin Fitzwater, the president's press spokesman,[9] that night at his home in Alexandria, Virginia, and urged that the president fly to Valdez to

8. McIntyre was elected to Congress in the Republican sweep in 1994. He persuaded Speaker Gingrich to appoint him leader of a congressional regulatory review process. The effort was quickly perceived by the public as anti-environment and contributed importantly to the voter backlash against the Republican Congress in 1996.

9. Marlin Fitzwater had been my press spokesman at EPA, and his performance had been consistently superior.

inspect the damage but, more importantly, to demonstrate that he cared. Marlin agreed and said that he had already suggested that course of action but that it was not happening. About two days later, Bill Reilly and the Secretary of Transportation went to Valdez but a major opportunity for Bush had been lost. (I once said that, when I was EPA administrator, I would pray for oil spills because they gave me the opportunity for wonderful press coverage. Obviously, I did not literally pray for such events because spills are often tragic affairs. However, the public likes to see its government leaders sharing their concerns and a major spill provided that opportunity.)

On national security matters, of course, Bush was very much engaged. Naturally, I had little opportunity to observe this but did so on one dramatic occasion. Early in January 1990 Bill Reilly called me in Hobe Sound to invite Aileen and myself to dinner at his and Libbie's home in Alexandria a few nights later. I said that was not really possible, as we were not driving north until two days after the date in question. Bill then said that a "very important person" was coming for dinner. I understood immediately that that meant the president and, after a quick consultation with Aileen, said we would be there. On the evening before the Reillys' party, we happened to be giving a dinner of our own at Hobe Sound. The 6:00 p.m. news announced the beginning of the Gulf War, and the next morning we took off for Washington, not knowing whether the dinner was canceled or not. What we discovered on arrival was that the Bushes could not come to dinner but had asked us for drinks at the White House that evening.

And so, the Trains, the Reillys, and Bob Grady (speech writer and advisor who later became an assistant director at OMB) and an attractive young woman with him joined the Bushes at the west end of the hallway that runs the entire length of the second floor of the White House. "Hallway" is something of a misnomer; "gallery" might be more appropriate. That particular area is furnished with sofas, comfortable chairs, and tables so that it makes a sort of adjunct living room. I remember it being similarly used by the Johnsons.

Barbara and I sat on the sofa that backed against the palladian window at the west end of the hall. The president sat in a large wing chair with Aileen next to him, with Bill Reilly on the sofa facing mine. A butler brought us drinks and we talked, as might be imagined, about the war which was then about 24 hours old. The CNN coverage of the war, continuing from Baghdad itself, was a topic.

A telephone sat on a small table at my elbow at the end of the sofa. Suddenly the phone rang. Conversation was instantly frozen. I remember having the mad thought: suppose it's Saddam Hussein? The butler immediately answered the phone, then proffered it to the president, saying, "It's General Scowcroft." The president took the phone and walked a few feet away, listening briefly with his back toward us. Then he brought the phone back and hung it up next to me. "That was Brent," he said. "The Iraqis have just fired a Scud missile at Israel. He'll call back as soon as we know where it lands."

He was perfectly calm and his tone was almost conversational. However, he went on to express his anxiety over Israeli reaction and his hope that they would not try to retaliate. If they did, it could radically change the entire character of the limited war we and our allies had undertaken. Minutes later, the phone rang again. This time the president picked it up and there was another brief conversation. When he was through, the president told us that the missile had landed in Tel Aviv.

We left soon after, having spent at least 45 minutes with the Bushes. It was extremely kind and generous of them to entertain us at such a time. They were relaxed and hospitable, although the president was clearly in a very serious frame of mind. We were privileged to have had an extraordinary glimpse of history in the making and from a vantage point that could hardly be equaled. Any thought of Bush as being "disengaged" at that time would have been ludicrous. When we left the White House, we went to the Reillys' for dinner. We had a lot to talk about!

There were other occasions with the Bushes that come to mind: the State dinner at the White House for Queen Elizabeth II and Prince Philip; going with the Bushes to the Kennedy Center and sitting in the presidential box; the award to me of the Medal of Freedom, which I have described earlier; their annual Christmas receptions at the White

House; the small farewell cocktail party in the "family quarters" at the White House for Antony and Jenny Acland as Antony was retiring as British ambassador and they were returning to England; Aileen's luncheon party for Jenny to which Barbara came; the award to Bush of a medal by Chancellor Kohl at the German Embassy.

When Bush's reelection campaign was organizing in 1992, I turned down the invitation to once again chair or co-chair an Environmental-ists for Bush Committee. It was an uncomfortable decision in which a long history of personal friendship conflicted with a perception of the Bush environmental record as increasingly negative. I found that the staff at WWF would be up in arms if I became publicly associated with the Bush campaign. Several members of the WWF board I con-tacted were equally negative. However, the most important considera-tion was that at the time I was chairing the National Commission on the Environment, as previously noted.

The commission was bipartisan and its members had tried to get our report released during the campaign. I insisted that it not be made public until after the election. Several sections of the report implied criticism of U.S. environmental policy and leadership and could have been used against Bush in the campaign. It was only my influence that kept this from happening, and I would have lost that influence if I had been identified with the Bush campaign in a partisan sense. Moreover, the impact of our report, it seemed to me, would have been signifi-cantly lessened if it had become the subject of partisan debate during the campaign. Nevertheless, whatever its rationale, my decision was not a happy one.

Sadly, while we continue to run into the Bushes from time to time, the easy friendship of earlier days seems gone. I am sure that George (and, of course, Barbara) puts personal loyalty above most other attri-butes and probably found me wanting in that regard. For my part, I too believe in the importance of personal loyalty but in this instance that sense was outweighed by loyalty to a cause which had been the central focus of my career for some thirty years. To do otherwise would have made a mockery of that career or, at least, so I felt—and still feel. As it was, I never took any part in criticizing Bush during the campaign but simply avoided endorsing his environmental record. The latter was doubly hard because Bill Reilly had done a superb job as EPA administrator under Bush.

Of course, the fact that I have gone to such lengths to explain and rationalize my decision not to chair an Environmentalists for Bush Committee in the 1992 campaign brings home what an uncomfortable decision it was and that there is lingering discomfort to this day. George Bush is a fine, decent man and a credit to his country.

President Clinton

THE ONLY CONTACT Aileen and I had with President Clinton was at a reception given by Secretary of the Treasury Lloyd and "B.A." Bentsen at Blair House to celebrate their 50th wedding anniversary. Clinton and his wife, Hillary, entered the crowded premises and immediately separated to "work" the crowd independently of each other.

We talked with both of them. I congratulated him on securing congressional approval of NAFTA that day. Aileen told him that she was a Republican but strongly agreed with his positions on abortion, gun control, and planned parenthood. Without doubt, he was an imposing, charismatic presence. Aileen talked to Hillary Clinton about Wellesley, and I talked to her about the importance of promoting bipartisan support for key legislative initiatives, citing my own experience with environmental legislation. Later, particularly during his second term and in the wake of revelations about his personal life, we became pretty thoroughly disenchanted with Bill Clinton.

CHAPTER 23

Travels to Far Places

I HAVE REFERRED frequently to various travels that Aileen and I have engaged in, either separately or together, over the years. Some of this travel was on official government business, some for WWF (or earlier, for AWLF), and a fair amount of it personal. To describe all of our journeys would require another book. However, our travels deserve more than just passing reference. Hence, this chapter is devoted to the subject. I have found it impossible to organize the material in any consistent fashion. Some of the narrative is organized chronologically and some geographically.

Visits to the U.S.S.R.

ON SEVERAL of my official visits to Moscow, all involved with the implementation of the U.S.-U.S.S.R. Agreement on Cooperation in the Field of Environment—to use its cumbersome, official title—I went to the Kremlin to give a report to President Podgorny, one of the triumvirate that then ruled the Soviet Union, Brezhnev being the principal member. I was accompanied by our ambassador, Walter Stoessel, on two occasions, and, after passing through the tight Kremlin security, we ascended in a small elevator along with a very smart guardsman. Podgorny would have met first with my Soviet counterpart, Yuri Israel, and the two of them would join Walter and myself in a formal conference room where we sat around a round table with interpreters.

The discussions were mostly pro forma and not very substantive although they generally lasted at least an hour. There was a certain amount of light banter. I recall briefing Podgorny on the new U.S.-

Soviet Migratory Bird Treaty[1] and explaining how U.S. scientists had banded waterfowl in Soviet Siberia which had then migrated down the West Coast of North America and been shot in California. Podgorny professed shock at this intelligence and exclaimed: "What? You Americans are shooting Soviet birds?!"

It was the period of détente and I was able to travel widely in the Soviet Union. Aileen and I went to Leningrad (now once again St. Petersburg) on the night train from Moscow and toured the Hermitage. We also visited the Piskarevskoe Cemetery, where 800,000 of the 1.5 million residents of Leningrad who died during the German siege, which lasted about three years during World War II, are buried in a common grave. From Leningrad we also visited Tsarskoe Selo and the fabulous palaces there—Pavlovsk, Peterhof, Catherine—which had been meticulously restored after their destruction by the German forces.

We were accompanied to Leningrad by the entire U.S. delegation which I headed, and we were given a gala dinner aboard a very large Soviet oceanographic research vessel in the harbor. The ship's officers and the enlisted men and women gave us a marvelous choral concert, at the end of which they invited us Americans to respond in kind. Fortunately, Shirley Temple Black, the world-renowned former child film star, was one of our delegation. After a hasty consultation, she and I did an impromptu song-and-dance routine to the lyrics of "The Good Ship Lollipop"! I clearly added little to the performance but it was a smash hit in any event and American honor was upheld.

On that particular trip in the autumn of 1972, Aileen and I went on to Irkutsk on Lake Baikal and then to Yakutsk, north of the Arctic Circle, where I visited the Permafrost Institute, of interest because of the plan to build an oil pipeline across permafrost terrain in Alaska.

1. Negotiated by E.U. Curtis "Buff" Bohlen under the general umbrella of the environmental agreement. Buff had been my immediate assistant at the Department of the Interior when I was Under Secretary. He later joined the World Wildlife Fund as vice president and, in the Bush administration, served as Assistant Secretary of State for Oceans, Environment, and Scientific Affairs (OES). He and his wife, Janet, are close friends and have a farm near us on the Eastern Shore. Buff continues today to be actively engaged in facilitating the conservation of lands in Alaska and the Everglades as a special consultant to the Secretary of the Interior.

On the shore
of Lake Baikal

(I did not learn anything there that we did not already know.) Lake Baikal is the largest freshwater lake in the world—it contains about one-fifth of the earth's fresh water.

A two-part *New Yorker* series by Marshall Schulman (later an Assistant Secretary of State) rang an alarm bell to the effect that Baikal, said to be the world's largest body of clear, pure water, was threatened by the effluent from two pulp mills on its shores. I visited the pulp mills and inspected their waste-water treatment facilities. From there we went to the lakeshore where the effluent was being discharged and I was invited to drink from a glass of the stuff. In the interest of détente I agreed and found it relatively clear and tasteless. Subsequently, I learned that the effluent also included the waste from the village where the pulp mill employees lived. Anyway, I survived.

There were many amusing and interesting incidents during our Soviet travels, more than space permits recounting here. In 1975, we took Bowdy and Errol with us to Moscow and then across Siberia to Khabarovsk in the Far East, on the Amur River border with China. We had our own Ilyushin 18 aircraft for the journey and visited Samarkand, Bokhara, Dushambe, Tashkent, Irkutsk, Yakutsk, and finally Khabarovsk. Yuri Israel accompanied us for much of the trip, along with a few other Soviet staff, including our inseparable KGB agent.

With George Bush at U.S. Liaison Headquarters in Beijing, 1976. Harry Thayer, Deputy Chief of Mission, is on the right, and Neil Bush in the left background.

The plane had a crew of eight. Aileen has kept a photographic record of all our trips and the photos of this trip, all carefully labeled, fill a large scrapbook.

People's Republic of China

FROM KHABAROVSK, we flew to Japan and spent a few days on Sado Island off the west coast and then on to Beijing. (One could not travel directly between the U.S.S.R. and China at the time.) The U.S. maintained a liaison office in Beijing, prior to the establishment of full diplomatic relations, and George Bush was the liaison officer. He and Barbara were our hosts for a week. Their children George, Marvin, Neil, and Dorothy (Doro) were also there, which filled the official residence, and we stayed at the Peking Hotel.

I had one meeting with Chinese environmental officials organized by George, and we visited and met with various agricultural and urban communes. Otherwise, we were tourists and Barbara shepherded us through the Forbidden City and the Summer Palace, where the Bushes gave a large dinner party. Our families dined together almost every evening. We picnicked at the Ming Tombs and visited the Great Wall.

With Barbara Bush
at the Great Wall

With Errol and Bowdy
at Nara, Japan

On one occasion, in an effort to reciprocate the Bushes' hospitality, the Trains took them all to dinner at the restaurant at the zoo, which was located close to the Bush residence. There were numerous courses, quarts of good Chinese beer, and my tab for ten of us came to about U.S. $17.

From China we flew back to Tokyo, spent two nights in a *ryokan* at the ancient capital of Nara, and finally returned home. It had been a wonderful trip from every standpoint and an extraordinary experience for Errol and Bowdy.

Iran

THE FOLLOWING year, 1976, Aileen and I visited Dick and Cynthia Helms in Teheran. Dick had retired as director of the CIA and was now ambassador to Iran. They gave us a wonderful time. We saw the sights of Teheran and dined at the White Palace with the Shah's brother, Prince Abdoureza, a big trophy hunter. We visited Isfahan, Shiraz, and the ruins of Persepolis, where I was delighted to find the initials of the great African explorer Henry M. Stanley carved on the entrance wall. With Eskander Firouz, head of the national parks, and his wife, Iran, we spent several days in the mountains north of Teheran, near Mount Demavend. We rode ponies and hoped to find the tracks of a Caspian tiger. Of course, we did not; the subspecies is almost certainly extinct. But it was beautiful, exciting country.

Spain

EARLIER, WHILE I was at the Council on Environmental Quality, Prince (now King) Juan Carlos of Spain had made a "non-state" visit to the United States. Prior to his arrival, I had a call from someone at the State Department who was arranging the prince's schedule. "The prince has listed you as one of the four people he wishes to meet while he is in Washington. [Pause] Why does he want to meet with you?"

Meeting Generalissimo Franco, c. 1971. Introducing us is López Rodo, Minister of Social and Economic Development.

"Perhaps he is interested in the environment," I replied. And, so he was. As the designated heir to the throne and constitutional monarch once Generalissimo Franco died, he was doubtless anxious to position himself as a modern man and not a throwback to Spain's feudal past. I spent an hour or more with him at Blair House, the president's guest house, where he was staying. He showed himself to be both knowledgeable and interested in environmental matters and invited me to visit Spain.

Aileen and I did so the following year. I met with Prince Juan Carlos at his residence outside Madrid and also had a private audience with Franco. The latter was old and infirm when I met him, suffering from both a stroke and Parkinson's disease. However, he had all of his marbles and we had a good conversation. He said that he had never had any problem controlling pollution. "I usually drive north on Fridays to my country estate," he said. "If I drive through a village and there is a lot of trash around, I have the car stopped and send for the mayor. I point out the problem to him and tell him to clean it up. You know, when I drive back through that town on Monday, it is spotless!" The absolute dictator, as Franco was, glanced at me with a guileless look of surprise on his face as he said this. At the same time, there was a twinkle in his eye. On my return to Washington, I sent the president a detailed description of my visit with Franco, including my observations about his physical condition. Nixon had a voracious appetite for news, including minutiae, of other heads of state.

There was an entertaining incident one morning during the Madrid visit. Aileen and I had each been picked up at the Ritz Hotel by separate limousines and police escorts—she to go to the Generalissimo Franco Foundation which produced textiles and other crafts, and I to my audience with Franco. She recounts that she was proceeding in her car down a highway, police sirens wailing, when suddenly, at an intersection, her car braked to a stop and she was thrown to the floor. She raised herself to her knees to look over the driver's seat and was just in time to see my entourage sweep grandly through the intersection, I reading a newspaper and oblivious of Aileen and her escort.

On that same trip Aileen and I visited Toledo and then flew to Sevilla and drove to the Coto Doñana in the great marshy estuary of the Guadalquivir River. Here was the last haunt of the rare Spanish imperial eagle and a concentration point for birds migrating between Europe and Africa, the winter home of hundreds of thousands of European ducks, geese, and waders. It was also one of the few remaining habitats of the Spanish lynx. The purchase of the Coto Doñana reserve had been one of the first projects of the World Wildlife Fund in the early 1960s and the hope was that it would eventually include 65 square miles of Las Marismas. We spent a day and a night there at an old hacienda, the reserve headquarters. I understood that the area had been the original home of the Texas longhorn cattle. When we were there, the reserve was being threatened by proposed resort development along the coast and by the runoff of pesticides from neighboring agricultural areas. Back in Madrid, I gave a lengthy interview which was published in one of the daily papers, seeking to rally public support for protecting this unique area.

At Trujillo with Tom Meyer, Fleur Cowles, and John Loudon. Tom is adjusting a stock around my neck and the others apear to be playing out a mutual grooming act.

Some years later, while president of WWF-U.S. and North American vice president of the International Union for the Conservation of Nature (IUCN), I attended an IUCN Congress in Madrid, staying at the U.S. Embassy with our ambassador, Tom Enders, and his wife, Gaetana. In 1992, together with our great friend John Loudon, we spent Easter in Trujillo, southwest of Madrid, as the guests of Fleur Cowles and Tom Meyer. It was a colorful, entertaining few days, with many fairly exotic characters. Trujillo is an ancient hill town, dating back to the Moors and probably the Romans, and it was from here that the conquistador Pizarro went to Peru. An equestrian statue of him stands in the plaza before the cathedral. Our hostess, Fleur Cowles, is a writer and artist of great talent and an international personage. She was a trustee of WWF-International for a number of years. She and Tom live at Albany in London, and we see them there or in Washington once or twice a year.

Alaska and the American West

WHILE Under Secretary of Interior in 1969, I visited Alaska several times in connection with the trans-Alaska oil pipeline. In addition, together with Errol and Bowdy, Aileen and I visited Glacier Bay

With Bowdy in the Brooks Range,
Alaska, 1973

National Park in Alaska and the Katmai Peninsula, where we fished for salmon on the Brooks River and had fairly close encounters with brown bears.

With our friends Rocco and Marian Siciliano and their children, Aileen and I plus Emily, Bowdy, and Errol rafted down the Colorado River from Moab, Utah, through Glen Canyon (then being wiped out by damming) and into Lake Powell.

A year or so later, Aileen and I, together with Elliot and Anne Richardson and Ernie and Helene Sargent, rafted down the middle fork of the Salmon in Idaho, ending at the Snake River where Governor Cecil Andrus, later Secretary of the Interior, flew in to meet us. That was a memorable trip, with trout fishing along the way, Rocky Mountain sheep on the slopes beside us, and golden eagles soaring overhead.

In the summer of 1972, Bowdy and I flew to Anchorage, Alaska, where we joined an old Washington friend, John Kauffman, and Bob Waldrop, who had worked briefly for The Conservation Foundation. We flew from Anchorage to Bettles, just north of the Arctic Circle, and from there flew north of the Brooks Range in a bush plane carrying two canoes strapped to our pontoons—illegally, I suspect—and landed on a small lake close to the Alatna River. I will never forget going in to land on that lake as a large bull moose was standing feeding in the shallows right under us. He raised his head, water and weeds dripping from his horns, as we passed by him. We carried our canoes

Sylvia and Bob Blake with
Charlie and Janet Whitehouse
at Silver Tip Ranch, Montana,
where the Trains have been
lucky enough to be guests

and gear to the Alatna and went down it for several days, camping as we
went. Bowdy and I shared a pup tent. It was a great wilderness experience. At the confluence with the Kobuk River, we were picked up by
another bush plane and, after flying around the spectacular Gates of
the Arctic mountains and landing a couple of times along the Kobuk,
we ended up in Kotzebue on the Chukchi Sea. Bowdy had been at
Kotzebue the summer before, working with Bill Sladen on his whis-
tling (now tundra) swan project.

While Bowdy and I were enjoying ourselves in Alaska, Aileen and
Errol did a wilderness trail ride for a week in Montana. A highlight of
that adventure occurred one night when Aileen and Errol bedded
down in their sleeping bags in their pup tent, located unwittingly on a
bear trail, forgetting that the saddlebags they brought into the tent
with them contained orange peels from the day's ride. In the middle of
the night a black bear stuck his head into the tent, attracted by the
smell of the orange peels. Aileen awoke, grasped the situation, and
then, raising both of her feet sharply upward, sleeping bag and all, gave
the bear a good, swift kick in the chin. The bear wisely beat a hasty
retreat and Aileen could feel his body brush by her along the length of
the tent as he retreated. Errol slept through most of the whole episode
but Aileen was pretty shaken by it.

Nepal and Bhutan

BOTH ALONE and with Aileen, I made about six visits to Nepal, where WWF-U.S. established major new programs under the direction of Bruce Bunting, WWF-U.S. vice president for Asia. With others, I urged the creation of a strong private conservation organization in Nepal and the King Mahendra Trust for Nature Conservation in Nepal (KMTNC) was established, chaired by King Bahendra's oldest brother, Prince Gyanendra. I had called on him at the Royal Palace to persuade him to support the concept, and I became one of three non-Nepalese members of the board. Aileen and I visited Tiger Tops, as well as the Royal Chitwan and Royal Bardia National Parks. We took part in several elephant drives, reminiscent of the great hunts of days gone by. On one of these an Asian one-horned rhinoceros was surrounded and tranquilized for the installation of a radio collar. The rhino was named "Russell." Another time, a line of elephants drove a recalcitrant tiger toward a tree in which Aileen and I occupied a *machan* with Hemanta Mishra, then managing director of KMTNC. Hemanta was supposed to dart the tiger with a tranquilizer as it passed just below us. The tiger did not cooperate and turned back through the elephant line, slashing one of them as it passed. (Our friend David Challinor, then assistant secretary of the Smithsonian, happened to be on the elephant that the tiger slashed.) There was much trumpeting and roaring.

We trekked in the Himalayan foothills near Pokhara and landed up the Everest Trail by helicopter, visiting the Tengboche Monastery, later destroyed by fire. I walked the Annapurna Trail from Jansemm to Muktinath with Bruce Bunting and Michael Wright of the WWF-U.S. staff. We made two trips to Bhutan, on one of which we became lost at sundown in the forests of Manas National Park while riding the king's own elephant. There was a visit to the remote valley which was the wintering ground of the rare black-necked crane. Bhutan was a beautiful, unspoiled country which we felt privileged to visit. We loved the Himalaya, and I can well understand how some of the world's great religions had their genesis there.

In Nepal, 1985. Both of us had mounted the elephant by facing it from the front, placing one foot against its trunk, grabbing an ear in each hand and then, on the mahout's command, landing on the elephant's head as it raised its trunk.

Thailand

Aileen and I went to Thailand several times to visit conservation areas and to meet with Thai conservationists, and, on one such visit, I had an audience with the king, accompanied by Aileen and our ambassador Bill Brown. Bill was a good friend and had worked with me at EPA where he had been detailed by the State Department to coordinate the U.S. side of the U.S.-U.S.S.R. environmental agreement. During the audience, the king did most of the talking, which was frustrating as I had a list of subjects to raise with him. The thing I remember most clearly was keeping both of my feet firmly planted on the floor, as I had been carefully instructed that to show the sole of my foot to His Majesty or to point my toes toward him would be a serious affront and a major breach of politesse. In the middle of the audience, a servant entered the room on his knees and offered refreshments on a tray. Behind the king, a pair of black elephant tusks stood on a stand, a remarkable and very rare trophy—the product, I believe, of a disease.

After the audience proper and in an adjoining hall, I presented a WWF award to Queen Sikrit in the presence of the entire royal family and Thai TV cameras. We had been accompanied to Thailand by our good friends Connie and Anne Sidamon-Eristof, and they joined us at the reception that followed. Along with the chief of staff of the Thai army, we formed a receiving line and each member of the royal family came along the line to welcome us. As each approached, the general prostrated himself on the floor, arms spread out before him, forehead to the floor. I am afraid that none of the rest of us followed his example. We were the guests of the Browns at the embassy residence and enjoyed the large guest house in the embassy compound.

New Zealand

WE TRAVELED to New Zealand in 1982—with several days in Bora Bora and a brief visit to Tahiti—for the biannual congress of the International Union for the Conservation of Nature, of which I was the North American vice president. After a visit with Gary and Judy Glazebrook on their 20,000-acre sheep farm near Hawke's Bay on North Island, we spent two weeks headquartered in Christchurch where the IUCN congress was held. With Charles de Haes, director general of WWF-International, we did a motor tour around the South Island, visiting Stewart Island off the south coast and then driving up the west coast to Milford Sound. We took a boat down the sound; we landed by plane on the snowfields of Mount Cook. On Stewart Island, we saw a single specimen of a tree never identified elsewhere in the world except in the Amazon Basin.

Back to China

FROM NEW ZEALAND, we went to Hong Kong and then to Szechwan Province in western China, where we visited the Wolong Reserve, home of giant pandas. There, George Schaller, world-renowned conservation biologist and research scientist, was leading a WWF project designed to further understanding of pandas and their environmental needs. Unfortunately, we never succeeded in coming up with a panda in the wild, although we found tracks and relatively fresh droppings. (Over the years, one becomes accustomed to plunging one's fingers into various "droppings" to assess their freshness and, thus, the proximity of the animals.) We did spot a troop of rare golden monkeys, an unusual sighting.

We went on from Wolong to Sian, where the Chinese have unearthed an extraordinary army of life-sized warriors—all sculpted as individuals—from burial mounds associated with early emperors. We flew from Chengdu (capital of Szechwan Province) to Sian in a Soviet-built Chinese aircraft in which the only seats were a metal bench running down each side of the plane's interior. An overhead rope down the middle provided the stewardess with a handhold as she moved back and forth. The flight was over mountains and very rough and almost all of the other passengers were sick. We had a portable backgammon set which diverted us sufficiently so that we had no problems of that sort. However, we were glad when we arrived in Sian.

We were amazed and delighted by the archeological remains which are among the wonders of the world. We were entertained at dinner by a group of officials and were served, among other delicacies, sea slugs (or sea cucumbers)—a repulsive dish if I have ever seen one. I succeeded in not eating mine but Aileen, ever eager not to offend, slid hers off her plate and under the table. Her Chinese dinner companion, spying the empty plate, exclaimed with delight, "Ah, you like!" and promptly put another serving of sea slug on her plate. This process was repeated several times until Aileen felt she could safely decline further helpings.

Toward the close of dinner, our host, who was seated across the table, pushed back his chair and started to rise to offer a toast. As he did so, his feet slid out from under him and he collapsed back in his chair. Understandably startled, he peered under the table and quickly took in what had occurred. He burst into laughter in which all joined, although most were clueless as to the cause of the merriment. It was one of our great dining moments.

Japan

ANOTHER SUCH moment came at Akon on the northern tip of Hokkaido in Japan. We were there during an official government trip, rather than under WWF auspices. As I recall, we were the only non-Japanese in the town. We had been to a national park that particular day and had been struck by the picturesque beauty of the place with its gnarled pines and little limestone islands in a lake, all looking to our surprise remarkably like the scenery on Japanese screens which we had always assumed was a figment of the artist's imagination. We were also struck by the fact that the little promontory jutting into the lake which provided our vantage point was knee-deep in tin cans and other rubbish. I have always been amazed at how fastidious the Japanese are about their personal cleanliness and about their "inner space" including their homes while at the same time often seeming totally oblivious or disinterested about conditions outside that space. I suspect that aspect of Japanese culture strongly affects the way Japan relates to world affairs.

Once back at our hotel, we had donned kimonos and walked down the main street to the public baths. Each hotel or inn in Akon had its own distinctively decorated kimono. Never having been in a Japanese bath before, I had no idea what to expect. I walked into the men's changing room only to be confronted by an elderly lady who stood in front of me while I removed every stitch of clothes I had on and handed them to her piece by piece. After this cultural shock, the rest of the bathing ritual seemed routine.

Later, sitting on the floor of our hotel room, I enjoyed an excellent dry, vodka martini on the rocks and Aileen a white wine. Dinner was brought to our room with great fanfare, accompanied by the hotel manager, the head chef, and a waiter who deposited a large, whole fish on a platter on the floor before us. The decoration was extraordinary. A vase of flowers stood at one end of the platter, the petals carved out of carrots and turnips. A wave sculpted from carrots broke over the fish which in turn was ensnared in a lacy net delicately carved out of turnips.

We stared at the production and then the chef bent over and with chopsticks deftly removed a bite-sized piece of raw fish from the side of the fish. It was only then that we noticed that the fish was still breathing, its gills opening and shutting as it gasped for air. The exterior flesh of its sides had all been cut into small squares and carefully replaced. Doubtless we had been done great honor by this culinary production but it was all we could do to keep from being sick on the spot. Finally, after profuse apologies by us, the fish was borne away, and we dined on something less exotic.

Later, as we lay on our futons on the floor, a masseur arrived and knelt between us. As he attacked me, I broke into uncontrollable laughter and Aileen pulled the futon over her head so as to avoid his ministrations. Finally, he left and another day in Japan was over.

India

I HAVE NO comparable memories of India although we spent two weeks there on our way to our first visit to Nepal in 1982. Historically and culturally, it was a fascinating experience. We stayed in New Delhi—a part of the time at our embassy, otherwise empty, as we had no ambassador in residence at the time. We visited Agra and the Taj Mahal—seeing the latter by moonlight, in the dawn, and during the day. We stayed at Jaipur and visited the Bharatpur Bird Sanctuary to see the small population, now probably gone, of Siberian cranes that wintered there.

The most unforgettable experience was a several-day stay in the Ranthambhore Tiger Reserve. We stayed in a small, ruined but semi-restored, marble temple which looked out over a lake. We and our host, Fateh Singh, the warden of the reserve and a great tiger expert, and his camp staff were the only people in the reserve. We could hear the sambar deer bark at night along the lakeshore and found a large male tiger while driving in an open jeep. It was unafraid and stood for photos. Tragically, many of the Ranthambhore tigers have been poached in recent years to feed the Oriental demand for tiger parts for traditional medicine.

Aileen and I walked a couple of miles along a dirt road out of camp and sat for an hour or so in a small temple ruin along the shore of another lake, hoping for the sight of a tiger. We did see sambar and crocodiles but no tiger. Walking back to our camp, we found tiger pug marks in the dust of the road, fresh since our earlier passage.

We dined at a table spread in the shade of a large banyan tree. During one breakfast, a monkey jumped from the tree, hit the ground once, leapt on to my shoulder, grabbed the toast I was lifting to my mouth, and disappeared back up the tree—all in the flicker of an eyelash. The old city of Ranthambhore, now abandoned and in ruins, stood on an escarpment behind the camp, and we climbed up to it on a narrow trail up the cliff.

The combination of natural and cultural wonders made Ranthambhore an enchanting place. When the tiger reserve had been established in the 1970s, the human population had been removed. Within the boundaries of the reserve, the vegetation was rich and lush. On the outside, right up to the reserve boundary, the land was a desert, the natural vegetation all but destroyed by overgrazing. It was an instructive example of how rich nature can be when left to its own devices and of how destructive humanity can be of the very natural systems on which its survival depends. Uncontrolled population growth is a crucial part of the problem. When more and more people try to squeeze a living out of a finite piece of the earth, a downward spiral of degradation occurs.

During the entire two-week stay in India, we traveled on our own and not as part of any tour group. We hired a car and driver to get from place to place and once traveled on an incredibly crowded train. Of course, we had made some arrangements in advance and there was usually someone to take us under their wing.

Malaysia

WITH BRUCE BUNTING and Caroline Getty, we traveled to mainland Malaysia where we had meetings with the WWF-Malaysia board and staff and made one short field trip. We then went on to the Malay-

Caroline Getty with
young orangutan, Sabah

sian states of Sarawak and Sabah on the north and northeast coasts of
Borneo. Those visits included meeting with local scientists and conservationists and an opportunity to observe firsthand the rampant destruction of native forests and their replacement with palm oil plantations.
In Sabah, we spent time on the slopes of Mount Kilabalu (over 4000
meters) and had our first experience with the several species of insec-
tivorous pitcher plants found there. We went to the port city of San-
dakan which my grandfather had visited almost one hundred years
before aboard his flagship *Ohio*. There we visited the orangutan rehabilitation center and enjoyed close contact with these engaging crea-
tures.

Tanzania

PRIMATES HAVE always held a fascination for both of us. I have
earlier described our encounters with mountain gorillas in Ruanda in
1958. More recently, we enjoyed seeing several species of lemur in
Madagascar. The reintroduction of golden lion-maned tamarins in the
Atlantic coastal forest of Brazil was a project I found highly rewarding. However, the primate highlight as far as I am concerned was a

Judy and Bob Waterman

several-day visit to the chimpanzees of Mahale National Park on the east coast of Lake Tanganyika in Tanzania.

Once again, our little party of Bob and Judy Waterman, Caroline Getty, and Aileen and me had the park entirely to ourselves, so far as visitors were concerned. We were guided by Roland Purcell and stayed at a beach camp managed by his delightful wife, Zoë. The chimpanzees had been observed for many years by Japanese scientists who never intruded on them in any way. For example, they never put out fruit to attract the animals or otherwise interfaced with them (unlike Jane Goodall's operation at Gombe Stream further up the lake).

As a result, once we found the chimps, we could sit and watch them, totally unconcerned about us, or stand as they trooped by, passing only a foot or two away on a forest trail, seldom even looking at us. It was a most unusual, moving experience. I was told that Bill Gates of Microsoft fame had visited there not long before, landing on the lake in a large amphibious plane together with a small party who went out to see the chimps. Gates apparently never left the camp and never tried to see the chimps while he was there.

Bruce Bunting

The Philippines

AS WAS THE case in Nepal and Bhutan, there had been essentially no WWF presence in the Philippines until I encouraged Bruce Bunting in 1982 to explore the possibilities. I had previously met with Celso Roque, then the energetic head of the Haribon Society, an environmental NGO in Manila, and the former Under Secretary of the Ministry of Natural Resources. We had met during an IUCN meeting in Madrid, and he had urged WWF-U.S. involvement in the Philippines. Celso is today a mainstay of WWF activity in Southeast Asia.

Over the years, I have made several visits to the Philippines to meet with the NGO community and the government officials concerned with environmental matters, to develop contacts with the Asian Development Bank and also with the private banks, such as J. P. Morgan, to meet with our own diplomatic and development assistance missions, and to visit projects in the field. Bruce Bunting, with his customary entrepreneurial energy, rapidly developed our base in the Philippines and we soon had an office in Manila, staffed almost entirely by Filipinos.

WWF-U.S. did one of its first debt-for-nature swaps in the Philippines. Using USAID funding, we bought up $20 million of depreciated Philippine debt which was conveyed to the Central Bank which in turn funded the endowment for the Foundation for the Philippine Environment. I served for two or three years as the only non-Filipino member of the foundation board and attended at least one meeting a year in Manila. The board is now entirely Filipino. On one visit, Aileen and I had a formal meeting with President Corazon Aquino, who was very responsive until I mentioned the need to curb population growth.

The U.S. Navy had given up its base at Subic Bay north of Manila, and WWF was trying to protect the natural areas, mostly original forest, around the base. Frank Wisner, who had been U.S. ambassador to the Philippines (then Deputy Secretary of Defense and ambassador to India), had come to see me to enlist WWF help in the effort. WWF responded and made the project a major priority.

With Bruce Bunting, we visited Palawan Island on the west side of the Sulu Sea and sailed up its west coast to explore an underground river that flowed into one of the bays; the area had been made a national park. We sailed on a *proa*, a Malaysian craft with outriggers. It was rigged for a lateen sail but used a sputtering engine. We were hit by a howling gale off the South China Sea and huddled on deck under drenching rain, trying to keep our belongings dry under a tarp. When we arrived at our destination several hours later, we had to take shelter in the lee of a headland and wait for the wind to subside before landing. As it was, we landed on a beach in the dark and with a heavy surf running. With an anchor to stern and a line to the beach, we jumped over the side in water to our shoulders, holding our belongings over our heads. The crew also jumped overboard, holding a large object over their heads which turned out to be a mattress, wrapped in plastic, for our use. I remember spending a good part of that night drying out the contents of my wallet over an oil lamp.

At the northern tip of Palawan was a small resort, El Nido, on the edge of a marine sanctuary that WWF had helped establish. We spent several days there snorkeling among the reefs. Unfortunately, Aileen developed an ear infection that caused her sheer torture on the flight back to Manila in a small plane. She had to go to a hospital and have a drain put into her ear.

New Guinea

IN 1994, we went on a fascinating trip to Papua New Guinea (PNG) with members of the WWF board, including Meg Taylor, the PNG ambassador to the U.S. We visited the north coast and the highlands, cruised the Sepik River, and visited the Kikori area where WWF was working with Chevron to minimize forest loss as a result of large-scale oil development. Weathered old crocodile-head dugout canoe prows and other mementos of our trip now add to the atmosphere of Grace Creek Farm.

Later, with a small group of WWF-U.S. directors and friends, we cruised from Ambon in Indonesia through the Banda Sea, snorkeling and diving and visiting some of the remote Spice Islands on our way to Irian Jaya, the Indonesian end of New Guinea, where we visited the home of the Asmat tribe on the south coast. It was there that Michael Rockefeller lost his life. Aileen and I have a beautiful Asmat war shield at Grace Creek. Before boarding our ship at Ambon, we and the Sants, Watermans, Helen Spaulding, and Judy Key had spent several marvelously hedonistic days on Bali, staying at the Amandari Hotel.

Romantic that I am, all of these places in Indonesia, the South China Sea, the Sulu Sea, and the Banda Sea reeked of Joseph Conrad. Aileen remembers my saying that at an early point in my life my ambition was to be a beachcomber in the area. I can see it now: I am wearing a rather worn and spotted white linen suit. I am unshaven. My hand trembles. My eyes are bleary. I lift my hand, and Amaya, my lovely young half-breed servant, brings me another Holland gin . . . Fortunately, I outgrew all that a long time ago but still . . . those faraway beaches and the tall, graceful palms strike a chord deep inside me.

The Indian Ocean

ACROSS THE Indian Ocean, we cruised with a WWF group among the Seychelle and Comoro Islands, along the coast of Madagascar, stopped at Reunion, and ended the trip at Mauritius where we stayed with the U.S. ambassador, Penne Korth, a friend from Washington. A highlight of the Seychelle part of the trip was a visit to Aldabra, home of a large tortoise and other endemic species. In the mid-sixties, Aldabra had been slated for development as a U.S. military base. I was the president of The Conservation Foundation at the time and had intervened with both Bob McNamara and Cy Vance, Secretary and Deputy Secretary, respectively, of Defense, to urge that Aldabra be left undisturbed.

It was, and the base was established further north at Diego Garcia. I doubt that my representations had anything to do with the decision, but, nevertheless it was satisfying to see the island atoll still in a relatively pristine state. We had a wonderful experience at Aldabra when we slipped over the side of a Zodiac (inflated rubber boat) in the middle of the vast lagoon to drift with the ebbing tide down a two-mile cut to the sea. We saw large fish as we were swept along by the current. Someone had said to me, "What will you do if you see a large shark lying ahead of you?" I said, "I will say, 'Hi there! I am from the World Wildlife Fund!'"

Africa

AFRICA, OF COURSE, has been the center of our travels for many years. I have already described briefly our two hunting safaris in Kenya. Many of our early WWF-related trips to Africa were with Rick Weyerhaeuser, who then headed the WWF-U.S. African program. Prior to joining WWF, Rick had worked with Iain Douglas-Hamilton on his Lake Manyara (Tanzania) elephant research project. We have been back to Tanzania several times: camping in the Serengeti in the midst of the migration, camping on the floor of Ngorongoro Crater, doing a two-week walking safari in the Selous Game Reserve complete with 30 porters. The latter safari was with Rod and Sukey Wagner and Fritz and Lee Link. Our guide was Richard Bonham. Along with Bob and Judy Waterman and Caroline Getty, we had an extraordinary visit with

Richard Bonham and Sukey
and Rod Wagner in the Selous
Game Reserve, Tanzania

Fritz Link

Lee Link

the chimpanzees at Mahale National Park on Lake Tanganyika, which I have already described. Walking instead of bumping along in a Land Rover has become our preferred way of seeing Africa today. We have walked several times in Zambia, usually in the South Luangwa National Park. Once, while accompanied by various of our children—all well grown by that time—we were entertained by Zambian President Kenneth Kaunda, since defeated for reelection and, even more recently, jailed for allegedly plotting a coup to overthrow the government. He gave each of our children an inscribed volume of his own writings.

Zimbabwe

Zimbabwe has become the focal point for many of our recent African adventures. Aileen and I have now been on five walking safaris along the Zambezi River, all with guide John Stevens. He and his wife, Nicci, who live in Harare, have become great friends and they have visited us in Washington and on the Eastern Shore. John is a licensed guide and in Zimbabwe that means he can carry a gun in a national park. On each trip we have camped principally in the Mana Pools National Park along the Zambezi. We either walk out from camp or drive to a new area and walk there. John leads, carrying his gun, and the rest of us—usually no more than six—follow closely in single file. It is an incomparable way to experience the bush—the sounds of the birds, the smell of the African earth, the animal signs that would go unnoticed from a vehicle, and the occasional close encounter. Stevens is the dean of Zimbabwe guides and an extraordinary "bushman."

We have done these Zimbabwe trips with Caroline Getty, together with her nephew Beau Perry and our grandson Alex Smith, the Watermans, the Sants (twice), John and Caroline Macomber, and all of our children (except Nancy and Chris), plus Emily and Allie Rowan along with their parents, Emily and Jim. Alex had gone with us to the Masai Mara in Kenya before our Zimbabwe safari and had celebrated his 15th birthday there, replete with Masai warriors doing the "lion dance" for him.

John Stevens,
guide extraordinaire

Family safari in
Zimbabwe, 1993.
From left: Jim and
Emily, Errol and J.C.,
Aileen and the author,
Marjory and Bowdy

Alex on his
15th birthday in the
Masai Mara, Kenya

Emily and Jim on their
own safari in Zimbabwe
in 1998 with Allie and
Emily and John Stevens

Botswana

There have been several trips to Botswana and the Okavango Delta with its marvelous bird life and animals. At least two of these trips involved WWF matters, as I was trying to lay the foundation for a WWF program. I met with President Masire, was given a reception by the U.S. ambassador, and generally made valuable contacts, but the WWF program never eventuated—largely stymied by the fact that Botswana was WWF-International's turf.

We camped once with Harry Selby, a fine person who had been Robert Ruark's professional hunter in Kenya. From Gabarone, the capital, we drove to Kolobeng where Livingstone had lived, found the foundations of his house, and looked out at the view which he described and which has hardly changed. On another occasion, in a small plane, we flew a circuit around much of the country, flying low across the breadth of the Kalahari.

In 1998, we went back, stopping briefly at the Maun airport where Harry Selby came out to greet us. He gave me a very upbeat report on the state of wildlife conservation in Botswana. We went on to "Abu Camp" in the Okavango Delta and spent five days riding African elephants through the bush with Emily and Jim Rowan and our granddaughters, Emily and Allie. What a joy it was to be with them on such an adventure!

Namibia

Namibia we visited three times, once with Caroline Getty when we had our own safari along the Skeleton Coast, guided by Louw Schoeman. We traveled and camped with Garth Owen-Smith who was pioneering concepts of local native responsibility for wildlife management. We found Des and Jen Bartlett, well-known wildlife photographers, living along the coast where they had made their base for a number of years. I went up with Des in his Ultra-Lite plane, flying over the gigantic dunes of that starkly beautiful landscape. I felt as if I were riding a bicycle at 2000 feet. It was cold and I was white-knuckled from gripping a metal strut.

We visited the Waterberg Plateau with the Sants and Watermans.

We have been to the Etosha Pan twice, once driving at night with a scientist to observe close-up a hunt by a large pride of lions. We used a red spotter light which the lions ignored and were able to stay in the midst of them at all times. Their hunt was a highly organized, disciplined affair. We watched two kills.

We visited Katy Payne's elephant communication project, supported by WWF, and spent a night on her observation tower as elephant passed within a few feet to drink at a nearby waterhole. Microphones picked up the low-frequency sounds—too low for human ears—by which they communicate. All of this information was recorded and later deciphered.[2] Caroline Getty recalls that after we had bedded down on the observation tower, all huddled together, there was a deep silence finally broken by my declaring to no one in particular, "I feel like I am sleeping in a compost heap!"

Aileen and I stayed in Windhoek with U.S. Ambassador Genta Holmes and her husband, Michael. We enjoyed immensely our exposure to the nearly independent country, and I was able to lay the foundation for what today is a very active WWF program in Namibia, largely funded by USAID.

The Amazon Basin

Caroline Getty, who accompanied us on several trips to Africa as already noted—including her first—is a young woman from San Francisco of whom we are very fond. We first met at Manaus on the Amazon in Brazil. She was there with her sister, Anne Earhart, and the latter's infant daughter, Sarah. Our small group, which included WWF scientist Tom Lovejoy, headed up the Rio Negro, which joins the Amazon at Manaus, in two small boats.

As luck (or poor management, which it was) would have it, our boat with Caroline and her sister and little niece ran out of gas. The other boat was ahead and went on, unaware of our plight. The Rio Negro was about a mile wide at that point and bordered by unbroken forest. The sun was merciless, and we rigged towels to provide shade for the

2. See Payne, Katy. *Silent ThunderL: In the Presence of Elephants.* Simon and Schuster, New York (1998).

baby. An occasional craft went by in mid-river, but our efforts to hail them were fruitless.

Finally, we succeeded in stopping a boat going upriver, and they took us in tow. It turned out that the probable reason none of the other boats stopped is that they suspected that we were river police. In any event, we finally reached our destination, a former lumber camp built on huge floating logs and spanning the area between the mainland and a nearby island. The river's powerful current flowed between the logs.

We fished for piranha; their snapping teeth made unhooking them tricky. When each of the fish was opened up, it turned out they had all been feeding only on vegetable matter. That was part of the story of why we had come to this place. For many months of the year, the Amazon and its major tributaries, such as the Rio Negro, are in flood and the water level rises 30 to 40 meters. As a result, the river floods for several kilometers back into the riverine forest. Research by Richard Goodwin, which was supported by WWF, had established that a high percentage of the many fish species of the Amazon system essentially only fed during the flood stage and did so by swimming into the flooded forests. We took dugout canoes and paddled through the tree-tops, the normal forest canopy. Orchids hung within reach. Freshwater porpoises surfaced ahead of us. And whenever a nut or fruit dropped from a tree, there would be an audible plop followed almost instantly by a fish rising to gulp it down. It was obvious that the water was teeming with fish.

The point of all this, at least to WWF, was that the human population in the Amazon Basin, including the large city of Manaus, relies on freshwater fish for a high percentage of its protein. Those fish, in turn, rely for their sustenance on the riverine forests that stretch along the shores of the Amazon and its tributaries. Thus, there is a direct connection between the food needs of the people in the Amazon and the continued existence of the riverine forests. This connection had never been demonstrated before the Goodwin/WWF project.

In addition to the river trip, we had a camping experience in the forest about a hundred kilometers from Manaus. All of this is a long-winded account of how we got to know Caroline Getty! In any event, we became close friends. Somewhat later, Caroline became a valued member of the WWF board, visited us at Grace Creek Farm, and we traveled together on a number of occasions. As I have mentioned, her first trip to Africa was with us. In our camp in the Selous Game Reserve of Tanzania, she had her first night in Africa in a tent and never slept a wink. Of course, Rick Weyerhaeuser, Aileen, and I, long accustomed to the sounds of an African night, slept like logs, oblivious of her misery in the next tent. First-timers are often in for rude shocks. Later on that same trip, while we were in Botswana, we stayed overnight in a hotel at Gabarone. Our young English guide, whose name I do not recall, had explained that we needed to make an early start in the morning. When we headed for bed, the guide escorted Caroline to the door of her room and then, as he turned to leave, said: "Good night! I'll knock you up at six o'clock!" I gather that Caroline had another restless night.

South Africa

WE HAD TWO splendid visits to South Africa. It is a beautiful country, though still torn by apartheid when we were there. The chairman of the South African Nature Foundation, the WWF national organization in the country, was Anton Rupert, the leading Afrikaner businessman, well known internationally. I knew him from our association on the WWF-International board. In Johannesburg, we were his guests at the large complex known as the Castle. Formerly the home of Charles and Jane Engelhard, it not only was a sumptuous residence but also included a conference center for the Rupert business enterprises, such as Rothman tobacco. Rupert was not there and we had the house to ourselves. Off our bedroom was a bathroom with an enormous, oval-shaped, marble bathtub which stood on a raised platform and sported gold fixtures. Naturally, I photographed Aileen in her bath.

We were the guests of honor at a dinner given by Harry Oppenheimer and his wife, Bridget, at their home, Brenthurst. The introduction to Oppenheimer, chairman of DeBeers (which controlled the world diamond trade) and of Anglo-American (which controlled a variety of other businesses), had come through Peter Johnson. Peter is one of the world's foremost wildlife photographers and has published a number of stunning books. He and his wife, Claire, lived just outside Johannesburg. I had met him at Long Point one fall where he had come at the invitation of Tony Coe[3] to photograph the Point for a book to be called *The World of Shooting*. (When the book eventually appeared, my cottage's living room provided a two-page photograph. Bowdy, who was a guest at the Point at the time, was extensively interviewed for the book.[4])

Oppenheimer was extremely cordial. Despite the obvious availability of numerous servants, it was evidently his practice to welcome his guests, give them an initial introduction to the others present, find out what they wanted for a cocktail, and then repair to a large table with liquors, ice, and glasses, make the drinks, and carry them over to the newly arrived guests. It was a good way of keeping engaged but without getting tied up in conversation with any particular guest. Having tried the same system myself at home, I find the difficulty to be that most of the guests arrive at about the same time. The Oppenheimers' dinner table was fairly baronial in size, with about 24 chairs, each with a servant standing behind it.

Oppenheimer learned that we were planning to visit Soweto the next day and strongly advised against such a visit at the time. There had been violence there during the day which continued on the next day. As a result, we never did visit this largest and best known of the black African townships.

The Brenthurst Library, a very modern facility on his property, houses Oppenheimer's Africana collection which had been started by his father, Sir Ernest Oppenheimer. The books in the collection are rather disappointing but the manuscript materials are outstanding. I

3. Henry E. Coe, 3rd. He had been a sailing friend of Aileen's as a girl on Long Island. Tony had represented Chase Manhattan Bank in South Africa and had there become a friend of Peter Johnson's.

4. Johnson, Peter, and Wannenberg, Alf. *The World of Shooting*. Photographex Inc. (1987). The text and photographs pertaining to Long Point are on pp. 292-307.

have found myself bidding against Oppenheimer for a Livingstone letter on at least one occasion—a losing proposition! His own personal interest lies with the Romantic poets. While in Johannesburg, I visited Thorold's bookstore, a rare-book enterprise owned and operated by Robin Fryde. I have bought a number of items from him over the years, and he has visited us in Washington.

We took the famous Blue Train from Johannesburg to Cape Town. I had reserved the one super-deluxe suite which consisted of a sitting room, a bedroom with twin beds, and a bathroom with an enormous tub that ran athwart the car. The club car where we had a drink before dinner was very congenial. The next morning when we awoke, we were crossing the vast barrens known as the Great Karroo. It was exciting to see a klipspringer standing on a rocky outcrop, a kopje, as we sped by. The trip took about 20 hours, from 4 p.m. to noon the next day, as best I can recall. In Cape Town, we again were the guests of Anton Rupert and his wife, Hubert. We again stayed at a great establishment, Fleur du Cap, a magnificent wine estate outside Stellenbosch. We had the splendid house to ourselves. The Ruperts live in a much more modest house in Stellenbosch but they gave us a dinner party at Fleur du Cap. Anton is a remarkable man whom I like and admire.

I attended a 25th anniversary meeting of the South African Nature Foundation at Groote Constanzia, a famous, old wine estate. I was welcomed and at some point in the proceedings was asked whether I would care to say something. After thanking them for their invitation to the meeting and offering my congratulations on their anniversary and on their many accomplishments over the years, I went on to recount my early involvement in African conservation, principally in East Africa and primarily involving the training of black Africans to undertake responsibilities in park and wildlife management. I went into this in some detail for my all-white audience, knowing that in the South Africa of that day essentially no black Africans had been trained for responsible positions in natural resource management at all. When I was through, there was dead silence, no questions, no comments. Finally, the meeting resumed as if I had never opened my mouth. All of this was at a time when apartheid was plainly coming to an end. I had not been aggressive, critical, or rude to my hosts but simply stated facts as I knew them. And those facts were certainly relevant to the South African situation. In any event, it was not a comfortable moment.

Stellenbosch and Cape Town were lovely places to visit. I got to know the principal bookstore, Clarke's, which specialized in contemporary South African books as well as rare books. We drove down to the Cape of Good Hope itself, a pretty bleak spot. We drove through Simon's Town, where over 100 years before my grandfather Train had called on the British naval commander while he was on his way to Kerguelen Island in the South Indian Ocean to observe the Transit of Venus.

On that first trip to South Africa, we visited Natal as the guests of Ian Player. Ian is recognized as the father of conservation in Natal and particularly as the savior of the white rhino. Of course, he may be best known as the brother of Gary Player, the internationally known golfer. Ian took us through the country of the first Zulu War, including the battlefield of Isandlwana where the British had been crushed in 1879. We visited some of the fine Natal national parks, particularly Umfolozi where the white rhino has made an extraordinary comeback.

Ian had instituted an effort to bring Afrikaners, English, and blacks together in the course of a wilderness experience. It was his conviction that stereotypes and ingrained biases tended to evaporate under such circumstances. He gave us a brief overnight demonstration in which a leading role was played by an old Zulu named Magqubu Ntobela. The latter spoke no English but Ian, who was fluent in Zulu, translated. Magqubu told us how the Zulu people used the various plants and about some of the history of his people.

We were joined by an English South African and by an Afrikaner who had been in the Green Berets and who spoke only limited English. The latter admitted that he could hardly remember ever having talked to an Englishman before and said that he had been brought up to hate the English. Much of this came out as we sat around the campfire at night.

During the course of the night, each of us took turns "on watch" by the fire for a couple of hours. The next morning, as we ate breakfast, Magqubu (pronounced "Makuba" with a distinct "click" after the first syllable) said the Lord's Prayer in Zulu—replete with all of the "clicks" that characterize that language. Then each of us was invited to say what the whole experience had meant to us. I have no recollection of what I said at the time but it had been a moving occasion. Ian founded his International Wilderness Leadership Foundation on the philosophy which he had demonstrated to us. An American, Vance Martin, became his right hand in this enterprise.

Aileen and I spent about four days in the West Cape area, centered on the town of Clanwilliam. It was the first week of September—early spring in the Cape—and the wildflowers were in full bloom. An American woman, Kay Berg, was our guide and she gave us an unforgettable experience. She had married a South African, and their daughter had married a local farmer at whose farmhouse we spent our first night on the way to Clanwilliam. Kay had taught herself botany and had published a guide to the Cape wildflowers. The flowers were unbelievably spectacular. We felt that we were viewing one of the wonders of the natural world. In some areas, the landscape was bright blue for a mile and then yellow, etc. In other areas, I counted 30 or more different flowering species within one square yard of ground.

We lunched at one farm where Anton Rupert joined us and where I heard an instructive story. It seems that the farmer, in order to protect the ground and the wildflowers, had removed all sheep from his land. Then he watched while over several years the diversity and profusion of wildflowers steadily declined. Finally, someone pointed out to him that for thousands of years and up to historic times, springbok had migrated through the area in their millions. Their sharp hooves had doubtless churned the ground as if it had been plowed. The farmer restored his sheep to the land and the wildflowers soon rebounded in all their glory.

Aileen playing croquet with
Dean Acheson at Mill Reef, Antigua.
Their opponents were
McGeorge Bundy and
Archibald MacLeish.

Vacationing in the
Dordogne, France,
1979, with Peter and
Deborah Solbert and
Mary and McGeorge Bundy

The Rowan house
on Nevis

Latin America and the Caribbean

I HAVE ALREADY described our honeymoon cruise aboard *Molli-hawk* in 1954, starting in Antigua and reaching the Tobago Cays in the Grenadines. In 1963, we chartered the *Caribee* with Kay and Crapo Bullard, old friends from Nonquitt, and sailed from Nassau down the Exumas in the Bahamas. In 1970, we spent a week with Laurance and Mary Rockefeller on board their large sailboat, *Sea Star,* cruising from St. Thomas to St. Martin. Then, in early 1977, we sailed as guests of Peter and Carol Black on board *Caroline* through the "out islands" of the Bahamas, the Turks and Caicos, and disembarking at San Juan.

After the Blacks bought Musha Cay in the Exumas, we visited them there once, fished for bonefish, snorkeled, and sailed aboard a later *Caroline.* On three different occasions, we rented houses at the Mill Reef Club, Antigua, together with Mac and Mary Bundy and Peter and Deborah Solbert. We were joined once by Kingman and Mary Louise Brewster. (Kingman had recently retired as president of Yale and was then U.S. ambassador in London.) With the Bundys and Solberts we also rented a condominium on Grenada for a visit one winter. These were fun times with old friends—rum punches on the beach, picnics on Green Island off Antigua, snorkeling, tennis, and a bit of dancing under the stars to tapes that Mac had brought with him.

More recently, we have visited Emily and Jim Rowan at their house on Nevis, spent a week snorkeling off Bonaire in the Dutch Antilles, and traveled on AES business to Puerto Rico and the Dominican Republic and with WWF to Dominica.

Mexico

Aileen and I have made many trips "south of the border." I first went to Mexico after law school with my friend Jack Castles and we spent about a week at Acapulco deep-sea fishing. We stayed at Las Brisas, the one and only hotel at the time. It was there that a torch-bearing diver leapt off the cliff into the sea at night. Subsequently, I returned to Mexico by myself to fish from Mazatlán further up the west coast.

Many years later, along with Kate Davis Quesada, Jane Dart, Alice Eno, Roger Payne (WWF whale scientist), Dave and Nancy Taylor, and Barney and Ginny Clarkson, we chartered a boat called the *Observer* out of La Paz on Baja California and cruised for a week in the Sea of Cortez, traveling overland to Magdalena Bay to see the gray whales on their calving ground. We returned there on the occasion of a WWF board meeting in Mexico City. Earlier I had called on Mexican officials to urge protection of the calving lagoons. We returned to Magdalena Bay with the WWF board in 1999.

As president of WWF, I made several trips to Mexico to visit WWF projects and to help strengthen conservation activities there. On one occasion, I traveled with Archie Carr, world-renowned conservation biologist whose specialty was marine turtles, to the coast of Michoacán southwest of Mexico City. We went to a stretch of beach which was a principal nesting area for the olive ridley turtle. Generations of human predation on their nests, not to mention predation by other animals, had reduced the nesting turtles to a mere handful of the original population. The eggs brought a high price and supposedly helped boost the virility of the Mexican male. WWF paid an equivalent price to local teenagers to collect the eggs, which were then relocated into protected nests, behind wire fences.

The WWF headquarters was simply a large thatched structure right on the edge of the beach. Eating, sleeping, cooking, and relaxation were all carried out in the one large open room. Sanitary facilities seemed nonexistent. Archie and I each had a hammock alongside local staff. Since turtles did not usually come ashore to nest until around midnight, he and I whiled away the time, sitting in our hammocks and sharing a bottle of rum. We managed to still be ambulatory at the appointed hour and went along the beach with our flashlights. We located several nesting turtles by their tracks up from the water and observed the entire egg-laying process. The eggs looked like nothing so much as Ping-Pong balls.

We visited the principal wire enclosure within which nests had been relocated, each with a small sign giving the date of relocation and the number of eggs. As we watched, little turtles were breaking the surface of the sand. They are genetically programmed to hatch at night so as to give them greater protection from predators, such as gulls, that prey on them during their perilous journey across the beach to the sea. They are also genetically programmed to head, when hatched, toward light. On the natural, undisturbed beach at night, the brightest area is the sea, the result of the reflected light of stars and moon.

The number and complexity of such natural arrangements, developed over evolutionary eons, never fail to leave me awestruck. In any event, taking advantage of this particular instinct, we placed a lantern on the ground by a corner of the nest enclosure where there was an entrance gate. A board stood on its edge across the opening. The hatching turtles lost no time heading for the light of the lantern and soon they were piling up in a windrow against the board. It was a simple matter to pick them up, determine their species (olive ridley or leatherback), and place them in a large, enamel wash basin.

When this was relatively full, I carried it down to where the waves were gently breaking and then, kneeling down in the moonlight, tipped the basin so that baby turtles spilled out and headed into the sea where they rapidly vanished. It was a moving moment that I will never forget. One senses the elemental forces that have driven this creature for millions of years. Of course, once in the sea their chances of survival were still not rosy but at least we had spared them the predation of gulls, raccoons, pigs, dogs, and humans. Of those that do survive, the females will return to this same beach to nest and repeat the age-old cycle.

At the conclusion of the visit to the turtle nesting area, I had gone to Morelia, the old colonial capital of Michoacán which lies almost due west of Mexico City, and paid a call on Cuauhtemoc Cardenas, the governor. He had been supportive of our project and had assigned a detachment of marines to help protect the beach. No matter that they were drunk most of the time! In any event, I wanted to thank him for his support and to give him a report on the project. He was a tall, somewhat austere figure, who listened attentively but had little to say and left the room where we were meeting quite soon. He has become a leader of the opposition to the ruling party and, in 1998, was elected the mayor of Mexico City.

Another WWF project in Mexico involved the monarch butterfly. Essentially all of the monarch butterflies of North America east of the Rockies migrate south in the autumn to half a dozen or so spots in the pine-covered hills of Michoacán. Each of these sites is about an acre or two in extent. Arriving in November and starting north in late February, there are in the neighborhood of 100 million monarchs at the height of the winter season. It is a most extraordinary sight, as whole trees are densely covered with clusters of the butterflies.

When the sky is overcast, the butterflies hang relatively motionless, conserving their energy. When the sun comes out, masses of the insects erupt into the air, swirling like autumn leaves in the wind. When the butterflies start north, feeding on milkweed along the way, the females mate as they leave. The males then die, and the female lays her eggs in a milkweed plant and then she dies. Her young absorb the toxicity of the milkweed, which protects the adult against most predators. The next generation moves further north and repeats the cycle.

Finally, in September, the fourth or fifth generation of monarch migrates back to the pine forests of Michoacán. And the individual butterfly that starts that journey is also the one that completes it. However, no butterfly that makes the great journey has ever made it before. It is removed by three or four generations from the ancestor that did so. So there is no experience or memory factor at work. A genetically implanted signal tells them to head for the wintering grounds, and they probably navigate using a variety of aids—perhaps celestial and perhaps orientation by electromagnetic lines of force around the earth. Whatever the explanation, the monarch life cycle and migration is truly an amazing phenomenon.

An organization named Monarca had been founded in Mexico City by Rodolfo Ogarrio to undertake the protection of the butterflies' wintering sites. Rodolfo was a young businessman-turned-conservationist. WWF not only shared his goals for the butterflies but also was anxious to encourage and assist the development of citizen conservation organizations in Mexico. Aileen and I visited Rodolfo and his attractive wife, Norma, and stayed with them at their country home. On the occasion of the WWF board meeting in Mexico City, Rodolfo took us to one of the monarch sites where we lunched and enjoyed the

butterflies once again. The threats to their wintering sites never seem
to cease. The principal threat is that of logging. Timber operations are
a main source of livelihood in the area, and WWF has sought to
develop alternative sources of income for the local people—tourism,
crafts, a trout hatchery, etc. It has so far proved impossible to buy the
land in question because it belongs to the local *ejido.*

On another occasion, Aileen and I paid a brief visit to Yucatán. We
had been on a two-week vacation aboard a chartered sailboat, sailing
and snorkeling along the barrier reef that follows the coastline of
Belize. We had flown in a small plane from Placentia in Belize where
we had left the boat to Belize City, where we had chartered a plane to
take us to Cancún, the resort at the northern tip of Yucatán. Unfortunately, the weather had grown very stormy and the pilot canceled our
flight. Having no alternative, we boarded a local bus which deposited
us 12 hours later at 1:00 a.m. in the town square of Puerto Morelos, a
small village on the coast not far from Cancún. We had not dared eat
or drink the roadside fare during the bus trip but had subsisted on a
couple of Cokes and a Hershey bar.

When the bus drove off into the night, leaving us with our small
pile of bags under the one naked bulb that lit the deserted square, we
felt pretty desperate. Suddenly I heard an auto start up. Sprinting in
the direction of the sound, I found a Land Rover just pulling away.
I hailed it down and persuaded the driver to take us to our motel a
couple of miles out of town, which he miraculously seemed to know.
When we finally arrived, WWF vice president Curt Freese had just
driven up after spending most of the evening at the Cancún airport,
trying to track us down.

We visited a Smithsonian-WWF project involving the mist-net-
ting of migratory birds in the Yucatán forests to help establish the importance of those forests as winter habitat for North American birds. It
has become plain that even though birds are fully protected on their
summer/breeding grounds, protection will not aid them if their winter habitat is destroyed or radically altered. Moreover, migratory birds
cannot simply shift to another forest habitat because these tend to be
already occupied at the optimum density. Thus, the birds simply vanish.

One of the root causes of forest destruction in the area was slash-

and-burn agriculture. At one time this kind of rotational agriculture left the land fallow sufficiently long for the forest to regenerate. However, because of human population growth today, the slash-and-burn cycle is repeated so frequently that there is little or no regeneration. Another project that WWF was supporting in Yucatán was a demonstration of the use of forest mulch as fertilizer to increase productivity and, hopefully, help stretch out the cultivation cycle.

We also visited a lobster fishery in a very large lagoon area called Sian Ca'an where WWF had introduced techniques to put the fishery on a sustainable basis. In any event, we crammed a number of WWF activities into our stay in Yucatán as well as a visit to Mayan ruins in the area.

Belize

We have been to Belize about four times, always enjoying the snorkeling on its barrier reef, second in size only to the Great Barrier Reef of Australia, which Aileen visited once with her sister Helen. Our two-week sailboat charter along the reef was memorable, in part, for the experience of swimming along with a school of barracuda. Twice we rented cottages on Salt Water Cay, once with Elliot and Anne Richardson and once with Roger and Vicki Sant and Sukey Wagner and her daughter, Lisa. These were fun occasions when we took our own cook and boatman (with boat) from the mainland. Another time, WWF had a board meeting at Belize City and we visited WWF projects in the mountainous jaguar reserve and on the reef off San Pedro Island.

Costa Rica

We have been to Costa Rica a number of times. The country has been a bright spot in Central America so far as conservation is concerned and has also succeeded in maintaining a non-military, democratic government and a stable middle-class society. Aileen and I visited the Monte Verde cloud forest reserve which WWF has played a major role in supporting over the years. There we had a fleeting glimpse of a quetzal. We spent several days at the Corcovado National Park on the

Pacific coast, enjoying the many birds such as toucans on walks through the forest.

In the capital of San José, I had a meeting with President Carazzo along with his government's senior environmental officials. (These men, Alvaro Ugalde, director of Costa Rica national parks, and Mario Boza, the country's first NPS director, received WWF's J. Paul Getty International Wildlife Award in 1983 at a ceremony with President Reagan in the White House Rose Garden.)

San José was also the scene of the first meeting of the parties to the Convention on the International Trade in Endangered Species of Fauna and Flora (CITES), the so-called Washington Convention, the U.S. delegation to which I had headed in 1973 when I was chairman of the Council on Environmental Quality. CEQ had been the principal proponent of the convention, and the U.S. had achieved endorsement of the concept by the Stockholm Conference in 1972. There were a number of environmentalists at the San José meeting, although not officially a part of any delegation, and by virtue of seniority of sorts I was the organizer of the non-governmental organizations. Using the Union Carbide office in San José, we were able to reproduce and distribute papers to the delegates, and each morning I assembled all the NGOs for a discussion of the day's business. TRAFFIC-USA, a small NGO concerned with wildlife trade issues, was an ally at San José and, following that meeting, became part of WWF-U.S.

Panama

Aileen and I made one trip to Panama. With USAID support, WWF was building an NGO network in the country. We visited Barro Colorado, an island in Gatún Lake where the Smithsonian had maintained a research program since the building of the canal and the flooding of the lake. The scientists had documented the steady erosion of species on the island due to its isolation. We spent a night with the San Blas Indians on one of their small islands off the Caribbean coast. These Indians cultivate crops in the mainland forest during the day and then withdraw to their homes offshore at night. Their age-old methods of cultivation make very little disturbance in the forest, and they venerate the trees as representing the spirits of their ancestors. The boundary of the Indian lands runs along the ridge of the Cordillera—the Continental Divide. It is instructive to see how lush the forest is on the Indian side of the divide and how overgrazed, eroded, and generally barren the land is on the Panamanian side.

One of our projects involved determining the exact location of the boundary and clearing a wide trail along it, hopefully as a bulwark against encroachment on the Indian lands. When we returned to Panama City, we attended a reception at which I had a conversation with the vice president of the country. I described our time with the San Blas Indians, and I commented on how much we could learn from them about ecologically sound cultivation. I found him totally insensitive to and disinterested in the Indians. As I recall, he said something to this effect: "Those Indians ought to give up their primitive way of life, move into the towns, and learn to live the way we do."

Guatemala

We had a WWF board meeting in Guatemala. I remember particularly the beauty of the countryside—the lakes and distant volcanos. We paid a brief visit to a small village on the Pacific coast where WWF was conducting a project. I asked the mayor what the population of the village was. "About 500," he said. "How long has the population been 500?" I inquired. "It has always been about 500," he replied. Looking at the crowds of young children, I said: "What happens to the surplus?" "Oh," he said, "they go either to Guatemala City or to the United States." One of my strongest biases is against the United States permitting itself to be used as a dumping ground for surplus people of countries that either will not or cannot control their own population growth.

One of the most interesting aspects of our time in Guatemala was our visit to Tikal, the great Mayan ruin close to the border with Belize. The ruins were quite spectacular, hacked out of the surrounding jungle. The Guatemalan government has set aside about 100 square kilometers of forest as a park surrounding the ancient city. Tikal is a World Heritage site and it was gratifying to see the combination of both cultural and natural values being protected at the same site.

Colombia and Ecuador

Following his graduation from Trinity College, Bowdy spent the following year in Bogotá, Colombia, taking university-level courses taught in Spanish and living with a Spanish-speaking family. I had recently (March 1978) become head of WWF-U.S., and we decided to put together a trip to South America. We chartered the *Beagle IV* in the Galápagos and our party was made up of Elliot and Anne Richardson, Henry Richardson, Aileen and myself, Bowdy, Errol, and Carter Christianson, an American girl in Bowdy's program in Bogotá. The *Beagle IV* was a converted research vessel. She was not a luxury craft but served our purpose very well. Her skipper was Fiddy Anglemeyer, whose parents had come from Germany prior to World War II and were sort of "earliest settlers" in the Galápagos.

After Aileen and I had spent several days in Bogotá, we had all met in Quito. There we met Roque and Pilar Sevilla for the first time. He had founded the principal conservation NGO in Ecuador, the Fundación Natura, which became over time a major collaborator with WWF and is today a WWF associate organization. The Sevillas are an attractive couple and have become good personal friends over the years. They ensured that we saw the principal sights of Quito, such as the Gold Museum. (Roque later became a member of the WWF-U.S. board, and, in 1998, he was elected mayor of Quito.) After little more than a day in Quito, we flew to the Galápagos via Guayaquil, landing on the island of Baltra, where we boarded the *Beagle IV.*

The Galápagos

We had a marvelous seven days. We saw few other boats and had almost all our landing sites entirely to ourselves. We were told that government policy then was never to permit more than 6000 tourists a year in the Galápagos. When we were last there in 1996—less than 20 years later—we were told that the government had set a final ceiling of 60,000 tourists a year and that the actual number was already close to 90,000. In any event, we loved snorkeling with the sea lions, visiting the blue-footed boobies' nesting colonies, and experiencing all the other wonders of the Galápagos. They are, indeed, magical isles. We visited the Charles Darwin Research Station on Santa Cruz where WWF was financing education exhibits at the visitor center.

We have been back to the Galápagos twice, and they were both wonderful trips. Aileen organized both trips and made all the arrangements. In 1994, we chartered the 100-foot ketch *Andando* (skippered by Captain Lenin) with a group of close friends: Antony and Jenny Acland from England,[5] Roger and Vicki Sant, Fritz and Lee Link, Gary and Joan Jewett, and Judy Waterman (Bob having had to drop out at the last moment due to a business matter). Then, in 1996, we again chartered the *Andando* and this time took all family: Chris and Nancy Gustin, Alex Smith, Jim and Emily Rowan, along with their daughters Emily and Allie, and J.C. and Errol Giordano. Bowdy had a business conflict so he and Marjory did not come.

On each trip, we did much that we had done before but it was a special treat to have such good friends and family share the experiences that we had loved so much. And there were special moments: sitting around our mess table on the afterdeck listening to Antony, after a sufficient number of glasses of wine, sing the Eton Boating Song; or six-year-old Allie playing with a sea lion pup in the shallows off one of the islands, both of them displaying that special empathy which the young seem to feel toward one another irrespective of species.

Gary Jewett was a good friend of President Sixto of Ecuador, having known him at the Inter-American Development Bank. As a result, following our cruise in 1994, we all dined at the Presidential Palace in Quito with the president and his wife. At the close of the dinner, after President Sixto made some gracious remarks about us and our visit, I took advantage of the opportunity to tell him—very politely and diplomatically, of course!—of all the problems that the Galápagos were fac-

5. Antony had been British ambassador in Washington in 1989-1992. He and Jenny were married not long after his arrival. He had lost his wife and she her husband, and they had known each other practically since childhood. They spent that Thanksgiving at Grace Creek Farm as the guests of Michael and Maxine Jenkins, Michael being the British minister at that time. We had gone to Florida for Thanksgiving and had lent the farm to the Jenkinses. The story which we enjoy is that Antony and Jenny became engaged at Grace Creek. Since his retirement from the Foreign Office, Antony has been provost of Eton, where we have visited them on several occasions—as well as at their farm in Somerset.

ing and the need for government action to regulate fishing, to control human migration from the mainland, to control tourism, etc. Sixto listened to it all with good grace and I followed up with a detailed letter when I returned to Washington. It will be a tragedy if the Galápagos are not protected. They are a World Heritage site. As it has turned out, most of our recommendations were included in Ecuadoran legislation in 1998.

The WWF board met in Quito in 1986. Bill Reilly had recently left the WWF presidency to become administrator of the Environmental Protection Agency and Kathryn Fuller had been named president of WWF. At a large dinner in Quito, with many Ecuadorans present, Kathryn made an impressive debut by giving a speech in Spanish. After the board meeting, there was a field trip to the Ecuadoran Amazon region. Traveling by plane, helicopter, and finally by dugout canoe, we stayed for several days in a small camp in the forest. All told, we have been to Ecuador four times.

Peru

Following our first trip to the Galápagos, we had flown to Lima, Peru, and spent about ten days in that varied country. In Lima, we stayed with Felipe Benavides, a well-connected Peruvian who was the country's best-known conservationist. He took us to the Paracas Reserve south of Lima, a large, arid promontory with concentrations of migrant shorebirds and sea lions. The guano islands just offshore, which we visited, had once been the base of a very profitable fertilizer industry. Enormous colonies of seabirds lived on the islands, feeding on the seemingly inexhaustible supply of *anchovetas*, a small sardine-like fish.

At one time the World Bank funded a modern fishing fleet to catch *anchovetas*. It was not long before the *anchovetas* had been reduced to noncommercial quantities through overfishing, the population of seabirds collapsed, the accumulation of guano no longer supported a fertilizer industry, and the fleet of trawlers lay rusting in a nearby bay. So far as I know, that remains the situation today. The whole fiasco was a demonstration of the folly of development projects which do not take appropriate account of ecological reality. One unforgettable moment on Paracas came when we kept out of sight behind a very large rock and sat there while several giant Andean condors, riding the air currents down from the mountains, soared a scant 20 feet above us.

We flew further south to Arequipa and from there drove up into the vast, arid foothills of the Andes to see herds of vicuña in the wild. They had been almost exterminated by hunters but Benavides had launched a personal crusade to protect them, and the campaign was having some success. Later we went to Cuzco and then on the train to Machu Picchu. The train, which has since been subject to occasional attacks by Peruvian terrorists, provided an appropriate prelude to that fabled city of the Incas, rediscovered in 1911 by Hiram Bingham. I remember my first view of torrent ducks in the rapids of the river alongside the train tracks. Errol and Bowdy were both with us, and we were all captivated by the wild and romantic situation of Machu Picchu.

Venezuela

On another trip, in 1985 or 1986, while I was wearing my WWF hat, we visited Venezuela. A member of our staff, Byron Swift, was working there at the time. He introduced us to Antonio and Aurita Branger, who owned a very large cattle ranch named Hato Piñero in the *llanos* (savannah) region of Venezuela. We flew there with Kathy Phelps, wife of William (Billy) Phelps, co-author of *A Guide to the Birds of Venezuela*.[6]

We spent three days at the ranch which was being developed to accommodate tourists, particularly birders. The bird life was extraordinary, especially the herons, egrets, ibises, and other species living among the many lakes and streams. We drove out at night to find a jaguar but failed. We did see the bright red eyes of many crocodiles reflecting the rays of our spotlight. There were herds of 20 or 30 capybaras, the largest of the rodents. They have semi-webbed feet and are so aquatic in their habits that one of the popes (or perhaps a local prelate) declared the capybara a fish so that good Roman Catholics could eat it on fast days.

6. De Schauensee, Rodolphe Meyer, and Phelps, William H., Jr. *A Guide to the Birds of Venezuela*. Princeton University Press, Princeton (1978).

WWF was interested in seeing to it that Hato Piñero achieved some sort of protected status, as was Don Antonio. However, after meeting at his apartment in Caracas with all of his relatives who also had an interest in the property, I decided it was too complex a matter for WWF to really help on. I served on an international advisory council for several years but eventually got off. (As of the end of 1998, Byron Swift tells me that a great deal of progress has finally been made in protecting the Hato Piñero lands.)

I met with the cabinet minister responsible for environmental matters and also with the board of Fudena, the leading Venezuelan NGO concerned with wildlife conservation and a WWF associate organization. With Fudena's longtime president, Cecilia Blum, we visited coastal areas west of Caracas.

Brazil

I have already touched on at least one visit to Brazil where I have been a number of times. There have been visits to São Paulo, Rio de Janeiro, Manaus, and Brazilia. At Brazilia, there was a presentation of the J. Paul Getty Wildlife Prize to two Brazilian citizens in the presence of the president. WWF Vice President Tom Lovejoy did the honors in Portuguese. Aileen was with me there as well as on visits to São Paulo and Rio and then up the coast to see the Atlantic coastal forest, which today remains only in fragments. It was there that the golden lion tamarin was being reintroduced in the wild in a joint project of the National Zoo in Washington and WWF. In Rio, we were given a dinner party by the internationally famous plastic surgeon Pitanguy at his hilltop home and clinic, replete with Picassos and comparable art. Pitanguy had "restructured" many of the famous faces of Hollywood. I recall sitting next to a woman at the dinner who told me proudly that she was a conservationist. I told her that was great. "Yes," she said, "I keep a pet parrot in my apartment!"

While in Manaus, in addition to our adventures on the Rio Negro, we visited a long-term project which was the inspiration of Tom Lovejoy, who was with us. The project, known then by the simple name of the Minimum Critical Size of Ecosystems Project, was designed to demonstrate the effect on biological diversity of isolating different-sized tracts of forest. Tom had taken advantage of a new Brazilian law requiring owners of large forest tracts to set aside at least 50 percent of the forest for protection. He persuaded several ranchers north of Manaus to accomplish this goal by setting aside a number of different tracts of varying sizes. Having established baseline data of plants, birds, mammals, etc., the project was monitoring the changes that occurred following isolation. So often, small natural areas are given protected status, but the reality is that they are not large enough to prevent a fairly rapid loss of species. Tom's project is designed to provide the scientific basis for understanding that phenomenon.

We spent a night at the project site, about 100 kilometers from Manaus on a dirt road slashed through the forest and deeply eroded by the heavy rains. We slept in hammocks slung close together under a thatched roof. It poured most of the night. There were a couple of other guests whom I did not know. In the middle of the night, an unfamiliar female voice spoke from the next hammock: "If you stick your —— knee in my back one more time, you'll be sorry!"

In 1992, I attended briefly the U.N. Conference on Environment and Development held in Rio on the twentieth anniversary of the Stockholm Conference. I was nominally a member of the U.S. delegation which was headed by Bill Reilly. My time in Rio happened to coincide with President Bush's attendance, and I took part in two meetings with him. The first was with U.S. environmental organization heads and I sat on his right. When he called on me first for remarks, I wished him a happy birthday and also expressed the hope that the U.S. would support and sign the Biological Diversity Convention being negotiated at Rio. (Bush did not really respond to our comments and the U.S. did not sign the convention.) The president met at lunch with international NGOs, and I was again asked to attend. This time I sat directly opposite Bush. As we were settling into our places, he said across the table to me: "Train, how do you keep so fit?" I replied: "Mr. President, I eat anything I want, exercise as little as possible, and have two good, stiff dry martinis before dinner every night." I do not recall the president pursuing the matter any further, and the international guests, all obviously awed by their luncheon meeting with the President of the United States, were visibly startled.

While Bill Reilly took a leading role in the conference, it was generally felt that the White House did not give him the support he needed. When Bush addressed the conference, I listened and watched on the TV in my hotel room. It was not a bad speech but equivocated on both the biological diversity and the global warming agreements. When I went down to the lobby after he had finished, I ran into then-Senator Al Gore. I asked him what he thought of the president's speech. "Disgusting!" said Gore. (Of course, the Clinton administration's position on climate change at the 1997 Kyoto meeting set out goals considerably more lenient than those suggested by the U.S. at Rio in 1992.)

In 1996, following the AES Corporation acquisition of a substantial part of the electricity-generating capacity of Rio, we had an AES board meeting there with a field trip to the hydroelectric facilities involved. On the same trip, we went to Buenos Aires and then to the AES San Nicolás coal-fired plant acquired as part of the Argentine privatization program. Having never visited Argentina prior to about 1990, I have been there four times since.

Argentina and Antarctica

ONE TRIP TO Argentina involved the annual meeting in 1993 of all the WWF organizations around the world, together with meetings of the WWF-International board and EXCO. It was not a particularly happy time, as the tension between me (and WWF-U.S.) on the one hand and Prince Philip and Charles de Haes (and WWF-International) on the other reached something of a climax during the meeting.

We stopped in Argentina twice on the way to Antarctica, always spending a night or more in Buenos Aires. With a WWF group, we visited Iguazú Falls, on both the Argentine and the Brazilian sides. Iguazú is one of the world's greatest cataracts and spreads over a very large area. To the south, we flew down the coast to Río Gallegos in

Iguazú Falls

Janet Fesler and Mel Lane
crossing Drake's Passage.
Janet is WWF's incomparable
trip organizer as well as
staff liaison to the
board and council.

Patagonia and then drove east across the vast, rolling plains to the Andes. We stayed at a little town on Lake Argentino and visited the face of the Moreno Glacier where Aileen took a marvelous photo that we have framed at home. I thought Patagonia very beautiful—enormous open spaces with the shadows of the clouds moving across them.

Mel Lane,
Connie Eristoff,
and Bill deRecat,
following a visit
to a Russian research
station, Antarctica

Our point of departure on both Antarctic trips was the Argentine port of Ushuaia on the Beagle Channel in Tierra del Fuego. This had been the jumping-off place for the Argentine invasion of the Falklands. We wandered the town, visited the small museum, went for a cruise along the Beagle Channel, enjoying the sightings of penguins, and spent a day in the Tierra del Fuego National Park. One trip to Antarctica was aboard the *World Discoverer* with a group of WWF members, many of whom were close friends. We had an extremely rough crossing of the Drake Passage and then a beautiful cruise through the Antarctic archipelago to Palmer Station, the U.S. research base.

We made many landings by Zodiac to visit nesting colonies of penguins—adele, macaroni, chinstrap, and gentou. The seabird life was wonderful. Peter Harrison, perhaps the leading expert on the seabirds of the world, was on board. We watched a leopard seal only feet from our Zodiac seize a penguin and literally shake it out of its skin before devouring it. It was spectacular cruising down narrow fjord-like passages with sheer mountains rising to the side and cliffs of ice in different shades of blue.

Our next trip to the Antarctic was at the end of 1994, also from Ushuaia, and was aboard a large Russian icebreaker, the *Kapitan Dranitsyn,* along with our old traveling companions, Bob and Judy Waterman and Caroline Getty. This time we sailed south into the Weddell

Penguin rookery,
South Sandwich Islands
in the Weddell Sea

Sea, our destination the breeding grounds of the emperor penguin. We found them in abundance on the shelf ice and visited several large rookeries. The chicks were already large fledglings, almost ready to strike out on their own. Our ship had two helicopters aboard, and these were used to ferry us from the ship to the rookeries.

One of those flights was particularly memorable, as we flew low amongst sparkling blue icebergs frozen into the ice shelf. Once we had landed, we hiked between ice cliffs on either side, emperor penguins sliding by us on their bellies, until we reached an open basin, surrounded by low ice hills, in the middle of which was the rookery. Our unanimous reaction was that this was the most beautiful place in the world. It had an extraordinary physical beauty combined with overwhelming silence, a sense of remoteness, of being at the ends of the earth—as, of course, we were—and wonder at the penguins and their extraordinary life cycle. Time seemed to lose its meaning as the sun dipped down to touch the earth and then rose again.

Among the number of professional wildlife photographers aboard our ship was Frans Lanting. We became good friends and have remained in touch since. Frans is one of the best wildlife photographers in the world and combines his technical artistry with a strong interest in the conservation of his subjects.

Traveling through the Weddell Sea was a great experience in itself.

I loved to stand on the silent bridge in the middle of the night—at least by the clock—and see the vast expanse of ice stretching to the horizon. The ship tried to take advantage of the open leads but frequently had to hit the ice head-on. She was designed to ride up on the ice and crush down through it. We stopped and went ashore in the South Sandwich Islands, first discovered by Captain Cook, and then went on to several stops along the north coast of South Georgia.

There we visited king penguin rookeries. Frans Lanting chartered a helicopter for a flight over South Georgia and invited us to join him. We flew up and over the central mountain range and traced the route followed by Ernest Shackleton in 1916 on his heroic journey to arrange a rescue of his polar expeditionary party which he had left on Elephant Island. From there he had traveled by small boat 800 miles through wild and icy seas to the south coast of South Georgia and then by foot over the mountains to a whaling station on the north shore. He succeeded in rescuing his party without the loss of a single man, an extraordinary story recounted dramatically in the book *Endurance.*[7] We visited a small island just off South Georgia and walked among nesting waved albatrosses. From South Georgia we went to the Falklands from where we flew to Santiago, Chile, and home.

Cruising Aboard Ivara

An account of our travels would be woefully incomplete if I did not include several delightful cruises in the Mediterranean with John Loudon aboard his motor yacht *Ivara.*

We first met John in about 1980 when he became president of WWF-International following the retirement of Prince Bernhard of the Netherlands and held the position until the election of Prince

---

7. Lansing, Alfred. *Endurance: Shackleton's Incredible Voyage.* Carroll & Graf, New York (1986). A more recent account illustrated by photos taken at the time is Caroline Alexander's *The Endurance: Shackleton's Legendary Antarctic Expedition.* Alfred A. Knopf, New York (1998). In July 1999, Aileen and I spent several days with Caroline Alexander as Joe Cullman's guests while salmon fishing in New Brunswick. She proved a delightful and extremely interesting person.

John Loudon

Doris Magowan

Michael and Maxine Jenkins

Aboard *Ivara* in the Ionian Sea

Philip about two years later. He had been chairman and CEO of Royal Dutch Shell, which he had built into one of the great companies of the world. We became fast friends and shared many perspectives on the management of WWF-International.

John stayed with us a number of times, both in Washington and at Grace Creek Farm, and we visited him in Holland. I have already mentioned our visit with him to Trujillo, Spain, but without doubt the most memorable occasions were our cruises with him aboard the *Ivara*. On at least two of these cruises, we were accompanied by our wonderful friend Doris Magowan—from Rhodes through the islands along the coast of Asia Minor, through the Dardanelles to Istanbul, and later from Antibes to Sardinia, Corsica, and back. Another occasion was a short cruise that included John's son, Johnny, and our mutual friends, Michael and Maxine Jenkins. We went from Piraeus (Athens) down the Peloponnesus and back. Our last cruise together was with his delightful new wife, Charlotte, through the Ionian Sea, ending at Corfu.

When I retired from WWF in 1994, John did me great honor by coming to Washington from Holland for the event. He died in 1996, and Aileen and I lost a dear friend. I once heard him described as "the greatest gentleman in Europe." He was an extraordinary human being, and we still feel his loss keenly.

———

Since we keep traveling, this book would never come to an end unless I stop adding new accounts of our visits to far places. We have been blessed by the opportunity to see more of the world than have most people. This is a good place to stop.

Chapter 24

Retirement

On my retirement from WWF, Roger Sant was elected my successor as WWF chairman. Roger, who is about 11 years younger than I am, is chairman of the AES Corporation, which he co-founded in 1981 with Dennis Bakke, now president and CEO. AES is an independent power company which builds, owns, and operates electric power plants around the world in a socially responsible way. Its current market value is over $10 billion. And, need I say, it designs and operates its plants to extremely high environmental standards. The company adheres to four core values which guide all of its activities: integrity, social responsibility, fairness, and fun. It is quite a remarkable operation, and it aspires to be "the global power company." It appears to be well on its way.

I served as a member of the AES board of directors from its inception until I retired (at my own insistence) in April 1997 and became a director emeritus. From the beginning, AES has provided a challenging, rewarding, and fun experience. The members of the board and of senior management have become good friends of Aileen and myself. AES has made me a relatively wealthy man—at least by any measure to which I have been accustomed!—and Aileen and our children and grandchildren are also stockholders. I said recently that I was going to tell our children that when they went to bed at night they should get down on their knees and thank God for Roger Sant!

Roger and I first knew each other in government during the Ford administration when he was assistant administrator for energy conservation and the environment of the Federal Energy Agency (forerunner to the Department of Energy), and I was EPA administrator. (Dennis Bakke was his deputy at the time.) In my battles within the administration over environmental policy when energy and environmental objectives often seemed in conflict, Roger was always a sympathetic

Roger Sant
and the author

and supportive participant. I don't believe I have ever held anyone in higher personal regard than Roger. Over the years, he and his wife, Vicki, have become close personal friends of Aileen and myself. Vicki is delightful and also highly motivated and effective in her own right. She is a leader in the field of human population control and a prime mover in the organization Population International. She heads the Summit Fund, a Sant philanthropy which focuses on the inner-city problems of the District of Columbia, chairs the board of the Phillips Collection, and serves on the board of Stanford University, among other involvements. Aileen is a director of the Summit Fund. We have been on two walking safaris in Africa with Roger and Vicki (once together with Bob and Judy Waterman and once with John and Caroline Macomber) and on other memorable trips.

In any event, it is important to give some emphasis here to the association with AES because, unless AES suffers a radical reversal of its fortunes, it is an association which will have a major influence on the lives of my family for generations. Moreover, in a purely personal sense, our friendship with Roger and Vicki has enriched our lives beyond measure.

One of the "other memorable trips" with the Sants occurred in 1990.

Vicki had arranged a surprise birthday party for Roger in Venice. The Watermans, Trains, and Chuck and Jane Ince made up the party in addition to the Sants, and we were all Vicki's guests. When Roger boarded the plane at Dulles with Vicki and Aileen, he knew they were flying to Frankfurt. I flew to Frankfurt from Kathmandu, Nepal—a typical Train itinerary—and spent the night in the Sheraton Airport Hotel.

I joined the Sants and Aileen at our flight gate, which is where Roger learned that he was going to Venice. Once in Venice, we went straight to Harry's Bar where we found four people sitting at a table wearing Roger Sant "look-alike" masks. It was only then that Roger learned that the Watermans and Inces were part of the group. We stayed at the Cipriani, toured Venice, dined along the Grand Canal, and had drinks on the roof of the Peggy Guggenheim Museum with the curator and his wife (arranged by Aileen with Peter Lawson-Johnson, chairman of the Guggenheim in New York). Our descent from the roof tested our sobriety, since the ladder had collapsed while we were on the roof.

From Venice we took the train to Florence. There we toured the Uffizi, dined at an outdoor restaurant close by, went to bed at our hotel, and were jarred by a heavy explosion. It turned out that the Uffizi had been bombed by an extremist political group minutes after we left our restaurant next door. The damage was extensive, and the Uffizi was closed for months.

Bachelor Point

IN LATE 1992, Aileen and I bought a marina called Bachelor Point Harbor at Oxford, on Maryland's Eastern Shore. Since, among the boating fraternity, it is well known that the only people crazier than a boat owner is a marina owner, a word of explanation is in order.

I have already mentioned that we owned a farm property called Lostock, which was close to Grace Creek Farm, although not contiguous. We occasionally walked there with weekend guests, and Bowdy hunted there with friends during the goose season. We grew soybeans and corn on the property. However, when a group of local youngsters "trashed" the old house on a lark, we decided that the place was more worry than it was worth, and we put it on the market. In the early fall of 1992 while spending the night at the Sheraton Airport Hotel at Frankfurt en route to Venice for Roger Sant's birthday party, I had a phone call from Chuck Benson, our real estate agent on the Eastern Shore, informing me that he had a buyer for Lostock who was offering close to what we were asking. I said that the offer was fine and then Chuck said something like, "Of course, you will have a large capital gain but I think maybe I can help you on that." He went on to say that he was the general partner of the Tred Avon River Limited Partnership which owned the Bachelor Point Harbor marina and had sold a number of home sites next to it. The asset owned by the partnership was simply the land, piers (with slips), and buildings. All operating personnel and equipment were in a corporation called the Bachelor Point Yacht Company, owned by John Todd. The Yacht Company leased the buildings from the harbor and, in return, the latter paid the yacht company a management fee. In Chuck's opinion, the purchase of the harbor assets would qualify as a "like-kind property exchange" with the Lostock farm property, and any capital gain on the sale of the latter would be deferred until the sale by us of the harbor. Legal counsel later confirmed this reading of the tax law, and we did carry out the exchange with Peter Pappas, the new owner of Lostock.

When John Todd indicated his desire to sell the yacht company, we ended up buying that as well in the spring of 1993. Thus, while the two entities continued to maintain their separate identities, we had, in effect, merged the entire operation.

It proved a very satisfying investment. While Aileen left overseeing the operation to me, we consulted on all major decisions. When we went with Chuck Benson to inspect the marina before purchase, the sight of the boats, particularly the sailing craft, stirred Aileen's sailor blood, and she was enthusiastic about the deal. Bachelor Point lies to your right as you enter the Tred Avon River from the Choptank, a broad river opening into Chesapeake Bay. It is prime yachting country. The marina is one of the most attractive of such facilities I have ever seen.

Bachelor Point's day-to-day management was entrusted to Jim Wagner, who did a superb job. We developed an excellent working relationship, and I left all routine decisions to him. Sarah Bradbury was the office manager, and she was outstanding. There has been, in addition, a highly skilled work crew of about 12. The workmanship at Bachelor Point is as good as it gets. My practice was to visit the marina about once a week on either Friday or Monday, depending on our weekend schedule, and to keep in touch otherwise by telephone. Of course, given our travel schedule, the above statement should be taken as "good intentions." However, I always felt complete confidence in Jim Wagner, Sarah Bradbury, and the rest of the crew.

In the spring of 1998, we sold Bachelor Point to David Pyles, an experienced businessman and marina owner. The sale made me quite sad. Aside from our ill-fated venture with the Talbot Printing Company, I have had no other experience of owning a business. It provided me with an involvement which was both fun and modestly rewarding financially. It also gave me a credible involvement in the Eastern Shore community. I will miss all that. However, the time came to sell and to do so while the business was still improving and I was still *compos mentis!*

Book Collecting

As MENTIONED much earlier, Aileen has always said that, when we married and set up our own home, I brought with me, among other things, about 200 books on hunting in Africa. That was probably a bit of an exaggeration, but I had started collecting early books on Africa a good many years before. That collection has now become one of my most engrossing interests. It comprises about 3000 items, mostly books but including manuscript materials, such as autograph letters and diaries, photographs, paintings and drawings, and also ephemera, such as cartoons, newspapers, and periodicals. In almost all cases, the books are first editions in very good to fine condition. The subject scope of the collection embraces early exploration, travel, and hunting (with, of course, considerable overlap among these categories) with some natural history. All books and other materials are dated 1950 or earlier, with some exceptions. The geographic scope is Africa, including Madagascar and Mauritius but excluding North Africa and West Africa. With very few exceptions, all items are in English.

I have four or five principal dealers in the United States, England, and South Africa. I also buy at auction in both London and New York and, when I do, have the good sense to leave the bidding to an experienced agent—Richard Sawyer in London and James Cummins in New York. I keep a card index of all items and periodically have turned out a typed catalogue to send to dealers. Currently, I am in the process of publishing a printed and illustrated catalogue with the professional help of Richard Sawyer in London.

The collection is a major physical presence in our home. It occupies all of the shelves in the living room, almost all of the library, and all of a former guest room on the top floor known as "the book room." The ultimate disposition of the collection remains a question mark. While all my children have a general interest in the collection, none of them are interested as collectors. One option is to sell it and, thus, realize the substantial appreciation in value that has occurred over the years. Another option is to give it to an institution, such as the Library of Congress, which has expressed interest.[1] For the time being, I get great pleasure out of maintaining and adding to the collection.[2]

Horse Racing

ANOTHER INTEREST of mine is horse racing but here I am very much the dilettante. In about 1950 I had invested with Orme Wilson in a two-year-old race horse which never started in a race. Moreover,

1. I expect to turn my personal papers over to the Library of Congress when I have finished using them. As noted in a previous chapter, copies of my father's and grandfather's journals have already been deposited in the manuscript division of the library.
2. An article describing the collection was published in *The Manuscript Society News* 16, no. 2 (Spring 1995), pp. 75-78.

In the winner's circle, Laurel Park, Maryland, with Gramercy, later our successful broodmare. My racing partner, Orme Wilson, is at left.

One of Gramercy's progeny, Winding Trail, winning the Cavalier Cup stake at Laurel Park, 1993. In the winner's circle are Mario Pino, the jockey, Midge Wilson, the author, and our longtime trainer, Charlie Hadry.

at about the same time, I was following the races and betting on them with great regularity. Many years later, knowing that Orme had a fairly substantial racing stable based on his farm at White Post, Virginia, I asked him whether he would sell me a part-interest in one of his horses. He sent me a list of options and I ended up buying for $13,000 a half-interest in a two-year-old filly named Gramercy (Castalle by

Dressed for Royal Ascot
and hamming it up a bit
with Harry Hambleden

Hagley). Gramercy won $144,000 over about four years of racing and
has been a broodmare since. Her first foal was a colt by Gilded Age
named Winding Trail, who won over $100,000 before his career was
cut short by a tragic accident and he had to be destroyed.

Others of Gramercy's progeny have been Grace Creek, Choo Choo
Baby, Kalorama Square, Primercy, and Gracie Gale. All those of racing age have been trained by Charles Hadry and have run in Maryland
at Laurel and Pimlico. Remarkable to those who know racing, all of
these horses have raced and all of them have won. While Orme and I
were 50-50 owners, the horses always ran under his name and colors.
Since Orme died in 1992, his widow, Mildred (Midge), and I have
continued this arrangement. As racing operations go, it is a modest
endeavor but it has been fun. Moreover, we have been in the black
every year except for a small loss in two years.

Several years ago, in association with Harry Hambleden, I bought a
small share in an English racing syndicate operated at Highclere Castle, the property of Lord Canarvon. The syndicate was managed by his

son, Harry Herbert. This venture has led to investment in other Highclere syndicates. In June 1997, 1998, and 1999 Aileen and I attended
Royal Ascot with Harry Hambleden and his wife, Leslie. One of our
horses, Heritage, won the King George V Stake in 1997—unfortunately
on the day we had had to return to the U.S.

Aileen's Activities

AILEEN, MEANWHILE, was engaged in a wide range of nonprofit
activities. For years she had been a regular nurse's aid at Walter Reed,
the military hospital in Washington. She was on the board of the St.
John's Development Services for Children (previously the St. John's
Orphanage). She became a member of the board of the Sulgrave Club.
In March 1970, she was a founder of Concern, Inc., formed as a
nonprofit, tax-exempt organization, staffed by volunteer Washington
women and designed to harness consumer power to help solve environmental problems. Its principal effort was to help citizens become
aware of environmental problems and to encourage intelligent prac-
tices in the marketplace, the home, and the community. Among the
founders of Concern, in addition to Aileen, were Mrs. Paul Ignatius
(Nan), Mrs. Richard Helms (Cynthia), and Mrs. Paul Mickey (Peggy).
The organization continues strongly today under the longtime chairmanship of Mrs. Anthony Lapham (Burks). When I was chairman of
the Council on Environmental Quality in the early 1970s, I had a fairly
active interface with Concern.

Later, Aileen became a member of the board of directors of WWF-
U.S., an involvement which she enjoyed immensely. From her background with Concern she brought to WWF a broad knowledge of
environmental matters. When I was elected president of WWF in
1978, she resigned from the board and became a member of the board
of WWF-International in Switzerland. Also in the latter part of the
1970s, Aileen became much involved with raising funds for Second
Genesis, a Washington-area drug rehabilitation program.

In the early 1980s, she joined the board of the Maryland chapter of The Nature Conservancy. She served for several years as chairman of the board, and in one of those years the Maryland chapter won the award as the outstanding TNC chapter in the nation. In more recent years, she has been a very active member of the board of the Friends of the National Arboretum, a fine institution that has developed many successful garden plant introductions in the U.S. Aileen has done a great deal to promote awareness of the arboretum in the Washington area, and its annual "cookout" has become a well-attended event. For several years, she has been on the board of the Chesapeake Bay Foundation, a highly successful organization dedicated to protecting and promoting the environmental quality of the bay and its watershed. In 1997-1999, she was vice chairman of a CBF capital funds drive. She is deeply engaged in cleaning up the Anacostia River. Thus, for many years, Aileen has been an environmental leader in her own right.

Among the many things for which I am grateful to Aileen is that she has always been enormously supportive of me in whatever job I was doing at the moment. That has been a priceless gift. She has never walled off her activities and interests from mine. Thus, when I was in government, we gave dinners that included other officials, including members of the Cabinet, the Chief Justice, Nixon's chief of staff, Bob Haldeman, etc. When visiting foreign dignitaries with environmental responsibilities came to town, we entertained them, including the British Minister of the Environment Peter Walker and the French Minister of the Environment (and mayor of Dijon) Robert Poujade, as well as the Spanish minister with environmental responsibility, López Rodo.

My appropriations subcommittee chairman, Jamie Whitten, later chairman of the full committee, came to supper with Aileen and myself. In fact, Aileen used to take boxes of tomatoes from our garden to Jamie and also to George Mahon, the powerful chairman of the House Rules Committee. Secretary of Transportation John Volpe got ripe figs from the farm. All this wasn't exactly bribery—or was it?—but it certainly helped build personal bridges to people with whom I often had difficult issues.

Likewise, when I became president and later chairman of WWF, Aileen played a key role in building the all-important collegiality of the board. Whether in entertaining at our home, contributing to the discussions of the WWF National Council of which she is a member, or helping lead WWF trips to various parts of the globe, Aileen's energy, warmth, enthusiasm, and knowledge have been all-important factors. There is just no question that she has contributed immensely to whatever success I have enjoyed, not only with WWF but in every other role of mine.

I know that there are those who might criticize Aileen and say that she was subordinating herself to the needs of my jobs. I don't think she ever felt that way and I am totally convinced that my performance in those jobs was immeasurably enhanced by her contributions. It was always a team effort.

Dogs and Other Pets

BELOVED MEMBERS of our extended family have been a long line of black Labrador retrievers. As I write this in early 1999, ten-month-old Sam is the sixth in an unbroken line of black Labs going back to 1952. Each one has been an integral member of the family and a close friend whose life with us has been a joy and whose ultimate death has left us deeply grieving. The first was Swift, whom I bought on Long Island shortly after I had met Aileen. He lived with me in my bachelor quarters on 35th Street in Georgetown and was the perfect companion—cheerful, devotedly loyal, impeccably mannered, and a fine retriever in the field. We had many a fine duck shoot together.

I was on the staff of the Joint Committee on Internal Revenue Taxation at the time, and Swift used to accompany me to work in the New House Office Building. He would spend the day quietly lying under a table in my office. At lunchtime, we would go across Independence Avenue to the Capitol grounds, where I would throw a retrieving dummy for him and he would perform other necessary duties. Alas, after several months of this, Swift and I were stopped one morning by

Swift, our first Lab, a wonderful dog

a Capitol policeman as we entered my office building. He told me that it was against the rules to bring a dog into the building. "But," I remonstrated, "Senator Byrd brings one to his office every day." "You are *not* Senator Byrd!" said the officer. That was the end of that arrangement. With Aileen's and my marriage, Swift became part of our household on Woodland Drive, and our children grew up with him as their gentle and long-suffering companion.

Swift was followed by his son, Razz (short for Razzmatazz), who was a fine dog in his own right. He in turn was followed by Mike, who left much less of an imprint, then Red, and then Judge. Judge was a gift from our friend Charlie Whitehouse and the son of his dog, Justice, an English Lab without papers. Hence, Judge was never bred and had no offspring. He was a handsome animal and our constant companion both in Washington and on the Shore. Unlike any other of our dogs, he slept in our bedroom in the city simply because he would not stay anywhere else. We drove back and forth with him to the Shore and to Hobe Sound over Christmas and New Year's.

Also unlike our earlier Labs, who were all *my* dogs, Judge was unmistakably Aileen's. She let him onto her lap once when he was a puppy, and he became hers, heart and soul. Probably our most common shared outdoor activity at the farm is a walk around the property or along a nearby road when the ground is soggy. Judge was our invariable companion on these walks, and he loved them as much as we. Sadly, Judge developed an aggressive cancer in his jaw and died at Hobe Sound in March 1998. The heart wrench is still with us as I write but young Sam promises to be a wonderful dog.

Other pets have included most notably two Norwich terriers, Casey and Toby, owned by Emily, who were important members of our household. Then, of course, there were hamsters, white mice, goldfish, turtles, etc. There was also a pair of hapless parakeets that got out of their cage one day and were "defeathered" by Razz. We found the totally naked little corpses on the living room rug and several million tiny blue feathers in every nook and cranny of the room.

Kalorama Square

IN 1977 WE moved from Woodland Drive to 1803 Kalorama Square, a four-story town-house condominium, one of 25 such houses at the corner of S Street and Phelps Place, N.W., in Washington. The houses stand in two north-south rows with a gas-lit mall in between. There is one entrance at 1824 Phelps Place and one garage entrance on S Street, with a guard on duty 24 hours a day. A garage underlies the entire complex and an outdoor swimming pool stands at our end of the mall. It is an attractive, secure place, convenient to shops and restaurants, and several of our good friends live in the other houses. WWF has generously provided me with an office and a secretary, Catherine Williams, and the WWF office, at 1250 24th Street, is only about a 12-minute walk from my house.

In the spring of 1996, we sold 1803 Kalorama Square and bought the house next door at 1801. Since the new and old houses have a common wall, I have always said that we moved about eighteen inches. Number 1801 is the end house and has marvelous views over the city to the south, the Washington Monument being the most conspicuous feature. Sunshine and light flood the house from three sides. We renovated the interior and re-landscaped the garden, which is considerably larger than those of the interior houses. Altogether, it is a delightful

1801 Kalorama Square

place and Aileen and I are both very happy there. We are blessed with three beautiful homes, counting the farm and Hobe Sound.

We entertain with some frequency, and Aileen loves to have friends in our new house. We also dine out with some regularity. I gripe about the amount of social activity from time to time but my young and energetic wife thrives on it, and it probably does me good. Our temperaments are simply different in this regard. She is basically gregarious and, while I am far from being antisocial, there is no doubt that I am a bit of a loner, as I have said before. However, I usually enjoy myself. At home, I am in charge of wines and take pride in serving good ones. Our house has a wine cellar, and keeping it stocked gives me pleasure.

Speaking of entertaining, Aileen and I have always enjoyed dances and have given a number of our own over the years. Emily's debutante dance at Woodland Drive in 1968, a surprise dance for me called "King for an Evening" at the Chevy Chase Club in 1974 (our 20th anniversary), and wedding anniversary dances at Chevy Chase in 1989 and 1994 with Neal Smith's orchestra come to mind.

Both a bit disheveled,
the author and brother
Mid at surprise
"King for an Evening" dance,
1974

Aileen with Alex at our 1994
(40th wedding anniversary) dance

I enjoy the Alibi Club, as did my father and grandfather and two brothers. I try to have lunch there every Friday but we sometimes go to the country on Thursday. There is an occasional poker game on a Monday night. On "non-Alibi" days, I generally lunch at the Metropolitan Club, usually eating in the grill room at one of the club tables; it is a pleasant way to keep up with old friends and meet new ones.

Aileen belongs to the Sulgrave Club but uses it less often. When we go to New York, we often stay at her Colony Club. I continue to belong to the Princeton Club and the Century in New York but seldom use them. I have been a member of the Boone & Crockett Club (founded by Theodore Roosevelt) since 1961 and was elected to the Alfalfa in 1994. I am a member of the Explorers' Club and a fellow of the Royal Geographical Society in London.

Aileen keeps herself in fine physical shape and has a figure that most women half her age would envy. She goes to a personal trainer twice a week (and has recently persuaded me to do likewise), plays tennis about twice a week throughout the year, and swims regularly in season. On her 70th birthday, with all the family gathered at the farm, she went waterskiing. I have always been a desultory exerciser at best. I have given up tennis entirely because of degenerative arthritis. I swim when I have the opportunity, and I walk quite a lot during the average day. I usually walk to and from my WWF office and from there to and from the Metropolitan Club. And, of course, our Labrador, Sam, takes both Aileen and me for several walks a day.

As I have already set out at some length, we have always traveled a great deal. A brief summary of our 1996 travels will demonstrate how intense our travel agenda sometimes becomes. In early January we were at our home in Hobe Sound, where we had gone before Christmas. We left for three days to attend the annual AES board and business review meeting at the Mauna Kea Hotel on Hawaii. In February (after returning to Washington January 15), we went for a week to the WWF winter board meeting and field trips on Dominica in the West Indies.

In March, we chartered the ketch *Andando* in the Galápagos for a ten-day cruise with ten of our family, including children, their spouses, and grandchildren. On the first of April, the tenants departed our Hobe Sound house and Aileen and I stayed there until about April 17, having two sets of six guests each for long weekends.

Almost immediately afterwards, I left by myself for Vietnam to attend and speak at a WWF-U.N.-Vietnam conference on Business and the Environment. AES asked me to stop on the way in Beijing, which I did for a day and two nights, to represent AES in a signing ceremony to do with a loan facility for a new power plant. I attended a banquet in the Great Hall of the People and sat on the right of the host, the Minister of Power. In Ho Chi Minh City (Saigon), I gave my speech at the conference and a press interview, spent a night in a national park where WWF was training personnel, and then spent several days in Hanoi, where I met with government officials and had a private meeting with General Giap, who had been the Viet Cong chief of staff during the Vietnam War.

I flew home via London, where I attended a meeting of AES Electric, the AES U.K. subsidiary. The trip home-to-home around the world took 12 days and I felt quite proud of myself, an old codger of 76. Not only did I travel alone the whole way but I carried all my gear in one carry-on bag. In mid-June, I went on an AES board trip to Argentina and Brazil. In July-August, we took a two-week walking safari in Zimbabwe with our friends John and Caroline Macomber and Roger and Vicki Sant. On our return, we went to New England for visits to daughter Nancy and Aileen's sister Helen Spaulding and a big clambake given by my sister-in-law Audry. Thence to Seattle and San Juan Island in Puget Sound for a visit with our friends Bill and Jill Ruckelshaus, followed by a visit near San Diego with former Senator and Secretary of the Treasury Lloyd Bentsen and his wife, "B.A."

Toward the latter part of September, we flew to Bali where we spent four days at the Amandari Hotel with Helen Spaulding, Al and Judy Key, Bob and Judy Waterman, and the Sants. All of us then joined a group of WWF directors and other friends (for a total of 38) and flew east to the island of Ambon. There we boarded a catamaran motor vessel for a cruise in the Banda Sea, with much snorkeling and diving, and then we went for several days along the south coast of Indonesian New Guinea (Irian Jaya) to visit the primitive Asmat people in their villages. Most of our fellow voyagers thought it was the best trip they had ever done. In October I went as usual to Long Point in Canada at least twice for duck shooting and then Aileen and I drove south to Hobe Sound in mid-December.

That, of course, was too much travel, though we would not have wanted to miss any of it, and I doubt we ever follow such an agenda again. In contrast, 1997 was largely a "stay-at-home" year. For many years, we have sent out a Christmas card recording a visit during the past year to some exotic spot—wearing fur hats on the shore of Lake Baikal, Siberia; sitting on the Great Wall of China; in an outdoor bathtub in Zimbabwe; on elephant back in the jungles of Nepal; or standing surrounded by near-naked headhunters in Papua New Guinea. Recently, I told Aileen that I had an exciting new idea for a Christmas card. "What's that?" she said, visualizing a visit to some far-off spot. "Sitting on the bench in front of our fireplace at home," I said. "It will get everyone's attention!"

Actually, we went to England and Ireland for ten days in June. I went salmon fishing on the Grand Cascapedia in Quebec in July. Aileen took our granddaughters Emily and Allie Rowan to the Eton Ranch in Wyoming in August, joined by Judy Key[3] and four of her grandsons. In October, Aileen went with a WWF group, including her sisters Helen and Judy, on a sailing cruise through the Marquesa and Tuamoto Islands in the South Pacific. Unfortunately, that trip fell in the middle of my Long Point season so I did not go. I treasure my days at Long Point, as has already become evident.

We see quite a bit of our children although never as much as we would like. After graduating from Wellesley, Nancy married St. John Smith (1946-) in 1968 and they were divorced in 1980. He is a graduate of Groton and Harvard and is a practicing architect in Boston. Since the divorce, he has remarried and has two children by that marriage. Nancy and St. John's son, Alexander St. John Smith (1975-), graduated with honors from the Pratt Institute in Brooklyn in June 1997 and is a graphic design wizard. Alex is a fine young man who paid for a substantial portion of his last year's college bills by his own earnings on the side.[4] In 1993, Nancy married Christopher Sage Gustin (1956-), a ceramic artist and professor at the University of Southern Massachusetts. Chris attended the University of California at Irvine

3. Sadly, Al Key died March 20, 1997, after a seven-year bout with cancer.
4. I particularly appreciated this, as I have assumed the job of paying for all of our grandchildren's educations. Some years ago, Aileen and I established a trust fund to do just that, funded by a gift of AES stock. At the time, AES paid a dividend. It ceased doing so several years ago in order to invest its earnings in further growth. Since the trust has no income, I have undertaken to pay all the education bills. When the trust assets are finally distributed, which will be when the youngest grandchild reaches 21, each grandchild will receive a pro rata share.

and received his bachelor's degree in fine arts from the Kansas Art Institute and his master's in fine arts from New York State University at Alfred, New York. They have a daughter, Leila (1993-). In 1997, Chris Gustin resigned his university post and is focusing on the development of a ceramic tile business.

In 1985, Emily married James Arthur Rowan (1948-), whom she met while both were in business in Washington. Jim is a graduate of Lawrenceville and Cornell and is now a managing director of the investment banking business of Legg, Mason and Company, a major regional brokerage, investment counseling, and investment banking firm, headquartered in Baltimore. They were married at Christ Church, St. Michael's, and Grace Creek Farm was the scene of their reception. They have two daughters, Emily Patterson Rowan (1986-) and Aileen (Allie) Schuyler Rowan (1988-), both of whom are at Potomac School. They live in Chevy Chase, Maryland. They are pillars of their church, St. Columba's, where Emily is a member of the vestry. Young Emily sings in the choir and is taking piano lessons. In recent years, Emily was at various times treasurer, secretary, director of financial services, and director of communication of Diginet Communications, Inc., a nationwide provider of Internet and Intranet services. However, she has given that up in the interest of home and family and other personal interests, such as drawing and painting.

Charles Bowdoin (Bowdy) Train (1955-) and Marjory Legare Hardy (1956-) were married in 1988 at Christ Church, Easton, Maryland. There was a reception afterwards at the home of her mother, Anne Legare, on Trippe Creek near Easton. Bowdy is a graduate of St. Albans School (1973), Trinity College (1977), and Georgetown Law School (1982), and Marjory is a graduate of Hollins College (1978). He practiced law with the firm of Shaw, Pittman, Potts, and Trowbridge in Washington for several years and then became a deputy assistant administrator of EPA for Solid Waste and Emergency Response. He loved the job and did well at it but, unfortunately, it came to an end with Clinton's election and the defeat of Bush in 1992. Bowdy's enthusiasm for the law had waned, and he has joined Bruce and Douglas Dunnan in the investment business. He is the managing director of the Grosvenor and Grosvenor Select Funds, venture capital funds. He and Marjory have three children: Julia Kent (1990-), Russell Bowdoin (1992-), and William Hardy (1994-). They, too, attend St. Columba's Episcopal Church. Bowdy is a director of the Maryland Chapter of The Nature Conservancy and of the D.C. Hospice and is a governor of the Metropolitan Club. Marjory has been active in the Mothers' Association of St. Patrick's School (where Julia and William go) and head of a fund-raising campaign in the Cleveland Park area to equip a playground. She was publicly honored for that effort in 1999. Sadly, as I write this in November 1999, Bowdy and Marjory have separated.

Errol graduated from St. George's School (1977) and Trinity College (1981) and in 1988 married John Carl (J.C.) Giordano (1957-) at Christ Church, St. Michael's. Their wedding reception was held at Grace Creek Farm. J.C. graduated from the Milbrook School and the University of Vermont (1980). He is with the national commercial real estate firm of Staubach Company in their New Jersey operation. They live on a ten-acre property near Lebanon, New Jersey, but are moving to Far Hills. They have twins, a son and a daughter, John Carl IV (Jake) and Schuyler Hamilton (Sky), both born in 1992, and a second son, Nicholas Bowdoin, born in November 1999.

My daily round has a fairly predictable pattern to it. Aileen and I get up about 6:45 to 7:00 a.m. She gives our young Lab, Sam, his breakfast and then takes him for a walk in the neighborhood. Georgina puts our breakfast on trays in the elevator along with the *Washington Post* and the *New York Times*. Aileen has her breakfast in bed and I have mine on a folding table in front of the French doors looking out over the city from the bedroom. In warm weather, we breakfast in the garden, usually after a swim in the Kalorama Square pool which lies just through a gate in our garden wall. I read the *New York Times* and she the *Washington Post*, exchanging items of interest that may not be in the other's paper.

I walk to the WWF offices at 1250 24th Street, about fifteen minutes away. I go straight down the steps at the head of 22nd Street up which I walked daily as a young boy with my nurse, Verena, on my way to Potomac School. At WWF, I have a fine office on the northeast corner of the fourth floor, the same I had had as chairman. I turn over my home mail to Cath, sign letters, meet with WWF staff, make calls, etc., and walk to the Metropolitan Club for lunch (or to the Alibi on Fridays).

I walk back to the office, perhaps stopping at a bookstore to browse a bit on the way. Unfortunately, "human-scale" bookstores where you know the salespeople are becoming things of the past in downtown Washington, as are used or rare book dealers, antique stores, art dealers, and other "browsable" establishments. Even my bank, where I stop to cash a check, is totally impersonal and the tellers seem to change by the month. I spend most of the afternoon at the office and walk home around five. About six, I feed Sam and take him for a walk. If Aileen is home, we go through the day's mail and catch up on each other's activities. On two mornings a week, we have a session with a personal trainer, and Aileen usually has a tennis match on two other days. She lunches often with a friend and occasionally with the Smithsonian Luncheon Group. At least once a week, she picks up a grandchild or two for a visit to an art gallery, another exhibition, or the zoo. And she takes them to lunch on a one-on-one basis. She recently took all her granddaughters to see a stage performance of "The King and I." She is a wonderful grandparent and has a much closer relationship with the grandchildren than I have.

Aileen checks her phone messages and inevitably spends a fair amount of time making calls. In season, we will have a swim in the pool at our front door and dress to go out for dinner. On the average, we dine out at friends' homes more often than by ourselves at home. We almost never watch television, which seems to set us apart from most of our friends. If we happen to be at home, Aileen does the cooking, and we clean up together. I may do a bit of writing or work on the book collection. We usually get to bed about 10:30 if we are alone at home or closer to midnight if we are out for dinner. I give Sam his final walk of the day before we go to bed. Bedtime usually seems to be our principal time for reading, but, unfortunately, it is hard to get through more than a very few pages before sleep calls.

Aileen continues to be an active trustee of the Chesapeake Bay

Foundation and of the Summit Fund of Washington, a philanthropic foundation established by Roger and Vicki Sant that focuses on the needs of the Washington area. She works hard on these responsibilities.

For my part, I have now succeeded in graduating from most such commitments, with one exception, although as chairman emeritus I remain quite engaged in the affairs of WWF. I am also an advisory trustee of the Rockefeller Brothers Fund in New York, on whose board I was a member for a number of years. The main exception is that I remain on the board of the Washington Monument Society, of which I am the first vice president. (My father was likewise a member.) Since the only officer senior to me is the president of the United States and that in an honorary capacity, I am in effect the chairman and CEO. The duties are not arduous. The society was chartered by the Congress to build the Washington Monument. After about one-third of the present monument was funded and built, the Civil War interrupted the work, and the society finally turned the task of completion over to the federal government. We meet at the monument on Washington's birthday. I deliver a short speech to a scattering of tourists, lay a wreath, visit the top of the monument (by elevator), usually with Jim Symington, second vice president, and then we repair to the Metropolitan Club for lunch and the business meeting of the society.

The cornerstone of the monument was laid in 1848. President James Polk, his Cabinet, the Senate, members of the House, the heads of the armed forces, the diplomatic corps, and Washington society all attended the event. Betsey Schuyler Hamilton—Aileen's great-great-great-great-grandmother, the widow of Alexander Hamilton—was on the platform that day, as was Dolley Madison. While I have no record of the fact, it seems likely that my own great-great-grandfather and prominent Washingtonian, Obadiah Bruen Brown, would have been in the audience as well. The oration on that occasion was given by Robert C. Winthrop, Speaker of the House of Representatives and the younger brother of Aileen's great-great-great-grandmother, Sarah Bowdoin Winthrop, who married George Sullivan, whose sons changed their name to Bowdoin. It was the eldest of those sons who married Frances (Fanny) Hamilton, the granddaughter of Alexander Hamilton and his wife, Betsey.

My own remarks on the 150th anniversary in 1998 borrowed heavily from Winthrop's speech. He had emphasized George Washington's moral character as the quality that most attracted his countrymen and I quoted him at length on the subject, which seemed particularly timely given the then-current public uproar over President Clinton's irresponsible personal behavior in the White House. The *Washington Post* picked up my remarks and published them in their entirety. (See Appendix.)

I mention the event not because of the Clinton scandal but because it links a current activity of mine with family associations going back many generations. It helps illustrate in a small way the inescapable interconnectedness of our past, our present, and necessarily our future. That, of course, is the whole point of this book, and it provides an appropriate point at which to close this account of my life.

Since our grandchildren represent the future, it seems appropriate to place their photographs here. Our eldest, Alex Smith, appears in earlier sections of the book.

Emily Rowan

Allie Rowan

Russell Train

Julia Train

William Train

Jake and Schuyler Giordano

Leila Gustin

Nicholas Giordano

Appendix

Remarks Given by Russell E. Train on the February 23, 1998,
Observance of George Washington's Birthday at the Washington Monument

LET ME OPEN these remarks by congratulating the National Park Service on undertaking the top-to-bottom renovation of the monument and by thanking the Congress and private sponsors for providing the necessary funds.

It was 150 years ago on July 4, 1848, that a distinguished group of Americans met on this same spot, joined by the largest crowd ever seen in the nation's capital up to that time, to do honor to the memory of George Washington and to lay the cornerstone of this great monument. We gather here today on the 150th anniversary of that historic occasion.

The president of the United States, James Polk, was here as well as the vice president; the members of the Senate and House of Representatives; the ambassadors and ministers of foreign nations; members of the judiciary; and the ranking officers of the Army, Navy, and Marines. The states were represented as well as many private organizations associated with the building of the monument, most particularly in that regard being the members of the Washington National Monument Society, to which the Congress originally entrusted the building of the monument and whose successors are here today.

In 1848 George Washington had only been dead 50 years, so his memory was still fresh and powerful to those gathered here. Indeed, among those present were some who had actually known Washington during his lifetime. Notable among these and seated on the platform that day were Dolley Madison, widow of President James Madison, and Betsy Schuyler Hamilton, widow of Alexander Hamilton, the first Secretary of the Treasury. And, of course, it was Madison and Hamilton together who had been the principal architects of the Constitution, which remains the supreme law of our land.

The featured speaker on that occasion—or the orator, as he was then called—was the Speaker of the House of Representatives, the Honorable Robert C. Winthrop of Massachusetts, a direct descendant of John Winthrop, the first governor of the Massachusetts Bay Colony.

Winthrop spoke in the place of John Quincy Adams, the sixth president of the United States and later a member of Congress, who had died shortly before the ceremony took place. In the tradition of the day, the address lasted close to an hour, although Winthrop described it as only "a few words." He reviewed the life of Washington and his many contributions to the founding of our country. But then Winthrop went on to say:

> It is, however, the character of Washington, and not the mere part which he played, which I would hold up this day to the world . . . [I]t is the glory of Washington, that the virtues of the man outshone even the brilliance of his acts . . . His incorruptible honesty, his uncompromising truth, his devout reliance on God, the purity of his life, the scrupulousness of his conscience, the disinterestedness of his purpose, his humanity, generosity, and justice . . . made up a character to which the world may be fearlessly challenged for a parallel . . . Everybody saw that Washington sought nothing for himself. Everybody knew that he sacrificed nothing to personal or to party ends. Hence, the mighty influence, the matchless sway, which he exercised over all around him.

Let us never think of Washington as simply one among many. At a time when we tend to lump all our presidents together on "Presidents' Day," let us remember Washington as towering above the others, standing alone, as does his monument, a man without whom this nation would not have come into existence. And, to the west, stands the memorial to that other towering American, Abraham Lincoln, who preserved our Union and brought freedom to all our people. The Washington Monument and the Lincoln Memorial face each other across uncluttered space.

However, I understand that plans are far along to build a World

War II Memorial in the middle of that vista. If I may be permitted a brief personal note: As a veteran of that war, I feel no need of a memorial, but, if others feel differently, let us for heaven's sake put it elsewhere. There are plenty of sites. Let us leave this section of the Mall to Washington and Lincoln, uncluttered by further memorials and their inevitable accompaniment of buses and cars and parking lots. Let us leave this space as it is—hallowed to the memory of these two giants of our history.

On safari, 1998, along the Zambezi River, Zimbabwe